INDIVIDUALIZING LANGUAGE INSTRUCTION
STRATEGIES AND METHODS

INDIVIDUALIZING LANGUAGE INSTRUCTION
STRATEGIES AND METHODS

RENÉE S. DISICK
Valley Stream Central High School

HARCOURT BRACE JOVANOVICH, INC.
New York / Chicago / San Francisco / Atlanta

To Fanny, Bernard, and David Disick

© 1975 by Harcourt Brace Jovanovich, Inc.

All rights reserved. No part of this publication may be
reproduced or transmitted in any form or by any means, electronic or mechanical,
including photocopy, recording, or any information storage and retrieval
system, without permission in writing from the publisher.

ISBN: 0-15-541404-6

Library of Congress Catalog Card Number: 74-21273

Printed in the United States of America

Excerpts from Abraham Maslow's *Eupsychian Management* have
been reprinted by permission of Richard D. Irwin, Inc., Homewood,
Illinois. Excerpts from Maslow's *Motivation and Personality* reprinted by
permission of Harper & Row.

FOREWORD

Many foreign-language teachers ask repeatedly for publications that help to answer the question "What shall I do Monday morning?" Although their question is symbolic of a general concern for techniques, too often it does not imply concern for relating what they do on Wednesday to what they did on Monday, nor for how their students may feel on Friday about what they have done all week. I am very pleased, therefore, that *Individualizing Language Instruction: Strategies and Methods* is not merely a "cookbook of techniques" for individualizing instruction. It is a successful attempt to consider the entire teaching-learning process; it is an unusually comprehensive blend of theory and practice. Although Renée Disick writes from the background and point of view of a classroom teacher, her very specific and practical suggestions for effective classroom behavior are more than the intuitive creations of a clever teacher. They are the thoughtful result of an understanding of theory that describes and clarifies the kinds of learning and interaction that can occur in a foreign-language classroom. Thus, the teacher can find in this book useful suggestions on widely ranging topics, from choosing Ditto masters to improving communication between teacher and student to helping students to satisfy basic motivational needs.

The book also contributes to our knowledge of the relationship between humanistic, or affective, goals and foreign-language learning. There is no doubt that these goals are assuming greater importance in today's society and that foreign-language learning may uniquely contribute to them. Indeed, students in any classroom that reflects the philosophy implicit in this book will learn much more than language skills. They will learn how to learn, how to be more independent, and how to work effectively in groups.

Individualizing Language Instruction: Strategies and Methods is important reading for today's foreign-language teacher. Teachers who are contemplating or practicing individualization will find many practical suggestions for initiating or modifying their curriculums. Even teachers who cannot individualize or who reject individualization will benefit from reading this handbook. In so doing, they must examine their assumptions, goals, and procedures—and from that we all benefit.

GILBERT A. JARVIS
The Ohio State University

PREFACE

Individualizing Language Instruction: Strategies and Methods is divided into three parts. The first treats some of the philosophical and ideological under-pinnings of individualized foreign-language instruction. Part Two deals with management considerations, such as staffing and equipping an individualized classroom, humanizing instruction, and making the transition to this style of teaching and learning. Part Three offers specific techniques for individualizing instruction in the four language skills as well as in culture and civilization. In addition, the extensive appendixes contain samples of actual classroom materials that may prove useful to teachers who are in the process of creating their own programs. Although the chapters may be read in order, each one is organized as a complete entity. This permits readers to begin as needed with the topics that are most relevant to their own particular teaching situations. In view of this, a moderate amount of repetition must be expected in the book, since some important ideas must be treated more than once.

The purpose of the book is to define individualized foreign-language instruction and to consider problems commonly associated with its implementation and management. Though it is hoped that the solutions proposed here are both realistic and practical, the author recognizes the impossibility of responding to all the contingencies that may arise in a given classroom. For this reason, the book is necessarily incomplete. It attempts, however, to define some basic issues, raise some important questions, and to suggest some answers. Ultimately, of course, readers must complete this book for themselves. In the final analysis each teacher is the expert in his or her own classroom. It is his or her responsibility to learn, to experiment, and to evaluate. No "expert" from outside the classroom can accomplish this better than the teacher. This book, then, is but a start. It can be of value only if its ideas are adapted and modified by individual teachers according to their own professional judgment. In so doing, they may promote growth in both their students and themselves.

The author wishes to express her gratitude to the following people who read and commented on the manuscript: Walter Brewer, Gilbert A. Jarvis, Gladys C. Lipton, Joan Robert, Philip D. Smith, Jr., and Rebecca M. Valette. She also appreciates the help of editor Albert Richards and copy editor Peter Kaldheim, with whom it has been a pleasure to work. Finally, she thanks her husband David for his tolerance, patience, and understanding while the book was being written.

RENÉE S. DISICK

CONTENTS

FOREWORD v

PREFACE vii

PART ONE   THEORETICAL CONSIDERATIONS

1 **INDIVIDUALIZED INSTRUCTION: AN OVERVIEW** 3

   1.1 General Considerations 3
   1.2 What Individualized Instruction Is Not 4
   1.3 What Individualized Instruction Is 5
   1.4 Individualized Instruction vs. Full-Class Teaching 6
   1.5 Some Reasons for Initiating a Program of Individualization 6
   1.6 Rationale for Individualized Instruction 8

2 **CONTEMPORARY THEORIES OF LANGUAGE LEARNING** 16

   2.1 General Considerations 16
   2.2 The Audio-Lingual Approach 16
   2.3 Reactions against Audio-Lingualism 18
   2.4 Linguistics in the 1970s 21

3 HUMANISTIC THEORIES OF MOTIVATION AND MANAGEMENT 24

3.1 General Considerations 24
3.2 Maslow's "Needs" Theory of Motivation 25
3.3 Meeting Basic Needs in the Classroom 26
3.4 Rogers: Facilitating Freedom to Learn 30
3.5 Glasser: Eliminating Failure 30
3.6 McGregor: Theory-X and Theory-Y Management 31
3.7 Maslow's Eupsychian Management 32
3.8 Eupsychian Management vs. Current Classroom Realities 33

4 DEVELOPING A CURRICULUM FOR INDIVIDUALIZED LEARNING 37

4.1 General Considerations 37
4.2 A Philosophy of Individualized Instruction 38
4.3 Humanistic Considerations vs. the Need to Uphold Standards 39
4.4 The Need for Diversified Course Offerings 41
4.5 Defining Curricular Goals 42
4.6 Performance Objectives in Foreign-Language Instruction 42
4.7 The Cognitive Domain 43
4.8 The Affective Domain 43

5 CREATING LEARNING PACKETS 47

5.1 General Considerations 47
5.2 Components of Learning Packets 48
5.3 Single Text vs. Multitext Program 48
5.4 Writing Unit Objectives 49
5.5 Writing Learning Steps 49
5.6 Creating Supplementary Materials 50
5.7 Avoiding Common Pitfalls 53

6 STYLES OF INDIVIDUALIZED INSTRUCTION 57

6.1 General Considerations 57
6.2 Choice of Objectives 58
6.3 Choice of Learning Rates 59
6.4 Choice of Learning Methods 62
6.5 Choice of Course Content 63
6.6 Selecting a Style of Individualized Instruction 65

PART TWO   MANAGEMENT CONSIDERATIONS

7   STAFFING AN INDIVIDUALIZED PROGRAM   71

    7.1 General Considerations   71
    7.2 Certified Teachers   72
    7.3 Native Informants   72
    7.4 Student Teachers and Teaching Interns   73
    7.5 Student Aides and Tutors   73
    7.6 Peer Teachers   75
    7.7 Secretarial Help   75
    7.8 Technical Assistants   75
    7.9 Positive Working Relationships among Classroom Personnel   76
    7.10 Caution in Staffing   79

8   EQUIPPING AN INDIVIDUALIZED PROGRAM   81

    8.1 General Considerations   81
    8.2 Paper and Paper Products   82
    8.3 Storage Facilities   84
    8.4 Audio Equipment   85
    8.5 Visual Equipment   88
    8.6 Classroom Furnishings   92

9   MAKING THE TRANSITION TO INDIVIDUALIZED INSTRUCTION   95

    9.1 General Considerations   95
    9.2 Acquiring Knowledge   96
    9.3 Finding Time   97
    9.4 Gaining Support   100
    9.5 Deciding Where to Begin   102

10   ORIENTATION   107

    10.1 General Considerations   107
    10.2 Orienting Department Members   107
    10.3 Orienting Oneself   108
    10.4 Orienting Students   110
    10.5 Orienting Aides and Paraprofessionals   112
    10.6 Orienting Supervisors and Administrators   113
    10.7 Orienting Guidance Counselors   114
    10.8 Orienting Parents   114

11 HUMANIZING RELATIONSHIPS BETWEEN TEACHERS AND STUDENTS — 116

- 11.1 General Considerations — 116
- 11.2 Promoting Synergy — 117
- 11.3 Improving Communication between Teachers and Students — 118
- 11.4 Humanizing and Personalizing Instruction — 122

12 OVERCOMING COMMON MANAGEMENT PROBLEMS — 127

- 12.1 General Considerations — 127
- 12.2 Heavy Teacher Preparation — 128
- 12.3 Efficient Student Use of Class Time — 130
- 12.4 Students' Demands for Attention — 133
- 12.5 Efficient Use of the Teacher's Time — 134
- 12.6 Problems Resulting from Student Misjudgments — 135
- 12.7 Neatness and Order — 136
- 12.8 Student Dissatisfaction with Individualization — 137

13 TESTING, GRADING, AND RECORD KEEPING — 138

- 13.1 General Considerations — 138
- 13.2 Guidelines for Test Construction — 138
- 13.3 Administering Written Tests — 142
- 13.4 Administering Oral Tests — 144
- 13.5 Establishing a Grading System — 146

14 PROGRAM EVALUATION — 151

- 14.1 General Considerations — 151
- 14.2 Feedback from Students — 151
- 14.3 Questionnaires for Student Evaluations — 153
- 14.4 Evaluation of the Individualized Curriculum — 155

PART THREE   TEACHING CONSIDERATIONS

15 TECHNIQUES OF INDIVIDUALIZATION I: PRONUNCIATION, SPELLING, VOCABULARY, GRAMMAR — 161

- 15.1 General Consideration for Part Three — 161
- 15.2 Pronunciation — 161
- 15.3 Spelling — 163
- 15.4 Vocabulary — 164
- 15.5 Grammar — 166

16 TECHNIQUES OF INDIVIDUALIZATION II: LISTENING, SPEAKING, READING, WRITING 170

16.1 Listening Comprehension 170
16.2 Speaking 171
16.3 Reading 178
16.4 Writing 180

17 TECHNIQUES OF INDIVIDUALIZATION III: CULTURE, CIVILIZATION, LITERATURE 183

17.1 Way-of-Life Culture 183
17.2 Civilization and Literature 186

APPENDIX A

Individual Interest Inventory 190
Example of Year-End Goals for a Foreign-Language Curriculum 192
Learning Packet Instructions for a Dialog 196
Learning Packet Instructions for a Reading Text 200

APPENDIX B

Learning Packet Instructions for a Grammar Topic 202
A Shortened Version of Learning Packet Instructions for a Grammar Topic 205
Sample Lesson Plan for a Flexibly Paced Grammar Unit 206
Learning Packet Instructions for a Culture Topic 211

APPENDIX C

Ten Criteria for Evaluating Commercially or Locally Prepared Learning Packets 212
Ideas for Developing Communicative Competence 214
Grammar-Based Exercises to Develop Speaking Ability 215
Ideas for Elective Enrichment Assignments 217

APPENDIX D

Form for Planning an Individualized Curriculum 223
Topics for Student Orientation 225
Foreign-Language Game Expressions (French) 226
Composition Correction Symbols 228

APPENDIX E

Self-Grading Form for Students 229
Program Evaluation Questionnaires 231
Useful Foreign-Language Classroom Expressions (French) 235
Evaluation Sheet for Oral Communication in the Foreign Language 236

INDEX 237

PART ONE
THEORETICAL CONSIDERATIONS

CHAPTER ONE
INDIVIDUALIZED INSTRUCTION: AN OVERVIEW

1.1 GENERAL CONSIDERATIONS

The enormous interest generated by individualization of foreign language instruction is, remarkably, the result of changes begun in the middle and late 1960s at the grass-roots level. Classroom teachers, of their own accord, chose to alter the structure of their classrooms and radically change their traditional teaching roles. In contrast with past reform movements, these changes occurred without the initial guidance and direction of the traditional sources of leadership: professional organizations and teacher-training institutions.

As individualization became more widespread, the foreign-language teaching profession began a serious examination of this approach to learning. What is individualized instruction? Does it work? The first major professional recognition of the movement came in 1970 when the second volume of *The ACTFL Review of Foreign Language Education*[1] focused national attention on its theme, "Individualization of Instruction." Definitions of it appeared in professional literature,[2,3] as did numerous testimonials from classroom teachers who found that individualization worked for them.[4-8] The topic sustained sufficient interest to merit treatment in subsequent volumes of the *ACTFL Review*,[9-12] and the professional journal *Foreign Language Annals* initiated a section devoted to articles on "Individualizing Instruction" that has appeared regularly since October 1971.[13] Just as the 1960s witnessed the audio-lingual era, so the 1970s appear to be the decade of individualized instruction.

1.2 WHAT INDIVIDUALIZED INSTRUCTION IS NOT

Despite the generally favorable press reaction enjoyed by individualized instruction in the early 1970s, some classroom teachers who have used this approach experimentally have met with failure so dismal that they have rejected it as merely another fad in education. Though individualization is not suitable for every teacher and every learner, many painful experiences may be avoided if some common misconceptions about it are exposed.

1.2.1 *Individualization vs. "Do Your Own Thing"*

Individualization is not synonymous with permissiveness. In fact, many early-level programs are characterized by a certain amount of rigidity. In the elementary stages of language learning, students clearly cannot choose whether or not they care to study the present tense. Even in upper-level language classes, a teacher wishing to individualize does not say, "Students, what do you feel like learning today?" (In many cases, the response might be, "Nothing.") Rather, the teacher presents a list of possible subject areas and solicits additional student suggestions.

1.2.2 *Individualization vs. "Let's Write Our Homework in Class"*

Individualization does not mean that the classroom is converted into a study hall. In some narrowly conceived programs, the oral skills have suffered because individualization was limited to different reading or writing assignments. When properly implemented, however, individualization can lead to marked improvement in listening and speaking by providing for small-group conversation practice and for oral testing.

1.2.3 *Individualization vs. Teacher Abandonment*

Individualization does not justify saying to one's classes, "Okay, kiddies, here are your packets. Now go and learn." Increasing students' responsibility for learning does not entail teachers abdicating their responsibilities for explanation, guidance, and direction. Students should not be left alone with their packets any more than they should be left unsupervised in the language lab.

1.2.4 *Individualization vs. Fragmentation and Isolation*

Individualization does not call for teaching the same lesson thirty times, nor does it call for the isolation of the individual learner. Intelligent use of large- and small-group instruction can reduce the necessity of explaining the same topic again and again. It can also provide students with needed opportunities to feel that they are part of a class and to communicate with their friends.

1.3 WHAT INDIVIDUALIZED INSTRUCTION IS

Briefly, individualized instruction is an approach to teaching and learning that offers choices in four areas: objectives of learning, rate of learning, method (or style) of learning, and content of learning. The extent to which choices are offered determines the degree of individualization in a particular program. If a wide variety of choices exists in all four dimensions, then the program may be considered fully realized. Programs that provide fewer areas open to choice may be called uni- or multidimensional. Within this broad category, the type of individualization carried on may be further specified. Programs featuring selection of course objectives are known as "independent study"; those emphasizing variations in learning rates are known as "continuous progress" or "flexibly paced"; those stressing a variety of learning methods or styles are considered "multimedia"; and those offering mainly a choice of content are labeled "mini-courses." Naturally, two or more dimensions may be combined in one program of instruction. One such combination would be continuous progress-multimedia, for example.

In order to bring about individualization, many—though not all—instructors have employed performance objectives, learning packets, and criterion-referenced testing, or all of these techniques.* Many programs—though again, not all—are characterized by some or all of the following features: Students move freely about the room and the school for at least part of the class period, and they learn in full-class groups, small groups, and alone. Testing occurs when students say they are ready to be tested. Classroom personnel includes paraprofessionals† and adult and student aides. Students play an active part in determining their learning activities and their grades. Relationships between teachers and students are personalized and humanized. A wide variety of learning materials and equipment is available for student use either in the classroom or in a resource or media center.** Credit is

---

* Learning packets are discussed at length in Chapter Five, and criterion-referenced testing is explained in Chapter Thirteen.
† A paraprofessional is a noncertified teacher's aide who assists the teacher in either language teaching or clerical duties. The role of paraprofessional personnel is discussed in Chapter Seven.
** A resource or media center houses books, periodicals, and audio-visual equipment and materials that are made available for the use of foreign-language learners.

awarded according to the amount of material mastered, not according to the length of time spent in class. A primary goal is the maintenance—and, it is to be hoped, the increase—of foreign-language enrollments by reducing the number of failures and appealing to individual needs and interests. Various classroom styles of individualization are discussed in Chapter Six.

1.4 INDIVIDUALIZED INSTRUCTION VS. FULL-CLASS TEACHING

Many teachers react to individualized instruction by noting that there is nothing new in its concept. Individualization, they say, has always taken place in the classroom: it is not unusual for a competent and concerned teacher to spend additional time helping an individual with a particular learning problem; it is not extraordinary for teachers to assign enrichment material to unusually capable students; it is not unheard-of to advance a bright class more rapidly through the curriculum. When provisions such as these are made for individual differences, then it is indeed true that the traditional classroom is individualized to a certain extent. However, there is still an important distinction to be made between traditional full-class teaching and a program of individualized instruction. In a teacher-centered situation, attention to individual needs is peripheral to full-class teaching and often must occur after the formal class session has ended. On the other hand, in a student-centered program of individualization, the major goal is to meet—*within* the classroom setting—the varying needs of the students enrolled. With individualization, there is a planned effort to maximize personalized teacher-student contacts and to provide instruction tailored to individual learning requirements. It is the preplanned aspect of individualized instruction that differentiates it from the spontaneous instances of individualization which may—or may not—occur in a traditionally taught class.

1.5 SOME REASONS FOR INITIATING A PROGRAM OF INDIVIDUALIZATION

Teachers who have chosen to change from full-class teaching to an "open-classroom" style of instruction have done so for a multitude of different reasons. Some have elected to change for the wrong reasons: desire to be innovative, compliance with administrative pressures, need to follow the latest educational fad, or fear of taking full responsibility for the success or failure of foreign-language learners. These reasons are termed "wrong" because they show a lack of understanding of what individualization means and a lack of commitment to making it work in one's own situation. There are, though, several "right" reasons for choosing to individualize, as demonstrated by the comments in the following paragraphs.

INDIVIDUALIZED INSTRUCTION: AN OVERVIEW 7

1.5.1 To Promote Student Involvement

Teacher A: "Though I tried my best to be a dynamic "ham actor," I felt that I couldn't maintain complete class attention day in and day out throughout the entire year. Once the novelty of my personality had worn off, I found that my best 'program' couldn't compete successfully with what my students saw on TV. I needed to find a way to involve students more in learning a foreign language."

1.5.2 To Reduce Discipline Problems Resulting from Inattention

Teacher B: "I hoped to remedy discipline problems arising from the need to keep thirty active youngsters quiet for forty-five minutes. If students had been free to talk among themselves for part of the class period, then perhaps they would have listened to me when I asked them to. I never enjoyed constantly having to tell students to pay attention."

1.5.3 To Increase Students' Oral Proficiency

Teacher C: "My students never developed oral fluency in the foreign language when I taught the full class for the entire period. How could they? I spoke at least 50 percent of the time. This left 22½ minutes to be divided up among twenty-five students, some of whom were too shy to talk in front of the whole class. But when I switched to small-group instruction, five students could talk at once without feeling embarrassed."

1.5.4 To Humanize and Personalize Classroom Relationships

Teacher D: "I wanted to get to know my students better and have closer relationships with them. It's hard to do this when you're standing up in front and they're facing you, like enemies almost. Once I moved away from the center, I began to have informal conversations with my students—in the foreign language! I got to know about their families, interests, and problems. They gave truthful, personal answers when in the small groups—not those phony statements they made up when talking to the whole class."

1.5.5 To Provide for Differences in Individual Learners

Teacher E: "I didn't feel comfortable teaching a single lesson to thirty different individuals. Even though my classes were supposed to be 'homogeneous,' there were many times when I knew I was boring the fast learners and confusing the slow ones. I wanted to find a way of permitting bright students to move ahead, while offering additional help—in class, not after school—to those needing it."

1.6 RATIONALE FOR INDIVIDUALIZED INSTRUCTION

As Altman points out,[13] concern for the individual learner is not a new phenomenon of the 1970s, nor is it unique to foreign-language teaching. Over a half century ago, educators devoted considerable attention to "individual differences" among learners and attempted to devise ways of providing for them. Nevertheless, the movement for student-centered instruction has now taken on an importance—even an urgency—that far surpasses that of the past. The reasons for this stem from social, economic, and intellectual changes that characterize contemporary society. Some of these are examined in the following pages.

1.6.1 *Demands of the "New Student"*

The launching of the earth-orbiting satellite Sputnik in 1959 propelled the United States into a feverishly competitive race with the U.S.S.R. for the conquest of space.[14] A key to winning, it was believed, lay in more education for more people. With the nation's honor at stake, Congress passed the National Defense Education Act. For a decade millions of federal dollars poured into all facets of education: textbooks and equipment, building construction and expansion, teacher education, curriculum research and experimentation. Education was viewed not only as a patriotic activity but also as a means for obtaining a good job, financial security, and the "Good Life." Students were urged to stay in school and learn as much as they could. The problem of dropouts became a topic of national concern. A high-school diploma or, preferably, a college degree was seen as a particularly effective avenues of upward mobility for ethnic and racial minority groups. This unity of national purpose, combined with optimistic faith in the value of education, characterized the early and middle 1960s—the period when record numbers of students, born during the postwar baby boom, were entering high school and college. In this expansive atmosphere foreign-language enrollments rose, language labs proliferated, and the value of foreign-language learning was unquestioned. Knowledge of a foreign language was considered valuable both for its intrinsic communication value as well as for extrinsic reasons: admission to colleges and fulfillment of degree requirements.

Toward the end of the 1960s, this situation changed considerably. The traditional values of social institutions—the family, the school, the church—became more and more the focus of doubt and rebellion among students. Severe disturbances on campuses—both in the United States and abroad—led to a reexamination of curriculum offerings. Along with requirements in other fields, foreign-language courses of study were now considered by many as irrelevant or as unnecessary barriers. As a result, these requirements were abolished at many colleges and universities, and enrollments in foreign language courses plunged dramatically at both colleges and secondary schools.[15] Alarmed at this turn of events, the language-teaching profession turned its attention to the so-called new student: "Most people will agree that today's student is of a new breed. He is more aware, more active, and more apt to challenge present practices and values."[16] Under pressure to maintain and increase enrollments as well as hold on to their jobs, educators at all levels of instruction turned to the study of students: their likes and dislikes, their needs and interests, what turns them on and what turns them off. Teaching, of necessity, became more student-centered.

1.6.2 Criticisms of Humanist Educators

The students were not alone in their protests against the form and content of the traditional school curriculum. Teachers, educators, and social thinkers joined in a rising tide of negative criticism. So-called romantic critics such as Holt,[17] Herndon,[18] Hentoff,[19] Kohl,[20] Kozol,[21] and others wrote movingly and persuasively about the harm elementary and secondary schools were doing to children. Schools, they said, stifled creativity, discouraged curiosity, and repressed spontaneity. They bred fear, distrust, and anxiety. Rather than offering students opportunities to explore and discover both the world and themselves, schools placed the highest value on rigid discipline and strict conformity. Instead of encouraging all students to develop their innate abilities, schools operated like Robin Hoods in reverse: They rewarded the rich and took from the poor. Students with intellectual talents succeeded under the system, but those whose socioeconomic or personal background rendered the school environment uncongenial to their needs were robbed—of their self-esteem and of their chances for advancement through education.

These criticisms were corroborated when Silberman, under a Carnegie Foundation grant, made a nationwide tour of schools at all levels and characterized most American classrooms as "grim and joyless."[22] In contrast, he cited the apparently successful "open classrooms" in British infant schools, whose free atmosphere and environment rich in varied resources produced happy, eager, alert youngsters who enjoyed learning. The most radical proposals for the improvement of education came from Illich, who suggested that schools were not necessarily the only or even the best places to learn. Many skills could be acquired elsewhere—in a factory, beside a master craftsman, or on a farm. Intellectual discussions need not be limited to duly enrolled students in certified institutions of learning; they can occur among interested participants in coffee shops or via computer-matched, multiparty telephone hook-ups.[23]

In response to the perceived wrongs of the existing educational system, many "free schools" sprung up as alternatives. Inspired in part by Neill's pioneering efforts,[24] these schools sought to create environments where students were encouraged to care about learning, not about good grades; where cooperation rather than competition was the rule; where the curriculum could be tailored to the needs and interests of individuals; where both students and teachers could participate in democratic decision making. Though financial difficulties caused some schools to close after operating for only a few years, the free-school movement nevertheless exerted considerable impact by pointing out the inadequacies of the established educational system. While a majority of students still seem to succeed under teacher-centered instruction, vast numbers exist whose intellectual and emotional needs are not being met in traditional classrooms. The legacy left by the critics of education and the free-school movement of the late 1960s is the challenge to reform standardized, monolithic institutions so as to provide learning opportunities that are student-centered and individualized.

1.6.3 *Predictions of Futurists*

In our electronic age of increasingly accelerated change, in which the innovations of tomorrow coexist alongside the artifacts of the past, the study of the future has taken on added importance as a means of understanding the present and directing it toward desirable social goals. Some futurist thinkers have contributed ideas on the nature of education in a modern society.

McLuhan[25] states that the printing press serves as the structural model for most contemporary educational institutions. Knowledge is presented in segmented, linear fragments much in the way that letters are arranged for printing. Just as these letters are uniform and interchangeable, so students, teachers, class schedules, and courses of study are divided into similar components to be put together in school-factories whose end product is mass education. The conveyor-belt process was suited to the industrialized society of nineteenth-century America, when large numbers of passive, receptive citizens willingly took their places on assembly and consumption lines. This model, however, is no longer appropriate in the postindustrial, electronic era in which people expect and demand more than minimal physical comfort in exchange for a robotlike existence.

Modern automation and computerization, far from turning men into machines as once feared, have increasingly liberated them from many mind-deadening repetitive tasks. By no means mere extensions of machines, men are increasingly called upon to exercise their powers of human reason on problems that go beyond the limited capacities of machines. By shortening the work week while maintaining or increasing productivity, automation has made possible for many people greater amounts of leisure time as well as more money to spend on recreational activities. Education for our twentieth-century society and beyond requires training in creative thinking and wise use of material and human resources.

Television, the most pervasive communication medium of the electronic era, has exerted considerable impact on the ways students learn. In contrast to the sharp-line clarity and well-defined information of "hot" media such as print, radio, and film, television is a "cool" medium. Its semidistinct image invites the viewer to complete what he sees by supplying connective lines between the myriad dots on the picture tube. Well before children enter school they are formed by television, not only by program content but by the manner in which the content is delivered. The message that television conveys is active participation and involvement in human affairs. It can exert a nearly hypnotic attraction on viewers because of man's natural fascination with himself and extensions of himself. Once accustomed to television's multisensory appeal—to its action, its immediacy, its integration of disparate bits of information into a whole—children may not respond positively in an outmoded classroom where they must passively learn isolated facts organized linearly by a teacher or textbook. To meet the competition from television, schools need to create multimedia environments in which students may interact with each other and become involved in the learning process.

Toffler[26] documents the highly transient nature of a rapidly evolving technological society where only change is permanent. New buildings are demolished to make way for the construction of even newer ones. Thousands of new foods, new materials, new products inundate the market each year. The once stabilizing influence of the family is dissipated as marriages become as disposable as paper tissues or last year's new car. In a world of constant obsolescence, knowledge is rapidly outmoded. Today's career may no longer exist tomorrow, and tomorrow's career may be unknown today. How can education prepare students to meet the challenges of the future?

Since a rapidly changing future promises only uncertainty, it is impossible to predict accurately the knowledge and skills an adult will require during the course of a lifetime. In view of this, Toffler calls for diversity in education and for training in learning how to learn. Society needs skilled people in highly diverse fields so that whatever the future may bring, there will always be a supply of workers with the needed proficiencies. If the skills developed in a person's area of preparation are not in sufficient demand, he needs the ability and resources to retrain himself for new types of work. The current emphasis in schools on memorizing facts is fruitless: Many facts soon become obsolete, and those that do not can be stored and retrieved much more efficiently by using mechanical rather than human memory banks. Instead of stressing memory, schools should place greater value on learning how to find and use available information. Training in research skills and techniques of inquiry should take precedence over rote repetition of the contents of a textbook chapter or a teacher's lecture.

The currently limited nature of most school curriculums is particularly unsuited to an education for the future. Though a common cultural heritage may have been needed during the eighteenth and nineteenth centuries to help assimilate immigrants into the American mainstream, this no longer holds true. Rather than maintaining their currently homogeneous nature, curricula ought to embrace a far greater diversity of courses to reflect the increasingly heterogeneous needs of today's students and tomorrow's citizens.[27]

1.6.4 *Insights of Psychologists*

The futurists' call for education that will prepare students for tomorrow is echoed by psychologist Carl Rogers, who states:

> Teaching and the imparting of knowledge make sense in an unchanging environment. This is why it has been an unquestioned function for centuries. But if there is one truth about modern man, it is that he lives in an environment which is *continually changing.* ... We are, in my view, faced with an entirely new situation in education where the goal of education, if we are to survive, is the *facilitation of change and learning.* The only man who is educated is the man who has learned how to learn; the man who has learned how to adapt and change; the man who has realized that no knowledge is secure, that only the process of *seeking* knowledge gives a basis for security. Changingness, a reliance on *process* rather than upon static knowledge, is the only thing that makes any sense as a goal for education in the modern world.[28]

Rogers states further that teaching is, in his opinion, "a vastly over-rated function."[29] He maintains that it has been traditionally concerned with trivial, inconsequential data. It falsely presupposes the superiority of one person in judging what another needs to know and concerns itself with covering this so-called essential material.

> This notion of coverage is based on the assumption that what is taught is what is learned; what is presented is assimilated. I know of no assumption so obviously untrue. One does not need research to provide evidence that this is false. One needs only to talk with a few students.[30]

What Rogers considers infinitely more significant than teaching is the act of *learning*, not "neck up" learning, which involves only the mind, but *experiential* learning. This more powerful, more significant, and more lasting type of learning involves the whole person—both his mind and his feelings.

> *It is self-initiated.* Even when the impetus or stimulus comes from the outside, the sense of discovery, of reaching out, of grasping and comprehending, comes from within. *It is pervasive.* It makes a difference in the behavior, the attitudes, perhaps even the personality of the learner. *It is evaluated by the learner.* He knows whether it is meeting his need. ... *Its essence is meaning.*[31]

Rogers' view of learning places the students squarely in the center of the educational process. Their goals, their needs, their feelings should be given primacy over institutional demands. The school exists for them; they do not exist for the school. The role of the teacher in this situation is to act as a "facilitator of learning." The teacher does this by providing classroom activities that promote experiential learning. The necessary teaching conditions that Rogers specifies will be dealt with in Chapter Three.

Another psychologist who emphasizes the student's role in the learning process is Abraham Maslow. He takes issue with the Skinnerian theories of operant conditioning, which have dominated educational psychology for the past several decades.* He criticizes stimulus-response learning theory because it takes entirely for granted the goals and needs of the learner. It is concerned solely with means of manipulation toward often unstated ends, ends that may be antithetical to the nature of the learners. What Maslow proposes instead is a "theory of basic needs," a theory of hierarchical goals and ultimate values of the organism. These goals are intrinsically valuable to the organism. It will therefore do anything necessary to achieve these goals, even to learning arbitrary, irrelevant, trivial, or silly procedures that an experimenter may set up as the only way to get to these goals.[32] The five basic human motivators that Maslow postulates are: physiological needs, safety needs, belongingness and love needs, esteem needs, and self-actualization needs. These basic motivators are arranged hierarchically in ascending order. For the most part, as a person moves toward the satisfaction of a lower need, the next higher one emerges to influence his choice of gratifications. A teacher wanting to motivate his students needs to find ways of appealing to their basic needs. Ultimately, student-centered teaching concerns itself with helping learners to develop their innate potentials and to become self-actualizing human beings. The five basic human needs will be discussed in greater detail in Chapter Three; suggestions will also be made for structuring a foreign-language classroom that encourages the satisfaction of these needs.

NOTES

[1] Dale L. Lange, ed., *The ACTFL Review of Foreign Language Education*, vol. 2 (Skokie, Ill.: National Textbook Co., 1970).

[2] Howard B. Altman, "Toward a Definition of Individualized Foreign Language Instruction," *The American Foreign Language Teacher*, vol. 1, no. 3 (Feb. 1971), pp. 12–13.

[3] Ronald L. Gougher, "Defining Individualized Instruction of Foreign Languages," in Ronald L. Gougher, ed., *Individualization of Instruction in Foreign Languages: A Practical Guide* (Chicago: Rand McNally, 1972), pp. 1–5.

[4] Mary B. Flynn, "Individualized Instruction—How I Tried to Resist and Couldn't," *Foreign Language Annals*, vol. 6, no. 2 (Dec. 1972), pp. 257–58.

[5] Marcia Harrell, "The Open Classroom in French," *The American Foreign Language Teacher*, vol. 2, no. 2 (Dec. 1971), pp. 21–22, 45.

[6] Sharon Hellman, "You *Can* Individualize the Teaching of Foreign Languages," *French Review*, vol. 45, no. 6 (May 1972), pp. 1152–60.

[7] Rita O. Kentz, "The Kids Are More Important than the System: An

---

* Skinner's theories as they apply to language learning are discussed in Chapter Two.

Experience with Personalized French Instruction," *The American Foreign Language Teacher*, vol. 3, no. 1 (Fall 1972), pp. 35–37.

[8] Carole L. Krill, "A Confession: We Need to Individualize," *Accent on ACTFL*, vol. 2, no. iv (1972), pp. 6–8.

[9] Ronald L. Gougher, "Individualization of Foreign Language Learning: What Is Being Done?" in Dale L. Lange, ed., *The ACTFL Review of Foreign Language Education*, vol. 3 (Skokie, Ill.: National Textbook Co., 1970), pp. 221–45.

[10] Theodore B. Kalivoda and Robert J. Elkins, "Teaching as Facilitation and Management of Learning," in Dale L. Lange and Charles J. James, eds., *The ACTFL Review of Foreign Language Education*, vol. 4 (Skokie, Ill.: National Textbook Co., 1972), pp. 61–96.

[11] June K. Phillips, "Individualization and Personalization," in Gilbert A. Jarvis, ed., *The ACTFL Review of Foreign Language Education*, vol. 5 (Skokie, Ill.: National Textbook Co., 1974), pp. 219–261.

[12] John F. Bockman and Ronald L. Gougher, "Individualizing Instruction," a section appearing regularly in each issue of *Foreign Language Annals*.

[13] Howard B. Altman, "Individualized Foreign Language Instruction: Ex Uno Plura," in Howard B. Altman, ed., *Individualizing the Foreign Language Classroom: Perspectives for Teachers* (Rowley, Mass.: Newbury House Publishers, 1972), pp. 2–3.

[14] A brief, highly readable account of foreign-language development in the United States prior to the early 1960s may be found in Frank M. Grittner, "Pluralism in Foreign Language Education: A Reason for Being," in Dale L. Lange, ed., *The ACTFL Review of Foreign Language Education*, vol. 3 (Skokie, Ill.: National Textbook Co., 1971), pp. 16–20.

[15] Two comprehensive reviews of foreign-language enrollment statistics are: John P. Dusel, "Surveys and Reports on Foreign Language Enrollments," in Emma M. Birkmaier, ed., *The ACTFL Review of Foreign Language Education*, vol. 1 (Skokie, Ill.: National Textbook Co., 1968), pp. 415–38; and Richard I. Brod, "Trends in Foreign Language Enrollments," in Dale L. Lange, ed., *The ACTFL Review of Foreign Language Education*, vol. 2 (Skokie, Ill.: National Textbook Co., 1970), pp. 341–62. See also Richard I. Brod, "MLA Survey of College Foreign Language Enrollments—Fall 1970," in "FL Notes," in *Foreign Language Annals*, vol. 5, no. 2 (December 1971), pp. 192–96.

[16] Introduction to James W. Dodge, ed., *Foreign Languages and the 'New' Student*. Reports of the Working Committees of the Northeast Conference on the Teaching of Foreign Languages (New York: Modern Language Association Materials Center, 1970).

[17] John Holt, *How Children Learn* (New York: Pitman, 1967); *How Children Fail* (New York: Pitman, 1967); both books also available in paperback (New York: Dell, 1967); *The Underachieving School* (New York: Dell, 1969); *Freedom and Beyond* (New York: Dutton, 1972).

[18] James Herndon, *The Way It Spozed to Be* (New York: Simon and Schuster, 1968); *How to Survive in Your Native Land* (New York: Simon and Schuster, 1971).

[19] Nat Hentoff, *Our Children Are Dying* (New York: Viking Press, 1966).

[20] Herbert Kohl, *36 Children* (New York: New American Library, 1967).

[21] Jonathan Kozol, *Death at an Early Age* (Boston: Houghton Mifflin, 1967).

[22] Charles E. Silberman, *Crisis in the Classroom* (New York: Random House, 1970).

[23] Ivan Illich, *Deschooling Society* (New York: Harper and Row, 1970); Illich et al., eds., *After Deschooling, What?* (New York: Harper and Row, 1973).

[24] A. S. Neill, *Summerhill* (New York: Hart, 1960).

[25] Marshall McLuhan, *Understanding Media: The Extensions of Man* (New York: New American Library, 1964); McLuhan et al., *The Medium Is the Message* (New York: Bantam Books, 1967).

[26] Alvin Toffler, *Future Shock* (New York: Random House, 1970); also available as a Bantam paperback, 1971.

[27] The language-teaching profession's awareness of the importance of diversity is expressed in Dale L. Lange, ed., *The ACTFL Review of Foreign Language Education*, vol. 3 (Skokie, Ill.: National Textbook Co., 1971), whose theme is "Pluralism in Foreign Language Education."

[28] Carl R. Rogers, *Freedom to Learn* (Columbus, Ohio: Charles E. Merrill Publishing Co., 1969), p. 104.

[29] *Ibid.*, p. 103.

[30] *Ibid.*, pp. 103-04.

[31] *Ibid.*, p. 5.

[32] Abraham H. Maslow, *Motivation and Personality* (New York: Harper and Row, 1954; 2nd ed., 1970), pp. 62-64.

CHAPTER TWO
CONTEMPORARY THEORIES OF LANGUAGE LEARNING

2.1 GENERAL CONSIDERATIONS

A program of student-centered foreign-language instruction needs some theoretical basis for the methods and procedures used in the classroom. Though no theory of language learning has been developed specifically for student-centered classrooms, some relevant insights may be gained from examining current, widely held beliefs.

2.2 THE AUDIO-LINGUAL APPROACH

During the post-Sputnik drive to improve the quality of foreign-language teaching, government-established National Defense Education Institutes promoted a new method considered more effective than the then-popular "grammar-translation approach."[1] It incorporated the findings of linguists and psychologists and came to be known as the audio-lingual approach.

2.2.1 *Linguistic Input*

During the 1920s and 1930s the focus of linguistics shifted away from historical studies of language development and toward research into living languages. Working in the field with native speakers of American Indian dialects, linguists set out to learn these languages and create alphabets and grammars for them. Their approach was essentially descriptive rather than prescriptive. From samples of native speech, they sought to discover the meaningful sounds (phonemes) and segments (morphemes) of the language and how they could be combined into acceptable structures (syntax). In their view, language was primarily an oral phenomenon that could and did exist independently of its written forms. Similarly, the patterns of daily living of the members of a society were valid expressions of its culture—even if written records were lacking. Each language, and the culture to which it is inextricably bound, is a unique and worthwhile subject of serious study within itself. It should not be evaluated in terms of other systems, nor should it be forced into models based on European languages and cultures.

As the findings of descriptive or structural linguists such as Bloomfield became more widely disseminated, their ideas and field methods influenced foreign-language classroom practices. According to these new principles, the oral skills of listening and speaking should receive greater initial emphasis than the written skills of reading and writing. Way-of-life culture should take precedence, in the early learning stages, over historical study of civilizations. Learners should progress from the basic sounds of the language to the combination of those sounds into meaningful units and, ultimately, into sentences. Pairs of words contrasting one sound difference would help students differentiate foreign language sounds and produce them. Dialogues would be preferable to narratives for introducing new vocabulary and structure, since they represent oral speech patterns. Practice in substituting given items for elements in a model sentence would help students infer the appropriate forms of the language as well as its structural rules. Spelling would be taught by showing what written symbols correspond to the sounds that have been learned. Initial reading texts would follow very closely materials that had already been practiced orally. Expressive, free writing would follow in later stages of learning. Since native speakers learn language through constant practice and use—not via memorizing rules or analyzing sentences—second-language learners would need to concentrate on talking the language, not talking about it. Similarly, they would acquire language skills in the natural order of listening, speaking, reading, and writing.

2.2.2 *Psychological Input*

During the period when the ideas of structural linguists were gaining greater currency, learning psychology in the United States was dominated by the behaviorist school. Skinner,[2] the leading proponent of behaviorist theories, claimed that language acquisition resulted from stimulus-response conditioning. Stimulated by physical needs for comfort, a baby makes random babbling responses. When certain combinations of sounds are rewarded by the satisfaction of the child's desires, they are reinforced and are more likely to recur under similar circumstances. Sound combinations not comprehended (and rewarded) by others are extinguished, that is, eliminated from the child's repertoire of behavioral responses. In Skinner's view, language acquisition is a matter of proper habit formation. Natives gain linguistic fluency by repeated practice, or conditioning, which develops in them automatic, reflexive response patterns.

Translated to an audio-lingual classroom, Skinner's ideas resulted in emphasis on automaticity, overlearning, and reinforcement. Dialogue lines had to be memorized and recited without hesitation at nearly-native speed. Responses to pattern practice stimuli needed to be immediate and rapid, with no time allowed for thinking. Major portions of class time were devoted to practicing oral responses, both chorally and individually. Language laboratories offered students additional practice of the same materials, but with taped instead of live speech models. Correct student responses were reinforced either through teacher praise or repetition. Incorrect responses were called to the students' attention for self-correction. Insofar as possible, the nature of student responses was carefully limited to what students already knew in order to minimize the possibility of their making errors. Not until students had gained automatic control over the sound and structural patterns of the language, through reinforcement, were they permitted to express themselves freely. Throughout the mimicry-memorization-drill phase, lexical meaning was subordinated to production of sounds and sentences. Students learned grammar inductively via analogy *after* practicing item-substitution drills. Comprehensive analyses and discussions of grammar rules were to come later, after students had become familiar with the patterns of the language and had developed automatic responses.

2.3 REACTIONS AGAINST AUDIO-LINGUALISM

Though classical audio-lingual methodology as expounded by Brooks[3] and Lado[4] generated considerable initial controversy and disagreement in professional circles, the movement, with its NDEA-conferred seal of approval, gained popularity and increasing numbers of converts in the early and middle 1960s. Toward the end of the decade, however, second thoughts arose as problems with implementing the method were encountered in the classroom. The renewed doubts and criticisms emanated from several quarters: teachers, linguists, and psychologists.

2.3.1 *Teachers' Reactions*

In the audio-lingual classroom, the teacher's position is absolutely central. As the source of authentic models of the foreign language, the teacher's role resembles that of the native speaker in the field studies done by descriptive linguists. When stimulating and reinforcing students' language responses, the teacher acts like a behavioral psychologist in the laboratory. Although this pivotal role appeals to the histrionic and authoritarian needs of some teaching personalities, it often may fall short of expectations in daily classroom use.

A serious flaw in Skinnerian learning psychology is that its original behaviorist approach is limited strictly to the study of observable physical phenomena; it excludes from consideration abstractions such as the feelings and attitudes of learners, which cannot be subjected to objective scrutiny. As it turns out, however, real-life learners are neither as well motivated as professional linguistic researchers nor are they as compliant as laboratory rats and pigeons. Though many students do indeed learn via the audio-lingual approach, scores of others do not. They are bored. They refuse to mimic, refuse to memorize, refuse to copy, and refuse to practice over and over. Even successful students rebel at times. They want to know the exact meaning of each word they are saying, not some generalized, overall notion of the ideas in each sentence. Many object to waiting periods of weeks or months before they are permitted to see the written text of the language they had to learn orally. Many need grammar explanations *before* they perform pattern drills, rather than afterward. Many want skill in reading and writing much sooner than officially sanctioned learning schedules allow.

As a matter of practical classroom survival, many teachers have been forced to abandon audio-lingual orthodoxy. In acquiescing to student demands for more meaning, they have reverted to some of the mentalist theories of the grammar-translation approach under which they themselves, for the most part, had acquired foreign language skills. Parallel trends, though for different reasons, have occurred among linguists and psychologists.

2.3.2 *Linguists' Objections*

In a devastating critique, Chomsky[5] took issue with Skinner's contention that verbal behavior does not differ significantly from other forms of human behavior. Stimulus-response conditioning was an inadequate explanation of innovative, creative uses of language. Behaviorist theory could not account for a speaker's ability to produce a novel utterance and be understood by others who have never previously heard that utterance. What may explain the stimulus-free nature of normal linguistic behavior is that

> ...the native speaker of a language has internalized a "generative grammar"—a system of rules that can be used in new and untried combinations to form new sentences.[6]

Generative-transformational theorists believe that a speaker, in communicating meaning, proceeds hierarchically from basic kernel sentences through subsequent transformations and refinements that lead to the appropriate surface forms.[7] Their approach contrasts with that of the traditional descriptive linguists, who concentrated on the formal features of sentence elements.

Linguists who adhere to the generative-transformational theory seek to discover the laws that govern the acquisition and creative manipulation of a native language and, ultimately perhaps, a universal grammar controlling all language learning. This view of language as a unique and innate human capacity is supported by Lenneberg.[8] He finds that all normal children gain control of their native languages to comparable extents at roughly the same ages, no matter how structurally complex those languages may be. While learning to speak, children select simple elements of communication that, as they mature, they become capable of incorporating into more complex structures. Language development is therefore predetermined by human biology, as well as by cultural and environmental factors; it is not purely a result of imitation and reinforcement.[9]

A basic idea of generative-transformational theory is the distinction between linguistic competence and linguistic performance. Competence refers to the native's knowledge of whether sentences he hears or produces are grammatical or not. This competence is innate and intuitive; it exists independently of the native's ability to articulate the rules governing correct language usage. Performance refers to actual production of utterances in real-life communication situations. This performance, however, does not reflect the speaker's basic competence. Inattention or emotional or time pressures may cause certain slips or lapses to enter into a native's speech. These are not errors, in the true sense, since the speaker is capable of correcting them when made aware of what he has said.[10]

Jakobovits[11] extends this distinction. Second-language students may demonstrate linguistic competence in their control of drill patterns yet may be completely incapable of communicating their own ideas in performance situations. Conversely, some students seem able to speak freely even though lacking completely accurate control of all grammatical features. This would seem to indicate that an effective language course must train students both in competence *and* in performance. This is a challenge to the imagination and ingenuity of the individual foreign language teacher, since Chomsky makes no specific suggestions for classroom methods. He believes that one role of an experienced teacher is to validate or refute, in his own classroom, the theoretical findings of linguistics.[12]

2.3.3 Psychological Considerations

In a careful, thorough, and scholarly work, Rivers[13] examines some of the basic premises of audio-lingual theory in light of what is known about general human learning. Briefly, her well-documented findings include these points: foreign-language learning is not exclusively a mechanical process of habit formation; a student's internal perceptions and understandings determine whether his motivational state promotes or inhibits language acquisition. Though habits are strengthened by repetition and reinforcement, overlearning can lead to boredom and fatigue, which reduce the desire to perform. Furthermore, the development of stereotyped, fixed answers can result in loss of flexibility in new and unfamiliar response situations. Rather than merely inducing students to behave for some external purpose, teachers need to appeal to intrinsic motivators: student desires to experience achievement, learning progress, and the satisfactions of communicating in another language. Contrary to common audio-lingual doctrine, there is no reason to believe that the conditions of second-language learning resemble those of native-language acquisition. Since the two situations are so dissimilar, it makes little sense to follow the "natural" developmental order of language skills. Rigid adherence to lengthy periods of pure aural-oral training denies the existence of students' reading and writing abilities and, worse, by appealing to only one sense modality deprives many learners of the visual support they need. The result is tension and anxiety. Furthermore, it has been shown that time lags of varying length between oral and written skills have less positive effect on the development of sound pronunciation and spelling skills than learner aptitude and teacher vigilance do. Finally, learning grammar solely through pattern practice and analogy breaks down on several counts: The unguided learner may make logical analogies that are nonetheless false. The inductive method ignores the fundamental human desire to understand what one is doing, to perceive the underlying structure and relatedness of a whole concept, or *gestalt*. This understanding, which must involve analysis, works not only as an aid to memory, but also promotes an ultimate teaching aim, the transfer of learning to new communication settings. Rivers believes that both analogy and analysis have a rightful place in foreign language instruction. "... Analysis, and the understanding of structure are essential for the overall direction of communication, whereas analogy is a useful procedure for automatizing the details of language structure at the manipulative level."[14]

2.4 LINGUISTICS IN THE 1970s

Quinn,[15] in reviewing and evaluating the accomplishments and limitations of linguistics during the 1960s, notes what he considers to be two areas of significant failure. First, the descriptions of grammar in commonly used language textbooks show remarkably little change during the 1960s; second, the attempts to sensitize teachers to the nature of linguistic phenomena have not met with widespread success. He further states that the high-level, abstract, and theoretical argumentation that dominates generative-transformational linguistic theory in the 1970s seems to offer little cause to believe that foreign-language instructors may soon base teaching strategies upon findings in this field. Research in the area of error analysis, though, does offer some promise of greater insight into the processes of foreign-language learning.

From the standpoint of practical classroom application, perhaps the most significant recent trend is the emphasis on teaching and testing for "communicative competence." In reporting the results of her research, Savignon states that discrete items that test specific aspects of grammar acquisition do not correlate with a student's ability to express ideas fluently and comprehensibly. In an experiment where a group was given specific training in communicating information—without regard to strict grammatical accuracy—it was shown that these learners expressed greater satisfaction with their accomplishment and were more highly motivated than students who had practiced in the language lab or had attended culture sessions presented in English. Savignon concludes:

> For some students, clearly, learning about a foreign culture in English can be a worthwhile adjunct or even alternative to the study of a foreign language. For others, the development of communicative competence offers a more meaningful experience with the cross-cultural context. There is no evidence, however, that the study of a foreign culture increases a student's interest in learning the language. Interest in learning the language appears, rather, to be a function of past success. To the extent that the student does well in his foreign-language course, he will want to continue. The teacher who is willing to broaden his own objectives, allowing for different interests and styles of learning, will increase the opportunity for the individual student to experience that success.[16]

NOTES

[1] Excellent discussions of pre–audio-lingual methodology, as well as extensive bibliographies, can be found in Kenneth Chastain, *The Development of Modern Language Skills: Theory to Practice* (Chicago: Rand McNally, 1971), pp. 7–29, and in Wilga M. Rivers, *Teaching Foreign Language Skills* (Chicago: The University of Chicago Press, 1968), pp. 1–24 and 30–31.

[2] B. F. Skinner, *Verbal Behavior* (New York: Appleton-Century-Crofts, 1957).

[3] Nelson Brooks, *Language and Language Learning* (New York: Harcourt Brace Jovanovich, 1960, 1st ed.; 1964, 2nd ed.).

[4] Robert Lado, *Language Teaching: A Scientific Approach* (New York: McGraw-Hill Book Co., 1964).

[5] Noam Chomsky, "Review of Skinner's 'Verbal Behavior,'" *Language*, vol. 35 (1959), pp. 26–58, reprinted in Jerry A. Fodor and Jerrold J. Katz, eds., *The Structure of Language: Readings in the Philosophy of Language* (Englewood Cliffs, N.J.: Prentice-Hall, 1964; also in L. A. Jakobovits and M. S. Miron, eds., *Readings in the Psychology of Language* (Englewood Cliffs, N.J.: Prentice-Hall, 1967).

[6] Noam Chomsky, "Linguistic Theory," in Robert G. Mead, Jr., ed., *Language Teaching: Broader Contexts*. Reports of the Working Committees of the Northeast Conference on the Teaching of Foreign Languages. (New

York: Modern Language Association Materials Center, 1966), p. 46; reprinted in John W. Oller, Jr., and Jack C. Richards, eds., *Focus on the Learner* (Rowley, Mass.: Newbury House Publishers, 1973), pp. 29–35.

[7] Noam Chomsky, *Syntactic Structures* (The Hague: Mouton, 1957) and *Aspects of the Theory of Syntax* (Cambridge, Mass.: M.I.T. Press, 1965).

[8] Eric Lenneberg, *Biological Foundations of Language* (New York: John Wiley and Sons, 1967).

[9] The fascinating topic of language acquisition by children is treated in greater detail in the following recommended sources: Wilga M. Rivers, *Teaching Foreign Language Skills* (Chicago: The University of Chicago Press, 1968), pp. 71–76, and bibliography, p. 101; Kenneth Chastain, *The Development of Modern Language Skills: Theory to Practice* (Chicago: Rand McNally, 1971), pp. 101–20.

[10] Brief treatments of generative-transformational linguistics may be found in Rivers (see note 1), pp. 64–67 and 73–74; and Chastain (see note 1), pp. 79–85 and 89–92.

[11] Leon A. Jakobovits, *Foreign Language Learning: A Psycholinguistic Analysis of the Issues* (Rowley, Mass.: Newbury House Publishers, 1970), p. 49.

[12] Noam Chomsky, "Linguistic Theory," in Robert Mead, Jr., ed., *Language Teaching: Broader Contexts*. Reports of the Working Committees of the Northeast Conference on the Teaching of Foreign Languages. (New York: Modern Language Association Materials Center, 1970), p. 45.

[13] Wilga M. Rivers, *The Psychologist and the Foreign Language Teacher* (Chicago: The University of Chicago Press, 1964).

[14] *Ibid.*, p. 129; another helpful and more recent review of research in language learning is found in Chastain (see note 1), pp. 124–42. Recent findings of cognitive psychology are presented in David P. Ausubel, *Educational Psychology: A Cognitive View* (New York: Holt, Rinehart, and Winston, 1968). A useful examination of several linguistic theories as applied to language instruction is presented in Karl Conrad Diller, *Generative Grammar, Structural Linguistics, and Language Teaching* (Rowley, Mass.: Newbury House Publishers, 1971).

[15] Terence J. Quinn, "Theoretical Foundations in Linguistics and Related Fields," in Gilbert A. Jarvis, ed., *The ACTFL Review of Foreign Language Education*, vol. 5 (Skokie, Ill.: National Textbook Co., 1974).

[16] Sandra J. Savignon, *Communicative Competence: An Experiment in Foreign-Language Teaching* (Philadelphia: Center for Curriculum Development, 1972), p. 65.

CHAPTER THREE
HUMANISTIC THEORIES OF MOTIVATION AND MANAGEMENT

3.1 GENERAL CONSIDERATIONS

In the preceding chapter some theories of language learning were examined. In developing an individualized, student-centered program, one cannot limit consideration solely to the intellectual (or cognitive) domain. The learner's feelings (or affective domain) must also command serious thought and attention. Reason and emotion are inextricably joined in each learner; both play active roles in the process of instruction. A teaching strategy that ignores or minimizes the importance of feelings, one which views students in narrow cognitive terms, not only underestimates the scope of human nature but seriously limits the strategy's classroom effectiveness. In the hope that the affective dimension of learning will receive more widespread emphasis in the future than it has in the past, this chapter is devoted to theories of motivation and ways of implementing them in the classroom.[1]

3.2 MASLOW'S "NEEDS" THEORY OF MOTIVATION

Maslow[2] proposes five basic needs—physiological needs, safety needs, belongingness and love needs, esteem needs, and self-actualization needs—that humanistic education should aim to satisfy. He lists these human needs in the following hierarchical order, proceeding from the lowest to the highest.

3.2.1 *Physiological Needs*

Physiological needs are the most "prepotent" of the five basic human needs. A person lacking food or water, or experiencing some other fundamental biological need, attempts to satisfy these primary needs before turning attention toward higher goals.

3.2.2 *Safety Needs*

If physiological needs are relatively well satisfied, then safety needs emerge. These include needs for security; protection; freedom from fear, anxiety, and chaos; structure, order, law, limits; and strength in the protector.

> The average child and, less obviously, the average adult in our society generally prefers a safe, orderly, predictable, lawful, organized world, which he can count on and in which unexpected, unmanageable, chaotic, or other dangerous things do not happen, and in which, in any case, he has powerful parents or protectors who shield him from harm.[3]

> Child psychologists, teachers, and psychotherapists have found that permissiveness within limits, rather than unrestricted permissiveness, is preferred as well as *needed* by children.[4]

3.2.3 *Belongingness and Love Needs*

Belongingness and love needs become more prominent once physiological and safety requirements are fairly well met. Maslow sees the spread of workshops that train participants to develop their sensitivity and ability to communicate as motivated in part by an

> ... unsatisfied hunger for contact, for intimacy, for belongingness and by the need to overcome the widespread feelings of alienation, aloneness, strangeness, and loneliness, which have been worsened by our mobility, by the breakdown of traditional groupings, the scattering of families, the generation gap, the steady urbanization and disappearance of village face-to-faceness, and the resulting shallowness of American friendship.[5]

He believes that to some degree the formation of rebel groups by young people, as well as some emotional disturbances, are caused by the thwarting of belongingness and love needs.

3.2.4 Esteem Needs

The esteem needs that emerge, usually, after belongingness and love needs are more or less satisfied fall into two categories.

> [First, there is] ... the desire for strength, for achievement, for adequacy, for mastery and competence, for confidence in the face of the world, and for independence and freedom. Second, we have what we may call the desire for reputation or prestige, ... status, fame and glory, dominance, recognition, attention, importance, dignity, or appreciation.... Satisfaction of the self-esteem need leads to feelings of self-confidence, worth, strength, capability and adequacy, of being useful and necessary in the world. But thwarting of these needs produces feelings of inferiority, or weakness, and of helplessness. These feelings in turn give rise to either basic discouragement or else compensatory or neurotic trends.[6]

> The most stable and therefore most healthy self-esteem is based on *deserved* respect from others rather than on external fame or celebrity and unwarranted adulation.[7]

3.2.5 Self-Actualization Needs

Even when individuals satisfy all the aforementioned needs, they may still be expected to develop a new restlessness and discontent unless they succeed in doing what *they*, as individuals, are suited to do.

> A musician must make music, an artist must paint, a poet must write, if he is to be ultimately at peace with himself. What a man *can* be, he *must* be. He must be true to his own nature. This need we may call self-actualization.... This term ... refers to man's desire for *self-fulfillment*, namely, to the tendency for him to become actualized in what he is potentially. This tendency might be phrased as the desire to become more and more what one idiosyncratically is, to become everything that one is capable of becoming.... *At this level, individual differences are greatest.*[8] [Italics in last sentence added by the present author.]

3.3 MEETING BASIC NEEDS IN THE CLASSROOM

For Maslow the most effective teachers are those who may be characterized as self-actualized human beings. Such teachers behave

> ... in a very unneurotic way by interpreting the whole [teaching] situation differently, e.g., as a pleasant collaboration rather than as a clash of wills, of authority, of dignity, etc.; the replacement of artificial dignity—that is easily and inevitably threatened—with the natural simplicity that is *not* easily threatened; the giving up of the attempt to be omniscient and omnipotent; the absence of student-threatening authoritarianism; the refusal to regard the students as competing with each other or with the teacher; the refusal to assume the professor stereotype and the insistence on remaining as

realistically human as, say, a plumber or a carpenter; all of these create a classroom atmosphere in which suspicion, wariness, defensiveness, hostility, and anxiety tend to disappear.[9]

Though Maslow does not offer specific suggestions on structuring the classroom environment so as to further the self-actualization of students, an attempt will be made here to extrapolate from his general remarks some concrete practices applicable to individualized foreign-language classes.

3.3.1 Meeting Physiological Needs

Except for some highly unusual cases, it may be assumed that students' physiological needs are largely met by their parents. It may also be assumed that the overwhelming majority of school plants provide adequate physical comfort in terms of space, heat, light, and so on. One area, however, to which a teacher might contribute is that of the students' needs for physical activity and movement. By providing students opportunities to get up and walk around during class, a teacher can minimize the restlessness and boredom that can, on a daily basis, become painful for students and inhibit their willingness and ability to learn.

3.3.2 Meeting Safety Needs

Here too, it may be assumed that the vast majority of school buildings provide adequate physical safety. The students' psychological safety, however, is equally important. They need to know what they may and may not do in class, and what the consequences of their various behaviors will be. They need assurance that the announced policies will be carried out fairly and consistently. They must have a clear idea of what they are to learn, how they can demonstrate their learning, and how their performance will be evaluated. They must feel protected from sudden, arbitrary, or random changes in class structure or procedure.

Teachers provide for these safety needs when they communicate to students their idiosyncratic classroom policies: on gum chewing, on talking, on coming prepared to work, on absences, and so on. Teachers may state the rationales for these rules and the punishments for not following them. They let students know the long-term and immediate short-term learning goals of the course and make clear their grading criteria.

This information may be communicated orally or it may be included in an orientation booklet to be given to each student at the beginning of the year. Performance objectives written for each unit of work help students understand clearly what they are to learn and how they will be graded. By specifying their expectations at the outset, teachers can reduce students' anxieties and uncertainties relating to classroom procedures and course requirements.

3.3.3 *Meeting Belongingness and Love Needs*

In a predominantly teacher-centered classroom it is difficult to meet students' needs for belongingness and love. When students sit in rows facing front, speak one at a time when called upon, and talk about factual material to the teacher—rather than to their peers—they have little opportunity to satisfy their affective needs. Students who *do* feel they belong are most often among the small handful of highly intelligent and successful class members. Those who feel loved are very likely the ones who have many friends outside of class or the relatively few who enjoy an unusually good relationship with the teacher. With the exception of this fortunate minority, the belongingness and love needs of most students remain unfilled in the traditionally structured classroom, though, for many, they may be filled by family members and friends outside of class.

If the affective needs of this majority are to be met in class, the very structure of the teaching situation must be changed so that it becomes student-centered. By promoting small-group activities and one-to-one relationships, a teacher can encourage the development of cohesive groups of friends who stick together and feel responsible for each other. Instead of just one focus of attention—the teacher—there are many to which students may turn. Feelings of belongingness and love are much more likely to emerge when pairs or small groups are actively involved in a task or problem that has particular relevance for them, rather than on some general, impersonal topic proposed for class discussion.

3.3.4 *Meeting Esteem Needs*

Though the first three human needs—for physiological comfort, safety, and belongingness and love—may be met largely in the home, this is less the case with esteem needs. As students broaden their social contacts, their self-concepts depend not only upon the judgments of their families but, to a considerable degree, on the evaluations of teachers and peers. Since students spend a large part of their waking day in school, beginning in early childhood and onward to late adolescence, the success or failure they encounter there is a vital element in the development of their self-esteem. It is in the school context, too, that learners seek to earn the esteem of others.

Esteem needs can be legitimately met in several ways in the classroom. Students' opinions of themselves and their feelings of worth in relation to a given skill are largely determined by their achievements in that area. A teacher can—and indeed should—promote a sense of adequacy and self-confidence in students by maximizing their opportunities for classroom success. This may entail: offering students greater responsibility for self-evaluation; tolerating grammar mistakes that do not interfere with comprehensibility; providing remedial instruction when difficulties are encountered; and permitting greater student freedom and responsibility in making decisions regarding use of class time, goals of instruction, methods of learning, and so on. Requiring students to master new material to 80 or 90 percent accuracy (with several retests offered) may confer a measure of self-confidence on learners accustomed to being satisfied with much lower achievement levels. Such a grading system, which encourages most learners to reach fairly high minimum standards, contrasts with the practice, in traditionally taught classrooms, of fostering competition among students for the few high grades that are awarded.

Students can gain the esteem of their peers through the status their knowledge and skills earn. Opportunities for self-distinction in traditional classrooms are usually limited to supplying correct answers and perhaps running errands for the teacher, activities which can lead as easily to alienation from one's peers as to the approval of the group. In a student-centered class, however, there is much greater diversity of acceptable, status-bearing roles. Students may demonstrate their competence, without arousing hostility, by serving as peer teachers or conversation-group leaders. If they choose, they may be freed from regular class activities to work on independent projects or even to play language-related games. The additional roles open to the competent learners need not arouse the jealousies or animosities of less able students, since they result naturally from demonstrated proficiency. The freedoms and privileges of successful learners result from their own individual efforts and achievements, not from the apparent favor of the teacher. The learners thus perceive that their objective accomplishments result in respect and recognition, and their self-images are enhanced.

3.3.5 *Meeting Self-Actualization Needs*

Helping students actualize their highest innate capacities is the greatest and most difficult challenge to classroom teachers, as well as, potentially, their most fulfilling reward. Teachers who aim to achieve their own professional self-actualization center not on themselves but on the learners in their classes. These teachers accept their students as they are rather than as how they wish the students were. They recognize their students' unique talents, interests, and limitations.

Acutely aware of the great individual differences among learners, these teachers aim to provide variety and choice in the classroom. Early in the year, they may ask students to complete questionnaires relating to their language-course goals, career ambitions, preferred leisure activities, and individual skills or interests. They may explain to students that the only purpose of the questionnaires is to help in promoting their success in the classroom, but, if any questions are considered too personal, they need not answer them.*
Having considered the information received, teachers may plan for a variety of classroom materials—texts, tapes, slides, flashcards, and so on, relating to

---

* An example of such a questionnaire may be found in Appendix A.

various areas of interest—and for a considerable number of learning choices: pace, nature of testing, subject matter, preferred method of learning, and so on. In dealing with their classes, these teachers respect the needs of their students and offer alternatives for learning suited to the individual. They suggest rather than impose; guide rather than lead; develop rather than mold. They seek not to impose their own personalities, interests, and goals upon the learners, but to work with them to discover ways they might move toward self-actualization in their learning activities.

3.4 ROGERS: FACILITATING FREEDOM TO LEARN

In *Freedom to Learn* Rogers focuses on the qualities teachers must possess in order to make possible self-initiated, experiential, "gut-level" learning. This significant type of learning is not brought about via special methods or textbooks or audio-visual equipment. Rather, it is the result of certain attitudes that characterize teachers' relationships with their students. Rogers cites research data[10] supporting his thesis that the following qualities enhance student learning.[11]

3.4.1 *Realness*

Teachers do not play roles. They are themselves and express their real feelings. They separate their honest reactions to students' work from personal judgments on the students themselves. They share their legitimate feelings with students in an honest, open manner. They communicate to students their anger or frustration as readily as their pleasure and satisfaction.

3.4.2 *Prizing, Acceptance, Trust*

The teachers value the learners as worthwhile human beings and care for them, though in a nonpossessive way. They accept the learners' feelings of fear, hesitancy, or rebellion as readily as their own feelings of satisfaction with achievement. They have a basic trust and confidence in the learners' capacities for development.

3.4.3 *Empathic Understanding*

The teachers are capable of placing themselves in the learners' situations and looking at the classroom from the learners' points of view. They do this without judging or analyzing the learners.

3.5 GLASSER: ELIMINATING FAILURE

A third psychologist whose ideas are beginning to influence contemporary education is William Glasser. He believes that a major cause of problems in the schools—truancy, disruptiveness, underachievement—is the fact that students fail. Repeated experiences of failure, he maintains, build up in students negative self-images that, if allowed to continue permanently, lock a student into a pattern of failure that may be impossible to break. Glasser proposes that schools eliminate failure by awarding only A's and B's, since these are the only two grades that are generally considered "good." In addition, he suggests regular class meetings of students seated in a circle in order to discuss scholastic or personal problems. In this context the teacher attempts to create an accepting, supportive atmosphere that helps build trust and self-confidence.[12] At least one foreign-language program that has adapted Glasser's ideas is reported in professional literature.[13]

3.6 McGREGOR: THEORY-X AND THEORY-Y MANAGEMENT

In *The Human Side of Enterprise*[14] Douglas McGregor postulates a theory of humanistic management based on Maslow's theory of basic human needs. According to McGregor, a manager who wishes to promote the creativity and productivity of his staff needs to create working conditions that tend to satisfy the needs of those working under him. Rewards such as higher pay, larger fringe benefits, and better working conditions serve as incentives only as long as lower needs for physiological comfort and safety have been previously met. Once these are fairly well satisfied, however, workers tend to seek fulfillment of their higher needs: belongingness and love, esteem, and self-actualization. Since an individualized, student-centered classroom must depend to a considerable extent on the willing participation of learners—as contrasted with the obligatory compliance of students in a teacher-centered classroom—then management procedures that motivate students to work productively in class assume considerable importance.[15]

McGregor identifies two major types of management views of human nature: Theory X and Theory Y. Theory-X managers have a negative, pessimistic outlook. They believe that most people dislike work and seek to avoid it. Therefore, they must be closely supervised and threatened with punishment if they do not perform up to job expectations. Since most people prefer to avoid responsibility and lack strong ambition, the rewards they desire fall mainly in the area of security. This outlook is easily translatable to the traditional school situation, where teachers mistrust students and view them as lazy and unwilling to learn, and where threats of low grades and failure are used as motivations for scholastic achievements.

By contrast, Theory-Y managers exhibit a more positive and trusting approach. They believe that most people enjoy stimulating and creative work, that they are capable of self-control and self-direction, and that they both accept and seek further responsibility as they strive toward the actualization of their innate talents and unique abilities. It is this humanistic outlook that is needed in an individualized program of foreign-language instruction.

3.7 MASLOW'S EUPSYCHIAN MANAGEMENT

In elaborating on McGregor's work, Maslow comes out in favor of Theory-Y management, which he terms "eupsychian," that is, that which moves toward psychological health. It also implies actions that may be taken by a manager, psychotherapist, or teacher to encourage such a movement.[16] Among the assumptions upon which eupsychian management rests are the following: everyone is to be trusted; all people have the impulse to achieve; there is good will rather than rivalry or jealousy in the organization; human needs are not satisfied at the level of safety needs; there is an active trend to self-actualization; everyone can enjoy good teamwork, friendship, and love; hostility is primarily reactive rather than character-based. Maslow contends that people are improvable and want to improve the things around them, and that they need to feel important, needed, useful, successful, proud, and respected. He maintains that people prefer meaningful work to idleness and that the wisdom and efficacy of a person's choices must be trusted. There is a preference for uniqueness as a person in contrast to being anonymous or interchangeable. Maslow suggests that people will get more pleasure out of loving than out of hating, that they would rather create than destroy, and that they prefer to be interested rather than bored.[17]

Maslow is aware that these assumptions are possible only in cases where social conditions are good, where there is no lack of essential goods and services, and where there are ample rewards for all. He also acknowledges that "a certain proportion of the population cannot take responsibility well and is frightened by freedom ... (and) ... will not respond well to good conditions."[18] He adds that

> ...we don't really have exact and quantitative information on the proportion of the human population which does in fact have some kind of feeling for workmanship...some sort of desire for efficiency over inefficiency.[19]

Nevertheless, he states

> ...there is insufficient grounding for a firm and final trust in Theory-Y management philosophy; but then I would hastily add that there is even less firm evidence for Theory X. If one adds up all the researches ... practically all of them come out on the side of... Theory Y; practically none of them come out in favor of Theory-X philosophy except in small and detailed and specific special circumstances.[20]

Though Maslow asserts initially that the assumptions of eupsychian management are "articles of faith rather than articles of final knowledge, or ... articles of faith with some grounding in fact,"[21] he ultimately comes to the conclusion that

> There is empirical evidence to support Theory Y for most American citizens, and there is empirical evidence to disconfirm Theory X for most American citizens. It can almost be called fact "X" and fact "Y."[22]

Despite his strong conviction that Theory Y is indeed a workable, and even preferable, management philosophy, Maslow is far from a wide-eyed liberal idealist. He is acutely aware that in some situations Theory-Y management principles should not be employed. "That management policy ... is best which best fits the objective requirements of the objective situation."[23]

Maslow pointedly illustrates this pragmatic and realistic attitude:

> The correct thing to do with authoritarians is to take them realistically for the bastards they are and then behave toward them as if they were bastards. That is the only realistic way to treat bastards. If one smiles at them and assumes that trusting them and giving them the key to the pantry is going to reform them suddenly, then all that will happen is that the silver will get stolen, and also they will become contemptuous of the "weak" [people] ... whom they will see as spineless, stupid, unmasculine sheep to be taken advantage of. I have found whenever I ran across authoritarian students that the best thing for me to do was to break their backs immediately, that is, to affirm my authority immediately ... Once this was accepted, *then*, and only then, could I ... slowly ... teach them that it is possible for a boss, a strong man, a man with a fist, to be kind, gentle, permissive, trusting, and so on. And there's no question about it, that if the authoritarian disease has not gone too far, this kind of management will actually change the world outlook and the character of these people and reform them, at least some of them, over toward becoming democratic rather than authoritarian.[24]

3.8 EUPSYCHIAN MANAGEMENT VS. CURRENT CLASSROOM REALITIES

Some readers may react negatively to the preceding section. "Where," they might ask, "are all those Theory-Y learners? There weren't any in the classes we've taught." It is true that the reality of most of today's classrooms is a far cry from the portraits drawn by McGregor and Maslow. Few students seem to exhibit strong yearnings to learn. For many, the name of the game seems to be earning the highest grades possible for the least amount of work. Many students neglect even to bring their books to class, much less to take them home for study. Homework seems to be hopelessly outmoded for large numbers of them. In such situations it seems both impossible and inadvisable to maintain Theory-Y management principles.

In instances where this seems to be the case, perhaps a compromise principle can be instituted: Theory Y over X ($\frac{Y}{X}$). Management then operates initially and overtly according to Theory Y: students enjoy freedom of movement in the classroom and exercise a measure of control or choice over their activities. They may decide, in a limited way, which among several assignments they will complete, and they may also select dates on which they feel ready to be tested. Opportunities for success are maximized through the use of individually prescribed remedial exercises, personal guidance and counseling, several opportunities for retesting, and extra-credit assignments. To supplement the teacher's efforts, peer tutors as well as paraprofessional personnel are available to help with specific learning problems. A wide variety of materials is provided to appeal to individual interests and learning styles, and so on. (These proposals are discussed in greater detail in Part Two, which deals specifically with classroom management considerations.) *Then*, if this doesn't work—if some students do not function effectively despite the attempts to appeal to their higher, creative natures—the teacher has little choice but to buttress the Theory-Y structure of the class with Theory-X principles: less freedom in class, more specific assignments, low or failing grades for those students who do not complete their assignments or who do not seek the extra help they need.

Alternatively, management theory can be X over Y ($\frac{X}{Y}$). In this case, the class is highly structured at the beginning of the year in order to establish respect and good working relationships. As teachers and students become used to each other, however, greater amounts of choice are given to students, and the class assumes a structure more in keeping with Theory-Y principles. (This topic is discussed more fully in Chapter Nine, which deals with making the transition to individualized instruction.)

In summary, though daily classroom realities may at times make adherence to Theory-Y principles very difficult, a teacher may nevertheless be better off holding this philosophical position, insofar as possible, rather than a Theory-X position. The Y attitude facilitates the creativity and self-actualization of at least a minority of students, while the X-type students can be accommodated through rules and regulations that supply them with the structure, discipline, and perhaps even coercion they legitimately need. On the other hand, a dominant Theory-X position irrevocably closes off to *all* students the opportunities for fulfilling their higher emotional needs. Finally, perhaps teachers should choose to conduct their classes a little more according to Theory Y than Theory X—as an act of faith, if not belief—simply because life is more pleasant when one trusts other people and believes in their basic goodness. Though it is true that Theory-Y teachers may experience many disappointments from students, they nevertheless have a much greater chance than Theory-X teachers of experiencing the satisfactions of helping another person grow and develop.

NOTES

[1] See also Renée S. Disick and Laura Barbanel, "Affective Education and Foreign Language Instruction," in Gilbert A. Jarvis, ed., *The ACTFL Review of Foreign Language Education*, vol. 6 (Skokie, Ill.: National Textbook Co., 1975).

² Abraham H. Maslow, *Motivation and Personality* (New York: Harper and Row, 1954; 2nd ed., 1970), pp. 35–47.

³ *Ibid.*, p. 41.

⁴ *Ibid.*, p. 40.

⁵ *Ibid.*, p. 44.

⁶ *Ibid.*, p. 45.

⁷ *Ibid.*, p. 46.

⁸ *Ibid.*, p. 46.

⁹ *Ibid.*, pp. 177–78.

¹⁰ Carl R. Rogers, *Freedom to Learn* (Columbus, Ohio: Charles E. Merrill Publishing Co., 1960), pp. 115–23.

¹¹ *Ibid.*, pp. 106–15.

¹² William Glasser, *Schools without Failure* (New York: Harper and Row, 1969). A tape of the speech he delivered at the 1970 ACTFL Pre-Conference Workshop is available from James Dodge, Middlebury School of Language, Sunderland Hall, Middlebury, Vermont 05753.

¹³ "Foreign Language without Failure," in F. William, D. Love, and Lucille J. Honig, *Options and Perspectives: A Sourcebook of Innovative Foreign Language Programs in Action, K-12* (New York: The Modern Language Association of America, 1973), pp. 65–77; also described in Virginia Wilson and Beverly Wattenmaker, "Teaching Foreign Language without Failure," in Herman F. Bostick and Gail Hutchinson, eds., *Dimension: Languages '72: Proceedings of the 1972 Joint Annual Meeting of ACTFL and SCOLT* (New York: The American Council on the Teaching of Foreign Languages, 1973), pp. 36–43.

¹⁴ Douglas McGregor, *The Human Side of Enterprise* (New York: McGraw-Hill Book Co., 1960).

¹⁵ For a more detailed treatment of this topic see John F. Bockman and Valerie M. Bockman, "The Management of Individualized Programs," in Ronald L. Gougher, ed., *Individualization of Instruction in Foreign Languages: A Practical Guide* (Philadelphia: The Center for Curriculum Development, 1972).

¹⁶ Abraham H. Maslow, *Eupsychian Management: A Journal* (Homewood, Ill.: Richard D. Irwin and The Dorsey Press, 1965), p. xi.

¹⁷ *Ibid.*, pp. 17–33.

¹⁸ *Ibid.*, pp. 42–43.

[19] *Ibid.*, p. 53.
[20] *Ibid.*, pp. 56–57.
[21] *Ibid.*, p. 55.
[22] *Ibid.*, p. 148.
[23] *Ibid.*, p. 71.
[24] *Ibid.*, p. 72.

CHAPTER FOUR
DEVELOPING A CURRICULUM FOR INDIVIDUALIZED LEARNING

4.1 GENERAL CONSIDERATIONS

After examining some theories of language learning,[1] motivation, and management, teachers can make some assumptions about how to promote learning in their classrooms. These assumptions may form the philosophical bases of their teaching strategies. Ideally, the decisions they make regarding texts and materials, class structure, and teaching methods should result directly from carefully chosen and well thought out hypotheses about the purposes of education, what it means to know a foreign language, and how a language may be learned efficiently. The assumptions made and the techniques chosen will of necessity be tentative. As of now, little firmly supported scientific data concerning second-language acquisition is available. The gaps left by researchers and theoreticians who do not concern themselves with methods of classroom teaching need to be filled by practitioners who will bring to bear on the problem the collective fruits of their research, their experience, their thought, their sensitivity, and their intuition. One such attempt will be made in this chapter. It is by no means definitive. Rather, it is an example of one way to answer basic questions regarding foreign-language education, questions that teachers must ultimately answer for themselves: What are the goals of foreign-language learners today? What is the purpose of the training offered them?[2] How should a foreign language be taught? What psychological needs can and should be met in the classroom? What are the bases for these beliefs? How may these beliefs be translated into the reality of the school situation?[3]

4.2 A PHILOSOPHY OF INDIVIDUALIZED INSTRUCTION

The philosophic positions stated below are intended to represent a classical view of individualized instruction. It is hoped that the somewhat idealistic positions presented here will stimulate readers to evolve beliefs consonant with the realities of their own situations.

4.2.1 *Belief in the Need to Humanize Mass Instruction*

Each learner is unique in personality, abilities, and needs. Education must be personalized to fit the individual; the individual must not be dehumanized in order to meet the needs of an impersonal school system. Educating students in a humane way can lead ultimately to a better society characterized by tolerance, cooperation, and greater concern for others.

4.2.2 *Belief in the Rights of Learners*

Students' educations belong to *them*, not to their teachers and not to their schools. It is *their* lives that will be deeply affected by whether or not they succeed academically. Consequently, all learners are entitled to *several* chances to demonstrate their mastery of basic skills. They are entitled to know what they are expected to do and how they will be graded. They deserve to participate actively in choosing learning activities and in evaluating their efforts. They deserve the right to sufficient time and personal help so that they do not fail. Their feelings of self-esteem should be encouraged and promoted, not destroyed, by the school.

4.2.3 *Belief in the Need to Learn How to Learn*

Learning is a lifelong task that must not end solely because a diploma is placed in a student's hands. In view of how rapidly knowledge becomes obsolete in an era of intensive technological development, it is nearly impossible to predict accurately what a student will need to know ten, twenty, or fifty years after graduation. Schools may best equip students to meet the uncertain needs of the future by teaching them how to learn on their own, how to learn from other people, and how to learn from various media—at any time and in any place.

4.2.4   Belief in the Need for Self-Discovery and Self-Actualization

During their years of schooling and throughout their lives, learners are engaged in a search for self-identity. They want to find out who they are, where they are going, and why. They move toward tentative answers each time they make choices regarding how to spend their time and with whom to spend it. School programs that offer a diversity of choices help individuals become aware of their specific talents or interests. A school system that allows opportunities for choice can promote the self-actualization of creative and gifted learners.

4.2.5   Belief in the Value of Foreign-Language Learning

The place of foreign-language learning in the curriculum is primarily justified by the satisfactions it can offer in the *present*, not by promises of future college admissions, future jobs, or, some day, improved international relations. Though knowledge of a foreign language and a foreign culture may at some time offer one or more of these and other benefits, the main reason for students to take a foreign language lies in its value for today, for here, for now. Learning a language is hard work, but it can be enjoyable. Language study can offer opportunities for self-expression, creativity, and originality that can at least equal those of other disciplines. Knowledge of a foreign language is a worthwhile and desirable skill. It enables one to communicate in new ways with other human beings; it draws people together for new tasks; it promotes new understanding and new insight. Language is the expression of man's highest faculties, the basic achievement that has made all others possible. In expanding the ability to communicate as well as the understanding of this process, a learner is engaging in the most human of activities. Language learning encourages the development of one's thoughts, one's feelings, one's humanity.[4]

4.3   HUMANISTIC CONSIDERATIONS VS. THE NEED TO UPHOLD STANDARDS

While the philosophy just presented reflects the humanistic concerns of the middle and late 1960s, a more conservative backlash has developed in the early 1970s. There has been a growing concern with the apparent lowering of national educational standards. A weekly news magazine carries an article stating that the mean verbal and mathematical scores on Scholastic Aptitude Tests administered from the school year 1962–1963 until the school year 1972–1973 show a steady and marked decline over the ten-year period.[5] Though the results are not clear-cut and any number of other noneducational factors might have contributed to the decline, many people are quick to blame the schools for being too lax in their requirements. A result of this pressure has been a tightening of administrative policies. On the same page of the magazine, there is a story about a large city school system that will no longer automatically promote fourth- to eighth-graders whose reading levels fall more than one year below the norm for their grade level.[6] A few months later, the same publication reports that pass-fail grading no longer enjoys the favor it once had on college campuses. Professors express dissatisfaction with the caliber of student work produced under this grading system; students say they would prefer to have the quality of their work evaluated.[7] Some programs of individualized instruction have been criticized for what is judged to be excessive concern for the students' fragile psyches and inadequate attention to their intellectual development. Courses in which students cover half as much work as normal but earn honor grades have been viewed with alarm by more conservative educators and parents.

The arguments on each side of the humanism versus academic standards controversy are persuasive. Ginott[8] cites a note that the principal of a private school distributed to the teachers at the start of the year. It eloquently expresses the humanistic belief that a "good" society depends more on the contributions of mentally healthy citizens than on the accomplishments of its skilled technicians.

> Dear Teacher:
> I am a survivor of a concentration camp. My eyes saw what no man should witness:
> Gas chambers built by *learned* engineers.
> Children poisoned by *educated* physicians.
> Infants killed by *trained* nurses.
> Women and babies shot and burned by *high school* and *college* graduates.
> So, I am suspicious of education.
> My request is: Help your students become human. Your efforts must never produce learned monsters, skilled psychopaths, educated Eichmanns.
> Reading, writing, arithmetic are important only if they serve to make our children more humane.

Those who favor more stringent academic standards maintain that a modern, complex industrial society depends on trained personnel. There must be a system of evaluating individual competence and distinguishing between minimal qualifications and outstanding abilities. Surely, the standard argument goes, one would not want to entrust one's life to a surgeon whose entire medical preparation has been rated on a pass-fail basis; nor would one be eager to cross a bridge or fly in a plane designed by people who possess only 80 percent mastery of the essentials of their trade.

This controversy cannot be resolved definitively one way or the other. There is truth in the case presented by each side. Perhaps, though, some accommodation can be reached in the area of foreign-language teaching. The essential question is: What is the purpose of the instruction offered? What use may the students enrolled in a particular course be reasonably expected to make of the material they have learned? In many beginning classes the high demands made in the areas of accuracy and achievement seem to presuppose that the students will become language majors. This elitist approach, with its insistence on maintaining high standards and weeding out students unable to conform to them, leads in effect to a lowering of standards, since large numbers of students are closed off from opportunities to learn a foreign language. Perhaps a workable approach is to employ pass-fail grading—with a minimum 80 percent standard of mastery—in beginning and early intermediate courses. At these levels affective considerations predominate over cognitive ones. It is more important that students in the early stages of learning experience success in communicating their ideas and value their achievements than it is that they conform to absolute standards of accuracy. After a basic pride in foreign-language ability is established, then students in more advanced courses can be encouraged to adhere to higher standards of correctness and can be graded according to how well they do so.

4.4 THE NEED FOR DIVERSIFIED COURSE OFFERINGS

Affective considerations can also determine in part the course objectives. While the vast majority of high-school foreign-language programs in the early 1970s stressed active mastery of the four language skills in the preparation of college-bound students for literary studies, there has been a small but growing trend toward meeting a wider diversity of student needs and interests.[9] Courses have been established that enable students to communicate in specific community situations (a policeman to a foreign-speaking traffic offender, for example) as well as in the context of travel abroad.[10] Jakobovits envisions a multitude of specialized courses ranging from "How to Speak to Strangers in French" to (whimsically) "How to Give the Impression of Being a Multilingual Person."[11] Perhaps the foremost example of course diversification is found in Gerald Logan's curriculum guide which lists over forty different German courses.[12] In addition to four-skill college preparatory courses, he offers less demanding ones that are limited to only one or two language skills. Students may also elect to earn credit as student aides, or by following interests they have in children's literature, speed reading, fine art, current events, creative writing, secretarial German, German literature, and many more. The descriptions of mini-course electives developed at Marshall-University High School also offer suggestions and ideas for developing a more flexible curriculum.[13]

It is important to note that there may be some reaction—at least at the college level—against too much diversity in course offerings. A *New York Times* article[14] reports that at Brown University enrollments in self-discovery and independent study courses have fallen off sharply as students opt for preprofessional training and courses that assure them acceptance into the graduate schools of their choice. The curriculum reform that aimed to make students responsible for their own education has also encountered difficulty due to a lack of funds that would permit smaller classes and to the resistance of some faculty members to heavier teaching loads and additional counseling responsibilities.

4.5 DEFINING CURRICULAR GOALS

Some basic questions facing curriculum planners are: What is the ultimate goal of the instruction offered? For whom is it intended? Is it designed for college-bound or career-oriented students? Are students enrolled in order to fill a minimum requirement or do they intend to major in the language? Do students wish to develop all four language skills plus culture, or are their goals more limited? How is it envisioned that students will profit from their possibly limited exposure to a foreign language? In what way can language study contribute to their enrichment as human beings? Specific answers to questions such as these can help clarify the nature of the courses to be offered.

Developing a curriculum for an individualized foreign-language program may start with a written statement of the year-end goals of each course expressed in terms of student behavior. Either alone or with departmental colleagues, teachers need to determine what they hope their students will be able to do at the end of the course that they are unable to do when beginning it. What grammar and vocabulary will they know? What language skills will they have? Teachers must decide what communication behaviors they may realistically expect from students who receive passing grades. A decision should be made as to whether students are to be held responsible for all four language skills or for only some of them. Expectations for student performances in the area of culture also need to be determined. If feasible, both parent and student opinions can be solicited, via questionnaires, so that teachers may become aware of the goals, values, and needs of the community in which they teach.[15] Examples of year-end goals may be found in Appendix A.

4.6 PERFORMANCE OBJECTIVES IN FOREIGN-LANGUAGE INSTRUCTION

Performance objectives can make clear to students, teachers, administrators, and parents what students should be able to do as a result of the instruction they receive. These statements give information regarding the purpose of an assignment, what students are required to do, the conditions under which they will be checked or tested, and the criteria to be used in evaluating their work. If needed, a sample test item may be included for clarity.[16]

Performance objectives may be written in terms of unit goals and also in terms of quarter, semester, or year-end goals. In all cases, comparison of actual student achievement with the originally stated goals can provide considerable useful information regarding the quality and quantity of student learning. This information may serve as a basis for the evaluation and improvement of instruction. An example of unit goals and year-end goals, as well as the learning steps leading to them, may be found in Appendixes A and B.

4.7 THE COGNITIVE DOMAIN

Learning tasks vary widely in difficulty. Repeating a model sentence in the foreign language is simpler than performing a question-answer drill, and that in turn is less demanding than creating an original sentence expressing personal ideas or feelings. While one's ultimate teaching goal may be to develop communicative competence, drills and exercises remain undeniably essential prerequisites to free communication. What is needed, then, is a means to classify student performances from the simplest toward the progressively more complex. In this way, language acquisition can be structured so that students are guided systematically toward increasingly liberated uses of the foreign language. A means of accomplishing this is to create objectives and learning steps that represent not only the lower but also the upper stages of a cognitive (or subject-matter) taxonomy such as the one presented here.[17]

Stage I. *Mechanical Skills.* Students make discriminations, repeat, recite, or copy without necessarily understanding the material they are dealing with.

Stage II. *Knowledge.* Students know and understand the facts and rules they have been taught. Their responses vary little from those originally learned.

Stage III. *Transfer.* Students apply their knowledge in new situations such as oral drills or guided writing exercises. Student performance is controlled and predictable. The drill and exercise material consists of recombinations of familiar vocabulary and structure.

Stage IV. *Communication.* Students use the language creatively either to understand new information or to express their own ideas. The material to be comprehended may contain unfamiliar linguistic elements. Student responses are not entirely predictable. Some performance at this stage should be a goal of all foreign-language courses.

Stage V. *Criticism.* Having largely overcome most major communication difficulties, students focus primarily on analyzing and evaluating material presented to them. Performance at this stage may be the goal of advanced language, literature, and culture courses.

4.8 THE AFFECTIVE DOMAIN

The attitudes, feelings, and values of foreign-language learners have nowhere received nearly as much attention as has been devoted to their cognitive achievements. It has become increasingly evident, however, that nonobjective factors play an extremely important role in successful foreign-language acquisition.[18] When students are highly motivated, they can succeed in foreign-language learning—even in spite of intellectual limitations or less than ideal classroom conditions. Conversely, even high-aptitude students can perform poorly when they attach little worth to second-language study.

Critics of the establishment of affective goals maintain that since attitudes, feelings, and values cannot be measured objectively, it is absurd to posit desired student behaviors in this area. Unfortunately, these critics ignore the fact that student feelings have always existed and will continue to do so. To deny their importance solely because they are not as conveniently measurable as objective cognitive attainments closes off from teachers an area in which they may potentially exert considerable positive influence on student performance. Since student feelings toward learning will never "go away," even if disparaged by advocates of strict objective measurement, classroom teachers face a choice: Either they ignore student feelings or else they actively attempt to develop more positive ones toward foreign-language learning.[19]

Just as the knowledge and skills demonstrated by students may be classified taxonomically, so may the attitudes, feelings, and values that they develop in a course. This affective continuum ranges from teacher-direction of learning activities to student self-direction in seeking out additional contacts with the foreign language and culture. The three stages of the following affective taxonomy lend themselves to development in the classroom.[20]

Stage I. *Receptivity.* Students are open to learning. They are cooperative, attentive, and complete their assignments. Behavior at this stage is a minimal prerequisite to classroom learning.

Stage II. *Responsiveness.* Students are tolerant of differences between the foreign language and culture and their own. They enjoy participating in classroom learning activities and demonstrate interest in them. Helping most students reach this stage of feeling may be an affective goal of a foreign-language teacher.

Stage III. *Appreciation.* Students, of their own accord, consider the study of foreign language worthwhile. They voluntarily seek additional out-of-class experiences with foreign-language speakers or foreign cultural events. Though it is unrealistic to expect all learners to reach this stage of behavior, teachers may seek to develop it in at least a few of their students.

Affective objectives may be best expressed as broad, end-of-year goals, rather than as specific short-range performance objectives. Attitudes, feelings, and values do not develop overnight or in a period of a week or a month; they take shape over a much longer time span. Also, they cannot be measured with the specificity that may be applied to cognitive objectives. Whereas behavior that demonstrates ability to communicate may be observed and described, actions that show that a student enjoys or appreciates a course cannot be predicted. For these reasons, teachers seeking to create more positive attitudes toward foreign-language learning would do well to diagnose daily classroom behavior and devise ways of improving what they see.[21,22]

NOTES

[1] An example of one such theory is Philip D. Smith, Jr., *Toward a Practical Theory of Second Language Instruction* (Philadelphia: The Center for Curriculum Development, 1971).

[2] An illuminating examination of curricula based on student needs, on society's needs, and on subject-matter demands may be found in Frank M. Grittner, "Pluralism in Foreign Language Education: A Reason for Being," in Dale L. Lange, ed., *The ACTFL Review of Foreign Language Education*, vol. 3 (Skokie, Ill.: National Textbook Co., 1971), pp. 36–48.

[3] The following recent surveys of developments in foreign-language curricula are highly recommended reading: Gerald E. Logan, "Curricula for Individualized Instruction," in Dale L. Lange, ed., *The ACTFL Review of Foreign Language Education*, vol. 2 (Skokie, Ill.: National Textbook Co., 1970), pp. 133–55; Ronald L. Gougher, "Individualization of Foreign Language Learning. What Is Being Done?" in Dale L. Lange, ed., *The ACTFL Review of Foreign Language Education*, vol. 3 (Skokie, Ill.: National Textbook Co., 1971), pp. 221–45; Theodore B. Kalivoda and Robert J. Elkins, "Teaching as Facilitation and Management of Learning" and Gladys Lipton, "Curricula for New Goals," in Dale L. Lange and Charles J. James, eds., *The ACTFL Review of Foreign Language Education*, vol. 4 (Skokie, Ill.: National Textbook Co., 1972), pp. 61–96 and pp. 187–218; June K. Phillips, "Individualization and Personalization," in Gilbert A. Jarvis, ed., *The ACTFL Review of Foreign Language Education*, vol. 5 (Skokie, Ill.: National Textbook Co., 1974), pp. 219–61; and Anthony Papalia and Joseph Zampogna, "The Changing Curriculum," in Gilbert A. Jarvis, ed., *The ACTFL Review of Foreign Language Education*, vol. 6 (Skokie, Ill.: National Textbook Co., 1975).

[4] For additional thoughts on this topic, see Jane N. Lippmann, "Rationale for Language Study," in Gilbert A. Jarvis, ed., *The ACTFL Review of Foreign Language Education*, vol. 6 (Skokie, Ill.: National Textbook Co., 1975); and Gerald E. Logan, *Individualized Foreign Language Learning: An Organic Process* (Rowley, Mass.: Newbury House Publishers, 1973), Appendix B, "The Foreign Language Department Philosophy at Live Oak High School," pp. 129–31.

[5] "Decline in the SATs," *Time* (December 31, 1973), p. 45.

[6] "They Shall Not Pass," *Time* (December 31, 1973), p. 45.

[7] "Downgrading No-Grade," *Time* (February 4, 1974), p. 66.

[8] Haim G. Ginott, *Teacher and Child* (New York: The Macmillan Co., 1972), p. 317.

[9] See Robert C. LaFayette, "Diversification: The Key to Student-Centered Programs," *Modern Language Journal*, vol. 56, no. 6 (October 1972), pp. 349–53.

[10] Albert C. Eyde, "Community Gets Its Goals," *Accent on ACTFL*, vol. 4, no. 3 (February 1974), pp. 10–12.

[11] Leon A. Jakobovits, "A Typology of Foreign-Language Education with Particular Emphases on Compensatory and Individualized Instruction," in Ronald L. Gougher, ed., *Individualization of Instruction in Foreign Languages: A Practical Guide* (Philadelphia: The Center for Curriculum Development, 1972), p. 37.

[12] Gerald E. Logan, *Individualized Foreign Language Learning: An Organic Process* (Rowley, Mass.: Newbury House Publishers, 1973), pp. 39–47.

[13] Barbara L. Gunderson, "Creating Elective French Courses," in Lorraine A. Strasheim, ed., *Foreign Language in a New Apprenticeship for Living* (Bloomington, Ind.: The Indiana Language Program, 1971), pp. 44–47; see also, "Course Descriptions 1970–71," pp. 48–56.

[14] Robert Reinhold, "Brown University Trend: Back to Old Curriculum," *New York Times* (February 24, 1974), pp. 1:6–7 and 47:1–7.

[15] An interesting effort along these lines is described in Anthony Papalia, "Students, Parents, and Teachers as Data Sources for Determining FL Instructional Goals," *Foreign Language Annals*, vol. 7, no. 1 (October 1973), pp. 117–19.

[16] For a more detailed discussion of this topic, see Renée S. Disick, "Performance Objectives," *Focus Report #25* (New York: American Council on the Teaching of Foreign Languages, 1971).

[17] This taxonomy is a highly condensed version of the one more fully explained and worked out in Rebecca M. Valette and Renée S. Disick, *Modern Language Performance Objectives and Individualization* (New York: Harcourt Brace Jovanovich, 1972).

[18] See Howard I. Aronson, "The Role of Attitudes about Languages in the Learning of Foreign Languages," *The Modern Language Journal*, vol. 57, no. 7 (November 1973), pp. 323–29.

[19] See Renée S. Disick, "Developing Positive Attitudes in Intermediate Foreign Language Classes," *Modern Language Journal*, vol. 56, no. 7 (November 1972), pp. 417–20.

[20] All five stages of the affective taxonomy, as well as ways of developing and measuring desired student behaviors, are presented in Valette and Disick, 1972 (see note 17).

[21] A succinct discussion of ways of developing and measuring affective achievements at each of the three taxonomic stages may be found in Renée S. Disick, "Teaching Toward Affective Goals in Foreign Languages," *Foreign Language Annals*, vol. 7, no. 1 (October 1973), pp. 95–101.

[22] A useful guide to clarifying goals in the affective domain is Robert F. Mager, *Goal Analysis* (Belmont, Calif.: Fearon Publishers, 1972).

CHAPTER FIVE
CREATING LEARNING PACKETS

5.1 GENERAL CONSIDERATIONS

The most important element in preventing an individualized program from degenerating into chaos is its underlying structure and organization. Since on occasion the teachers will work with individuals or small groups, they will be unable to supervise directly at all times the classroom activities of each of their students. To compensate for the loss of the teacher's direct presence, other, indirect controls need to be instituted in the classroom. One means of accomplishing this is to hold students accountable—via oral and written testing—for certain specific achievements. These objectives may be communicated clearly to students in learning packets that contain statements regarding what students must accomplish and how they may go about it in class. Before designing learning packets, however, teachers need to know what their end-of-year goals are for each class so that the unit objectives may contribute to the development of those goals. In other words, teachers hoping to initiate a successful program of individualized instruction need to establish clearly in their students' minds, as well as in their own, both the long-term and the short-term goals of the course.

5.2 COMPONENTS OF LEARNING PACKETS

Basic constituents of learning packets are performance objectives and the learning steps that students must complete in order to achieve each objective. The steps consist of assignments such as oral pattern drills, written drills and exercises, and oral or written quizzes to provide feedback on daily student progress. Other items that may be included in the packet are: conversation practice materials, topics for compositions or oral presentations, culture assignments, lists of additional learning sources—such as slides, tape cassettes, filmstrips, books, and magazines—or any teacher-created material that supplements available textbooks.

5.3 SINGLE TEXT VS. MULTI-TEXT PROGRAM

If teachers base their programs on a standard textbook, then it is convenient to gear the learning packets to each unit or chapter taught. If teachers create their own materials or if they intend to use material from several different texts, then each objective is in itself an entity and any number of objectives may be grouped together for convenience. Samples of learning activity packets with performance objectives and learning steps for mastering a dialog, reading selection, and a grammar unit of study are presented in Appendixes A and B. A culture unit is presented in Appendix B.

The teacher who chooses to adapt a standard grammar book for individualization will enjoy the advantages of a well-integrated text that systematically reenters grammar and vocabulary. A basic text can also relieve the teacher of the considerable burden of writing as well as reproducing material. A disadvantage, though, is the often unchanging, predictable format that occurs throughout one book or even a series of books. After a while, students become bored with doing the same things in the same ways. It is the teacher's responsibility to introduce sufficient variety into the learning materials and develop formats that are suitable to the students' learning styles.

By selecting the best dialogs, grammar explanations, or reading selections from several different texts, the teacher can remedy the monotony of reliance on a single book, but the burden of selecting and reproducing material becomes overwhelming. An additional problem is that reproducing copyrighted material is illegal without the publisher's written consent. Moreover, the attempt to create entirely original teaching materials, though admirable, can result in a considerable drain on a teacher's time and energy. It is also extremely difficult for hard-working, full-time teachers to equal the combined expertise of a team of professional writers and editors.

A viable compromise solution could entail adapting a basic grammar text for individualization and then supplementing it with additional readers and cultural materials. Though the book's format may vary only slightly, the performance objectives that students must complete may change from unit to unit. If feasible, sample copies of textbooks from the departmental library may be moved to the classroom so that students can elect extra-credit assignments based on material in them.

Several new textbooks in French,[1] German,[2] and Spanish,[3] that claim to be designed for individualized instruction, have appeared recently, and others are likely to follow. Whether or not these books indeed do prove appropriate in all teaching situations remains to be determined. In the meantime, teachers who must use conventional texts or those who are not completely satisfied with commercially prepared learning packets will need to find ways of adapting existing materials for individualized instruction.[4] Criteria for evaluating either commercially or privately prepared learning packets are presented in Appendix C.

5.4 WRITING UNIT OBJECTIVES

After examining the contents of a chapter or unit of study, teachers should ask themselves what their students should be able to do after they have learned the new material. How do they show they know the new vocabulary? How do they demonstrate their ability to pronounce correctly? How do they prove that they can use the new grammar? How can they demonstrate reading comprehension? spelling accuracy? writing ability? What will oral and written tests be like? Under what conditions will they be taken? What is the minimal acceptable performance? Answers to questions such as these form the basis of the performance objectives for the unit.*

Ideally, the performance objectives, even those for the early phases of language learning, should be written at the *Stage 4: Communication* behavior level. Minimally, however, they can be written at the *Stage 3: Transfer* level. By focusing on communicative competence from the very beginning of the language-acquisition process, teachers may ensure the relevance of the foreign-language course and in this way enhance student motivation.

5.5 WRITING LEARNING STEPS

In a way, specifying learning steps for each objective is like making the teacher's daily lesson-plan book available to students. Learning steps inform students of what they must do to prepare themselves to achieve a stated objective. Steps may include: reciting dialogs, reading grammar explanations, memorizing dialogs or vocabulary words, listening to taped explanations,

* Cognitive and affective taxonomies are discussed in the preceding chapter.

practicing drills with a classmate or a cassette, writing exercises, attending explanation groups in class, or reading a basic text for comprehension. Some steps could require an oral or written check of an individual's progress. Students might have to pronounce certain words without error, or perform pattern drills with accuracy and fluency, or submit a written exercise that has been self-corrected according to a key. The signature of a teacher or teaching aide may be required before the student advances to the next activities.

Learning steps like those just described will fall at the lower three stages of the cognitive taxonomy: *Mechanical Skills, Knowledge,* and *Transfer.* Though student behavior at these stages does not constitute the ultimate goal of language instruction, these intermediate steps are nevertheless important in the process of foreign-language acquisition.

In some packets, all the performance objectives for a given unit are written on the first page or two, while all the learning steps appear on succeeding pages. An approach that may be more effective is to place the learning steps immediately after the objective for which they are intended. In this way, students are made aware of the communicative purpose of the otherwise meaningless series of drills and exercises they are asked to perform.

5.6 CREATING SUPPLEMENTARY MATERIALS

A learning packet need not consist only of performance objectives and learning steps related to the unit under study. Other materials that supplement the dialogs, grammar presentations, drills, and readings of the basic textbook may also be included at the teacher's discretion.

5.6.1 *Material for Developing Communicative Competence*

Many of the major textbooks currently available devote considerable space to oral exercises at taxonomic Stage III, *Transfer,* but are relatively lacking in exercises at Stage IV, *Communication.* A teacher interested in developing student skill in communicative competence could devise conversation questions or skit situations based on the new vocabulary, grammar, or reading that would encourage students to listen closely and to express their own ideas. For example, a lesson on double object pronouns could culminate in a series of personalized questions such as: What present have you received recently? Who gave it to you? When? Why? Or, if a dialog or reading selection concerns a sporting event, students may prepare skits in which they take the part of spectators or participants. Skits may also be impromptu. A conflict situation can be proposed into which students may project themselves into specified roles. For example, a young couple returns from a date at 3 A.M. The girl's parents want an explanation. Four students spontaneously act out the parts assigned. Additional samples of this type of material are presented in Appendix D.

A highly promising innovative technique involves creating grammar-based conversation questions that touch on student attitudes, feelings, and values. Instead of emotionally neutral questions such as, "What did you do last weekend?", a teacher might ask, "What did you do that made you happy?" Rather than ask students, "Do you like to dance (or sing, or draw)?" a teacher might say, "I like to dance. I like to sing. I like to draw." Individual students in turn repeat the sentences in order of their preference and may explain their responses if they wish to do so. This practice can enable students to clarify their values—at a time in their lives when this is often a central concern.[5] A different exercise involves having a student repeat—or "reflect"—the answers given by the group members. One student might answer, "I am happy when I am alone." A second student reflects, "You are happy when you are alone." This active, nonjudgmental listening builds feelings of self-worth and feelings of group acceptance and trust.[6,7,8,9] Samples of communication materials with a high affective content are presented in Appendix C. Methods of developing oral fluency are treated further in Chapter Sixteen.

5.6.2 *Vocabulary Lists*

Where vocabulary lists are not provided in the text or where they are incomplete, teachers may choose to provide explanations of the new, difficult, or hard-to-remember words—especially abstract ones such as prepositions, adverbs, and negations—or they may wish to indicate active or passive vocabulary words. The nature of these lists will vary according to the language and maturity level of the students for whom they are intended. They may consist of pictures and printed equivalents, foreign-language words and native-language translations, or foreign-language words and foreign-language explanations. The lists may serve as the basis for checking knowledge of vocabulary—a basic element of successful foreign-language communication. This topic is discussed further in Chapter Fifteen.

5.6.3 *Pretest Exercises*

Unless students in one class have had widely divergent foreign-language preparation the preceding year, true pretests do not play a major role in day-to-day foreign-language instruction. However, a pretest exercise that follows an explanation of new material and is actually an alternate—though somewhat longer—form of the written exam to be taken can exert considerable positive influence on student learning. While students often neglect to complete workbook exercises that seem to bear little relationship to the written test they must ultimately take, this is rarely their tendency with pretests. When students know that an exercise directly prepares them to succeed on a test, they take an interest in performing well and in understanding and correcting their mistakes.

5.6.4 *Answer Keys*

Developing student responsibility for self-evaluation and self-correction is a major goal of individualized instruction. Answer keys printed either in the space below oral and written exercises or on the reverse side of the page can facilitate student self-correction. Some teachers object to providing the keys at the same time as the exercise; they fear that students will simply copy the answers, rather than work them out for themselves. Instead, they provide keys only when students have completed the required work. Several problems are inherent in this system: Keys are often lost, and some fall into the hands of students who have not yet done their homework. At times, there may not be a sufficient number of keys available to all the students needing them. In addition, the process of finding a key and then returning it to where it belongs is often time-consuming and inefficient. For these reasons, including answers with exercises seems preferable. Though copying is still a clear possibility, it is just as easily accomplished when keys are withheld. Actually, the problem solves itself when students learn that copying pretest answers without understanding their underlying principles will inevitably result in failure to pass the tests based on them. Once students experience this a few times, they learn to write out the exercises before checking their answers with the key.

5.6.5 *Explanations of New Concepts*

Individualized programs that enable students to proceed completely at their own rate must depend to a considerable extent on written or taped explanations of new concepts, since the teacher and the teacher's aides may not be free to offer an oral explanation at the moment it is needed. If the grammar discussions in the textbook are clear, comprehensible, and suited to the maturity level of the students, the teacher need do little more than refer students to the appropriate pages. If, however, some students cannot easily understand the text, the teacher might consider creating his or her own written or audio- or video-taped grammar explanations. If these alternatives prove unsuitable to the learning styles of too many students, the teacher needs to reconsider the type of individualization appropriate in the class. Some students and some classes may well profit from less individualized pacing and more personal attention and explanation from the teacher. Various styles of individualization are considered in the following chapter.

5.6.6 *Enrichment Activities*

A language course that limits itself to a basic text or solely to exercises in the four skills runs the risk of becoming highly monotonous. Student boredom, in turn, may result in lack of motivation and underachievement. The variety needed in an effective foreign-language class may be introduced through enrichment activities. Once students have completed the basic work required, they may elect any of a number of communication or cultural activities: Students might prepare speeches or skits to be presented in class. They might put together scrapbooks of new vocabulary words or newspaper items relating to the foreign country or culture. They might browse through foreign-language magazines and note cultural similarities and differences. They might keep personal diaries in the foreign language or record in English instances of their coming into contact with the foreign language or culture outside of class. Bulletin board displays for classrooms or halls are another possibility. Supplementary reading and writing activities offer additional opportunities for enrichment. Some enrichment activities may have cognitive objectives: vocabulary expansion, greater oral fluency, or increased reading or writing skill. Other enrichment activities may aim primarily at the affective domain: development of greater awareness of the foreign culture, tolerance of cultural differences, or increased enjoyment of interesting, non-text foreign language materials.

Some teachers may choose to create learning packets devoted to cultural topics, which might include performance objectives, realia such as maps, floor plans of homes, food labels and so on, as well as exercises and tests. When time permits this preparation, or when these packets are available from outside sources, this approach is suitable for enriching a foreign-language class. If, however, such packets cannot easily be prepared or obtained, the teacher might make available to students simple lists of activities the could elect for extra credit. An example of a shortened packet is presented in Appendix C.

5.7 AVOIDING COMMON PITFALLS

While well-designed learning packets can greatly facilitate the individualization of instruction, their preparation can become a nightmarish experience for teachers unless common pitfalls are avoided.

5.7.1 *Avoid Overly Long Packets and Instructions*

Packets should be as long as necessary but as short as possible. Some teachers make the mistake of writing overly long and overly specific objectives. While the first learning packet should be fairly complete, subsequent ones can be considerably shortened once students become accustomed to the teacher's expectations. Another common error is the assumption that *all* materials must be included within the packet. This leads some instructors to reproducing pages and pages of material from basic texts or from workbooks. A less time-consuming practice would be simply to refer students to the appropriate places for the drills or exercises that they are to do.

5.7.2 *Provide a Balance of Activities*

Some packets prove unsatisfactory because they provide too little oral practice for students who spend most of the class time writing or, less fortunately, talking in English to their friends. Other packets provide for too many checkpoints, so that the teacher feels too confined to a testing role and enjoys few opportunities for individual explanations and guidance. Therefore, in preparing successive packets, each teacher needs to determine by trial and error what balance of activities proves workable in the classroom.

5.7.3 *Prepare Only as Much Material as Feasible*

Teachers beginning to individualize may believe it necessary to have on hand complete packets for an entire unit or an entire year's work. This need not be the case. Though students will be unable to proceed vertically at their own rates unless materials are prepared in advance, horizontal enrichment activities can nevertheless be provided for individuals who work faster than others in the class. If necessary, the teacher may distribute just a page or two of the packet at a time, which may contain objectives for a period of only one or two weeks. This is a workable alternative for teachers with several different daily preparations. The following year, however, a greater degree of individualization may be carried out, since considerable material has already been developed.

5.7.4 *Make Sure Students Understand Instructions*

In some instances, teachers may find that students do not want to read the instructions in the packet. Any one of several factors could be the cause. The wording may be too complicated or abstract for the age level of the students. Explanatory material might be too long or too crowded, so that it looks unattractive. Perhaps the printing is faint or hard to read. To remedy this, a teacher needs to shorten and simplify the instructions and provide for adequate spacing and clarity. It might also be helpful to read the first packet aloud to students and answer questions they may have. Student suggestions may also be solicited for ways to improve the packets.

5.7.5 *Provide for a Variety of Activities*

A common shortcoming of many packets is that their unchanging format makes them monotonous and boring. To provide needed variety, packet pages can be printed on colored paper, and cartoons, drawings, proverbs, humorous messages, or words of encouragement to students can be included. The teacher should vary objectives from unit to unit so that students need not do the same types of activities over and over. Some units might require compositions to display knowledge of grammar, while others could ask students to prepare oral speeches or skits. Tests should also be varied. Techniques for accomplishing this diversification are suggested in Part Three of this book.[10]*

NOTES

[1] Katharine M. Clarke and Holt Editorial Staff, *A la Française,* First Level Program and Alice Langellier, Katharine M. Clarke, and Holt Editorial Staff, *Nous les Jeunes,* Second Level Program (New York: Holt, Rinehart and Winston, 1973); Rebecca and Jean-Paul Valette, *French for Mastery* (Boston: D. C. Heath and Co., 1975); Charles A. S. Heinle et al., *Voix et Visages de la France* (Chicago: Rand-McNally, 1974); and David E. Wolfe, *Workbook and Study Guide* (Chicago: Rand-McNally, 1974).

[2] Harry Reinert and Jack Moeller, *German Today: Personalized Learning, A Continuous Progress System,* Level One and Level Two (Boston: Houghton Mifflin, 1974).

[3] Enrique E. Lamadrid, William E. Bull, and Laurel A. Briscoe, *Communicating in Spanish,* Level One (Boston: Houghton Mifflin, 1973); and Francisco Gaona and Jonathan Tibbets, *Basic Spanish* (P.O. Box 3383, San Rafael, Calif. 94902; 1971).

[4] Additional reference sources that may prove useful to the classroom teacher are: Ronald L. Gougher, *A Teacher's Guide to the Adaptation of Basic Texts for Individualizing Instruction: German* (Detroit: Advancement Press, 1974); Ronald L. Gougher and David E. Wolfe, *A Teacher's Guide to the Adaptation of Basic Texts for Individualizing Instruction: French* (Detroit: Advancement Press, 1974); and Ronald L. Gougher and Philip D. Smith, *A Teacher's Guide to the Adaptation of Basic Texts for Individualizing Instruction: Spanish* (Detroit: Advancement Press, 1974).

[5] Two indispensable sources of ideas and techniques in the area of values clarification are Louis Raths, Merrill Harmin, and Sidney B. Simon, *Values and Teaching* (Columbus, Ohio: Charles E. Merrill, 1966); and Sidney B. Simon, Leland Howe, and Howard Kirschenbaum, *Values-Clarification: A Handbook of Practical Strategies for Teachers and Students* (New York: Hart Publishing Co., 1972).

[6] These techniques are described in greater detail and a wealth of affective questions is offered in Virginia Wilson and Beverly Wattenmaker, *Real Communication in Foreign Language* and *Real Communication in Spanish* (Upper Jay, N.Y. 12987: The Adirondack Mountain Humanistic Education Center, 1973); Phyllis S. Stoller and Joanne Tuskes Lock, *Real Communication in*

---

* Criteria for evaluating locally or professionally prepared packets are presented in Appendix C.

French (Upper Jay, N.Y.: AMHEC, 1973); and Stefano Morel, *Human Dynamics in French* and *Human Dynamics in Spanish* (Upper Jay, N.Y.: The Adirondack Mountain Humanistic Education Center, 1974).

[7] A brief, but highly useful treatment of this subject may be found in Toni Gabriel, "Mind Expanding," *The American Foreign Language Teacher*, vol. 4, no. 1 (Fall 1973), pp. 25–26.

[8] See also James W. Dodge, ed., *Sensitivity in the Foreign Language Classroom*. Reports of the Working Committees of the Northeast Conference on the Teaching of Foreign Languages. (New York: Modern Language Association Materials Center, 1973).

[9] A college text that emphasizes developing the student's ability to communicate feelings and thoughts in full-class and small-group settings is Paul Ostyn, Bernard Le Texier, and Bruce G. Campbell, *Fluent Spoken French* (New York: Harper and Row, 1973).

[10] For another discussion of creating learning packets, see Gerald E. Logan, *Individualized Foreign Language Learning: An Organic Process* (Rowley, Mass.: Newbury House Publishers, 1973), pp. 15–35. A detailed treatment of how to write performance objectives is presented in Rebecca M. Valette and Renée S. Disick, *Modern Language Performance Objectives and Individualization: A Handbook* (New York: Harcourt Brace Jovanovich, 1972).

CHAPTER SIX
STYLES OF INDIVIDUALIZED INSTRUCTION

6.1 GENERAL CONSIDERATIONS

There is no optimum way to individualize foreign-language instruction.[1] The amount and type of responsibility that students can comfortably assume will vary with the ability and maturity of particular learners. Techniques of classroom management will also differ according to the readiness and preferred learning styles of the students. What is taught and how it is taught will depend on a host of widely divergent factors: level of language learning, personnel and resources available, student interests and aptitudes, as well as the teacher's own individual preferences. There are also several ways in which a course may be individualized—according to course objectives, rate of learning, method of learning, content of learning, or a combination of two or more of these approaches. This chapter will describe several styles of instruction, each of which can justifiably be labeled "individualized." The appropriateness of each one to various learning situations and the type of individualization the approach facilitates will be considered. Advantages and limitations of each approach will be discussed so that teachers and administrators may decide which style or combination of styles is most suited to local classroom conditions. The following chart presents the styles of individualized instruction that will be discussed.

STYLES OF INDIVIDUALIZED INSTRUCTION

Areas of Individualization	*Instructional Style*
Choice of Course Objectives	Independent Study Development of Preferred Skills
Choice of Rate of Learning	Continuous Progress Flexible Pacing
Choice of Methods of Learning	Multimedia Program
Choice of Content of Learning	Mini-Courses Interdisciplinary Studies Elective Assignments

6.2 CHOICE OF OBJECTIVES

When students bear the major responsibility for selecting course objectives, the resulting program is known as independent study. These students may enjoy as well opportunities for choice in the three other areas of individualization. A more limited way of offering choice of objectives is to permit students to emphasize the development of preferred skills within the framework of an established curriculum.

6.2.1 *Independent Study*

Independent study involves primarily the individualization of course objectives, though variations of rate, methods, and content may also come into play. In this style of individualization, students assume the primary responsibility for their learning and consult with their teacher or advisor from time to time to check their progress and to chart new directions for their studies. This style of individualization has been used both in the initial acquisition of a foreign language and for study at advanced levels.

As reported in the professional literature, self-instruction has enabled students to acquire a second language through standard or programmed texts, oral practice with tapes, weekly meetings with a program advisor, and periodic conferences with native speakers who evaluate their performance. Experience seems to indicate that the most important factor in promoting achievement is the motivation of the learners, though high language aptitude, self-discipline, strong academic ability, and intellectual maturity also play important roles. The age of the learners, apparently, is not crucial, since success has been reported with sixth- and eighth-graders as well as with high-school students.[2] Comparable results have been achieved with college-level language beginners.

Though less widely publicized, independent study also takes place at the upper levels of the curriculum. In cases where enrollments are not sufficient to support advanced courses or when students cannot fit a language course into their schedules, programs have been set up to permit students to study on their own and attend weekly tutorial conferences. In some institutions, one faculty member assumes the responsibility for all students electing individually directed studies. In others, teachers volunteer to set up additional meeting hours to accommodate these students.[3]

Self-instruction in the initial and intermediate stages of foreign-language acquisition can make it possible for schools to teach a greater number of foreign languages, since minimum class enrollments are no longer needed for exotic or less commonly taught languages. At advanced levels, courses featuring an independent study component can also be instrumental in maintaining enrollments by appealing to individual student interests. Successful independent study programs, which require that students be able to work comfortably some or most of the time alone and without direct supervision, allow for little variation. The potential monotony and loneliness inherent in this approach must be counterbalanced by student self-motivation. The key to successful implementation of independent study is selection: administrative or teacher selection of students at beginning stages and the natural selection that operates at advanced levels. While this approach can lead to highly gratifying achievements for a certain percentage of students, it is unlikely that it can be considered appropriate for the vast majority of today's school population.

6.2.2 *Development of Preferred Skills*

Though not widely discussed in the professional literature, another way of enabling students to choose course objectives is to allow them opportunities to develop further the language skills they prefer. For example, 70 or 80 percent of a beginning or intermediate course may consist of core material that all students are to master. The remaining 20 or 30 percent may consist of elective assignments in the areas of listening, speaking, reading, writing, or culture. Students choose to emphasize the skills they feel are most relevant to their own individual reasons for studying a foreign language.

6.3 CHOICE OF LEARNING RATES

Many of the programs of individualization established in the middle and late 1960s began by providing for differences in student learning rates. This resulted in the "continuous progress" style of instruction. As this movement gained momentum and increased in popularity, some teachers who lacked some or all of the conditions necessary for "continuous progress" found themselves unable to transfer this instructional style to their classrooms. Instead, they developed a more conservative approach to meeting individual needs for different learning rates; we shall call it here "flexible pacing." Both styles of individualizing learning rates are described below, and the advantages and limitations of each are discussed.

6.3.1 *Continuous Progress*

In a program of continuous progress instruction, students advance "vertically" in the course as far as they can and as fast as they can. As reported in the professional literature, successful implementation of this approach usually involves differentiated staffing, modular scheduling, resource centers, student learning packets, nongraded classes, and a system for awarding credit whenever new material is mastered.[4] Successful implementation of this approach requires close cooperation between teachers and administrators in order to effect these far-reaching changes in school policies and procedures. Ideally, the school's physical plant should provide facilities for large- and small-group instruction as well as carrels for independent study. Resource centers should offer students easy access to tapes, films, filmstrips, slides, cassettes, records, language masters,* and any supplementary materials designed to promote learning. Scheduling procedures should facilitate grouping of students according to their needs and should enable them to meet individually or in weekly groups for conversation practice sessions, conferences with a teacher, and personalized guidance. Funds may be needed to provide adequate differentiated staffing for the program: master teachers, teaching interns, paraprofessional aides, secretarial help, and personnel to maintain the books and equipment in the resource center. Additional funds may also be required for orienting and training staff members, for developing curricula, writing learning packets, and creating supplementary materials such as tapes or cassettes, visuals, and cultural units. Grade reporting procedures need to be modified so that students receive credit as it is earned.

Evaluations of continuous progress individualized programs have been generally favorable. Students and teachers have indicated preference for individual pacing over lockstepped procedures,[5] and some programs have reported lower attrition rates and higher enrollments.[6] In terms of subject-matter achievement, though some students may master only half the year's normal work, proponents nevertheless claim that on standardized measures, students in individualized programs generally perform at least as well as

---

* Language masters (also called audio-flashcards) are cards with foreign-language words or a sentence on a strip of magnetic tape and the corresponding written text printed alongside. As students push the cards through a specially designed machine, they both hear and see the foreign-language material. Language masters are used primarily for drilling pronunciation, spelling, and structural patterns.

their counterparts in traditionally taught classes, and in some cases they perform better.[7]

6.3.2 Transferability of Continuous Progress Instruction

As a result of favorable publicity, more and more language teachers have begun experimenting with continuous progress in the early 1970s. While many have written glowing testimonials to the effectiveness of this approach,[8] others have abandoned this class style because it has proved unworkable in their teaching situation. Major criticisms include: the inability of many students to assume responsibility for their own progress; the sacrifice of listening and speaking skills when students work alone; the sheer impossibility of providing sufficient individual attention within the limitations of existing student-teacher ratios; the extraordinary burden of preparing packets and correcting papers; and the difficulty of articulating continuous progress classes with those taught by traditional methods.[9]

A major drawback for some teachers who have established continuous progress instruction is that to many students "their own pace" results in almost no pace at all. In some cases, self-paced students have finished only half the material they might have completed had deadlines been imposed. Students themselves have frankly admitted their inability to exercise sufficient self-discipline and have asked that learning schedules be established for them. Though on one hand this defeats the purpose of developing individual responsibility and initiative, on the other it is hard to justify conferring on students greater freedom of choice than they can comfortably handle. For this reason, some continuous progress programs have adopted minimum levels of accomplishment that students must meet each quarter or semester.

Though the continuous progress model of instruction has enjoyed considerable attention and interest in the late 1960s and early 1970s, some teachers have begun to admit private reservations about it. In some schools students' oral skills have suffered under this model of instruction, and mastery of grammar has been incomplete due to excessive learning speeds. A further objection arises when acceleration in foreign-language learning results in decreases in enrollments. For example, some students who finish a three-year language sequence in only two years may elect to end their foreign-language studies rather than continue to more advanced courses. In an era of cutbacks in foreign-language positions, many teachers are reluctant to contribute further to this situation, especially when they have serious reservations about the quality of students' learning under continuous progress.

Experience so far seems to indicate that the continuous progress model of instruction is successful only when it is thoroughly understood, when teachers can devote sufficient time and energy to necessary planning, and when administrators provide the support and funds necessary for its implementation. There are, however, some programs that lack some or many of the ideal conditions required and that nevertheless are successful.[10]

6.3.3 Flexible Pacing

A more conservative solution to the problem of allowing for individual differences in learning rates has been the establishment of deadlines for each unit of study or, where necessary, for each unit objective. This approach, which we call "flexible pacing," has proved attractive to teachers who want to individualize pace but must ensure at least minimal rates of progress.[10] Students who in flexibly paced classes finish their assignments ahead of their classmates work on "horizontal" enrichment materials or serve as peer teachers, rather than proceeding "vertically" to new grammatical topics. In a typical flexibly paced class, roughly the first half of the period might be used for full-group presentations of grammar, culture, skits, or for small-group conversation practice. During the second part of the period, students could request additional explanations or help, practice with tapes or with friends, report for oral or written testing when ready, or engage in extra-credit enrichment activities. In addition to fostering group cohesiveness and spirit, the full-class sessions provide needed direction and guidance for students who are not yet prepared to work on their own without direct teacher contact and supervision. This style of instruction can also provide for greater attention to the listening and speaking skills, which may risk being neglected in classes where students proceed at their own rates.

A system of flexible pacing offers advantages: Teachers can more easily keep up with their class preparations; students may be grouped on a daily basis according to their individual learning needs without recourse to special administrative scheduling procedures; articulation is no longer a problem, since at the end of the year all students have completed roughly the same amounts of basic material; if the minimum rate of progress set is a reasonable expectation for the majority of students, failure rates can be reduced considerably. A significant feature of flexibly paced programs of individualization is that they can function effectively within the framework of a traditional school system. Special provisions are not required for grade reporting, extra funding, additional staff, or special learning facilities. These considerations are important for teachers who want to begin individualizing but lack initial administrative cooperation and support. The greater amount of structure and control inherent in the large-group, small-group, and independent activities of flexibly paced classes has led two prominent educators to suggest this learning style as a means of combatting the fragmentation and loss of oral skills that may occur in some continuous progress situations.[11] A sample six-day lesson plan for a flexibly paced grammar unit is presented in Appendix B.

6.4 CHOICE OF LEARNING METHODS

While providing for differences in learning rates is an important first step in the process of individualization, it is by no means final in meeting the needs of all students; individual differences in preferred methods of learning must also be considered. Though some students enjoy oral practice, others would rather read or write. Many are satisfied with basic textbook presentations, but others need the visual stimuli of flashcards, overhead transparencies, films, filmstrips, and slides. Certain students become restless when the teacher explains grammar to the entire class and would rather learn it on their own; others in the class, however, insist on these explanations in order to feel they really understand the new material. Mechanically inclined students enjoy working with the various machines that may be available for their use: tape or cassette recorders, language masters, or overhead, slide, or film projectors. Other students may become impatient with these learning aids. In view of these differences, a well-developed program of individualized instruction should provide choices not only in the area of learning rate, but also in the area of learning method. Several such programs with well-developed multimedia components are described in the literature.[12] Possibilities for incorporating various media into an individualized program are treated in Chapter 8 and in Part Three of this book.

6.5 CHOICE OF COURSE CONTENT

There are three principal ways in which course content may be individualized to meet students' interests. At intermediate and advanced levels, both mini-courses and interdisciplinary studies have become popular alternatives to the traditional curriculum. At beginning and early intermediate stages of language learning, carefully prepared elective assignments can in some measure provide flexibility of course content. Each of these approaches is discussed in the following sections.[13]

6.5.1 *Mini-Courses*

Once students have acquired a basic working knowledge of the foreign language, flexibility of content is possible. Mini-courses have thus become an extremely popular way of appealing to varied student interests in intermediate and advanced courses.[14] Lasting from a few weeks up to an entire semester, these courses are offered in areas of need and interest that students have indicated, sometimes by voting during the previous semester. When enrollments and staffing permit, two or more mini-courses are scheduled for the same hour, so that students may choose the one they prefer. A few popular mini-course topics are conversation and composition, cooking, art and music, foreign language for travelers, current events, poetry, short stories, novels, and major historical developments. An advantage of mini-courses is that they can significantly reduce attrition rates at upper levels of language study. They also offer the possibility of combining intermediate and advanced students in one class so that enrollments will be sufficient to justify these classes in the curriculum.[15]

Mini-courses are taught in a variety of ways. While some are handled in a lockstepped, full-class fashion, others are characterized by large-group meetings, together with small-group activities and independent research. Continuous progress, however, does not normally characterize the teaching style in these classes. At this stage of language learning, most students need to meet in small or large groups to discuss the new material with the teacher and exchange ideas on it. Students who enjoy working alone would enroll in independent study, rather than in a mini-course. The purpose of media used in mini-courses differs somewhat from what it is in beginning and intermediate classes. Though tapes, records, films, slides, filmstrips, and video tapes may occupy a significant portion of class time, these media are used because they happen to constitute the best available means of making certain presentations to the entire class. They are not employed as alternate resources designed to appeal to individual methods of learning, as is the case in earlier levels.

6.5.2 *Interdisciplinary Studies*

The recognition that not all foreign-language students wish to pursue linguistic, literary, or cultural goals at intermediate and advanced levels has led to the development of interdisciplinary studies. Depending upon the facilities and personnel available in each school, foreign languages have been the principal means of communicating instruction in subjects as diverse as elementary math and science, history and techniques of historical research, ethnic and cultural minorities, vocational guidance, and human dynamics.[16] Teaching may be full-class or in small groups. In some schools students take courses in the foreign language two or more periods a day in order to enjoy a "total immersion" experience and in some cases agree to eat lunch together in order to benefit from additional opportunities for conversation. Media may or may not be essential parts of the course. When scheduling and teacher background make interdisciplinary courses feasible, they can greatly increase student interest in foreign-language study and offer exciting and stimulating ways to individualize intermediate and advanced courses.

6.5.3 *Elective Assignments*

In beginning classes, the possibility of appealing to individual students' interests is somewhat limited, since most course content is determined by the necessity of teaching basic language concepts and specific vocabulary items. Even so, once students have mastered the core material they may elect extra-credit assignments in areas of their particular interests. Though their foreign-language reading ability is at an elementary level, there are, nevertheless, activities suitable for them. They might, for example, select simplified reading texts on sports, fashion, or food in the foreign culture from language magazines published monthly and written specifically for beginners.[17] Students might correspond with a pen pal[18] or follow current events in local newspapers or magazines. They might browse through foreign-language publications available in the classroom or learning center and list the new words they learn. Older publications might be cut up and assembled in scrapbooks. Artistically inclined students might make flashcards, grammar charts, or even create foreign-language games based on material learned. Written or oral reports in English in the areas of art, music, literature, or science are other possible choices. Sample assignments of this nature are included in Appendix C.

6.6 SELECTING A STYLE OF INDIVIDUALIZED INSTRUCTION

The model selected for an individualized program ultimately depends upon a number of factors: community pressures, student needs, and administrative policies as well as available personnel, equipment, physical resources, and funds.

If there is community pressure for accelerated learning and the development of advanced placement courses, the vertical individualization of the continuous progress, nongraded approach is a likely choice. If parents and students seek courses in languages not included in the curriculum, or if enrollments cannot support certain specialized advanced classes, independent study may fill this need. In school districts where teachers and administrators are receptive to change and where financial support is available for training staff members, hiring additional personnel, developing special materials such as learning packets, and acquiring audio-visual equipment, the independent study and continuous-progress-multimedia approaches will have a good chance of succeeding.

In situations where declining enrollments, student underachievement, discipline problems, and individual learning differences are of concern, either continuous progress or flexibly paced instruction coupled with multimedia presentations offers viable solutions. Teachers who must deal with conservative administrators, lockstepped grading and grouping policies, generally passive and dependent students, and the prospect of increasingly tight budgets may find the flexible pacing model more suitable to their situations.

Another factor that may determine the style of individualization chosen is the maturity and language level of students. Since most beginning students need some supervision and correction if they are to develop accurate pronunciation habits and speaking proficiency, the controlled oral group work that is possible with flexible pacing may be more effective than the freer structure of an individually paced continuous progress style of instruction. Younger, less mature, less independent students might meet with greater success in a program offering full-class teaching, guided small-group activities, and a selection of structured assignments than in a program where they must bear the major responsibility for their own progress. Once students have learned how to learn a language, however, they might very well benefit from the wider choices offered by continuous progress or independent study.

Finally, the level for which the individualized instruction is intended also influences the choice of classroom style. As has been stated, while independent study can be used at any language level, the continuous progress, flexible pacing, and multimedia models are relevant mainly at beginning and early intermediate levels when students are still acquiring fundamental language skills. Once these skills have been acquired, however, programs that center on providing for individual differences in interest, such as mini-courses and interdisciplinary studies, are more relevant to the needs of intermediate and advanced students.

NOTES

[1] A contrary view is expressed in Frank M. Grittner and Fred H. Laleike, *Individualized Foreign Language Instruction* (Skokie, Ill.: National Textbook Co., 1973), pp. 1–21.

[2] For program descriptions, see "Guided Individualized Study in Foreign Languages," "Managed Self-Instruction Using Programmed Materials," "Self-Instruction in FLES Spanish," and "Computer-Assisted Independent Latin Study," in F. William D. Love and Lucille J. Honig, *Options and Perspectives: A Sourcebook of Innovative Foreign Language Programs in Action, K-12* (New York: Modern Language Association of America, 1973), pp. 97–104, 153–62, 331–33, and 265–67.

[3] Stephen L. Levy, "John Dewey High School: Individualization in an Inner-City School," in *Foreign Language Annals*, vol. 5, no. 3 (March 1972), pp. 346–48; also described in Stephen L. Levy, "Foreign Languages in John Dewey High School, New York City: An Individualized Approach," in Ronald L. Gougher, ed., *Individualization of Instruction in Foreign Languages: A Practical Guide* (Philadelphia: Center for Curriculum Development, 1972), pp. 130–48.

[4] See Harry Reinert, "Practical Guide to Individualization," *The Modern Language Journal*, vol. 55, no. 3 (March 1971), pp. 155–61; Robert A. Morrey, "Individualization of Foreign Language Instruction Through Differentiated Staffing," *The Modern Language Journal*, vol. 56, no. 8 (December 1972), pp. 483–88; see also "Individualized German Instruction," "Individualized Instruction in Foreign Languages," "John Dewey High School Foreign Language Program," "Individualized Foreign Language Islands," and "Individualized Instruction," in Love and Honig, 1973 (see note 2), pp. 105–16, 132–42, 296–98, and 299–301. For further information, see Grittner and Laleike, 1973 (see note 1).

⁵ See Robert A. Morrey, "The Attitudes of Students and Teachers to Individualized Foreign Language Instruction," in Howard B. Altman and Robert L. Politzer, eds., *Individualizing Foreign Language Instruction: Proceedings of the Stanford Conference* (Rowley, Mass.: Newbury House Publishers, 1971), pp. 21–51.

⁶ Gerhard Clausing and Klaus A. Mueller, "Individualized Instruction Increases Enrollment at Berkeley," *Foreign Language Annals*, vol. 6, no. 4 (May 1973), pp. 532–33.

⁷ "Individualized Foreign Language Instruction," in Love and Honig, 1973 (see note 2), pp. 125–29.

⁸ Sharon Hellman, "You *Can* Individualize the Teaching of Foreign Languages," *The French Review*, vol. 45, no. 6 (May 1972), pp. 1152–60; Rita O. Kentz, "The Kids Are More Important than the System: An Experience with Personalized French Instruction," *The American Foreign Language Teacher*, vol. 3, no. 1 (Fall 1972), pp. 35–37.

⁹ A useful list of factors to consider is presented in John F. Bockman, "A Checklist for Development and Control of Individualized Instruction," in Gougher, 1972 (see note 3), pp. 79–85.

¹⁰ Flexibly paced programs that have been described in the professional literature are: Nancyanne Fitzgibbons, "The Open Classroom: A Case Study," in James W. Dodge, ed., *Leadership for Continuing Development. Reports of the Working Committees of the Northeast Conference on the Teaching of Foreign Languages.* (New York: Modern Language Association Materials Center, 1970), pp. 97–107; Joan S. Freilich, "French in a Flexible Classroom," *The French Review*, vol. 46, no. 6 (May 1973), pp. 1172–77. See also "Student-Centered Classroom," "Flexible Foreign Language Classroom," and "Coordination of Skills in an Individualized Program," in Love and Honig, 1973 (see note 2), pp. 215–24, 282–84, and 272–74.

¹¹ Nelson Brooks, "Introduction" to *A-LM in the Individualized Classroom* (New York: Harcourt Brace Jovanovich, 1973), pp. 2–5; and Florence Steiner, "Individualized Instruction Revisited: A Progress Report," *American Foreign Language Teacher*, vol. 4, no. 1 (Fall 1973), pp. 3 and 38–40.

¹² "Middle School Foreign Language: A Media Approach," "Spanish Culture," and "Latin, Horseshoe Style," in Love and Honig, 1973 (see note 2), pp. 306–10, 338–41, and 302–05; see also Gerald E. Logan, *Individualized Foreign Language Learning: An Organic Process* (Rowley, Mass.: Newbury House Publishers, 1973), pp. 48–51.

¹³ See also Logan (1973), pp. 37–47.

¹⁴ See Robert C. LaFayette, "A Foreign Language Option: The Mini-Course," *Curriculum Report* (Washington, D.C.: National Association of Secondary School Principals), vol. 3, no. 1 (October 1973).

[15] Program descriptions are found in: Donald C. Ryberg and Marcia Hallock, "Development of Mini-Courses at Marshall-University High School: Individualization and Interest," in Gougher, 1972 (see note 3), pp. 119–29; "Mini-Course Curriculŭm," and "Quinmester Program in Foreign Languages," in Love and Honig, 1973 (see note 2), pp. 163–72 and 185–92; and Warren C. Born, ed., *Toward Student-Centered Foreign-Language Programs*. Reports of the Working Committees of the Northeast Conference on the Teaching of Foreign Languages. (New York: Modern Language Association Materials Center, 1974), pp. 79–85.

[16] For program descriptions, see: "Butler Area Language Saturation Program"; "The French in Delaware"; "Minority Studies in Foreign Languages"; "The Skyline Center: World Language Clusters and Career Development Center"; "Total Immersion Language Program (TIP)"; and "Saturation Program"; in Love and Honig, 1973 (see note 2), pp. 15–25, 78–85, 173–84, 193–203, 243–52, and 327–30.

[17] Two sources of foreign-language publications for students are: Scholastic Magazines, Sylvan Cliffs, Englewood, N.J. (French, German, and Spanish); and Xerox Education Publications, Education Center, 1250 Fairwood Avenue, Columbus, Ohio 43216 (French and Spanish).

[18] Some sources of foreign pen pals are: World Pen Pals, World Affairs Center, University of Minnesota, Minneapolis, Minn. 55455; International Friendship League, 40 Mt. Vernon Street, Boston, Mass. 02108; Student Letter Exchange, Waseca, Minn. 56093; and International Youth Service, 20101 Turku, Finland. Tape Pals sources are: World Tapes for Education, P.O. Box 15703, Dallas, Texas 75215; and The Voicepondence Club, P.O. Box 14452, Long Beach, Calif. 90814.

PART TWO
MANAGEMENT CONSIDERATIONS

CHAPTER SEVEN
STAFFING AN INDIVIDUALIZED PROGRAM

7.1 GENERAL CONSIDERATIONS

As is commonly acknowledged, it is extremely difficult for one classroom teacher working alone with 25 students and a textbook to individualize foreign-language instruction successfully. If teachers intend to offer additional help to slow learners as well as guidance and attention to all students, they need assistance in the classroom. They must be released from some of their more mechanical duties, such as clerical work, passing out papers, and leading practice drill groups, so that they can help with individual problems. One means of accomplishing this goal is to employ additional teaching personnel.

The primary concern regarding extra staff members must be financial. Some schools may be willing to support a program that requires higher expenditures for salaries; many are not. Where budgets permit, additional staff may consist of paid native informants, teaching interns, secretaries, and technicians. If extra funds are not available, then the supplementary personnel —student teachers, adult volunteers from the community, and student aides—must be unpaid. A compromise approach that has enjoyed some administrative favor involves replacing some certified teachers with less expensive, noncertified personnel who report to the team leader or master teacher. This practice, however, has been vehemently opposed by some teachers' organizations fighting to preserve positions in rapidly dwindling language departments.

No attempt will be made here to prescribe particular staff or staffing structure[1] for an individualized program. Rather, various types of teaching personnel will be considered and some of their instructional roles described.[2] From this list, the reader may determine the number and type of people that can fit into the individualized program envisioned for his or her school.

7.2 CERTIFIED TEACHERS

Certified or credentialed teachers, whether they belong to a differentiated staff as master teachers, team leaders or assistants, or whether they manage their classrooms alone, are at the heart of the entire instructional process. They work with administrators to establish an individualized program, request needed equipment and personnel for it, provide for learning packets and supplementary materials, and assume overall responsibility for maintaining and improving the quality of instruction. Within the classroom, their duties include presenting new material as necessary, leading conversation groups, evaluating the students' oral and written work, and guiding them toward activities suited to their individual abilities and interests. These teachers seek to promote interest and enjoyment by demonstrating genuine concern for students' success, by providing help for those having difficulty, and by encouraging them to actualize their potential abilities.

7.3 NATIVE INFORMANTS

Native informants may be either paid or unpaid. In some communities there are residents willing to donate several hours a week helping in foreign-language programs. Notices printed in a PTA bulletin or in the local newspaper can help bring these people into the classroom. If funds are available, native informants might be recruited from among students in nearby colleges or universities. Securing personnel through agencies such as Amity Aid Program[3] is another popular alternative. This agency arranges for college-age foreign students to exchange their help in the classroom for room, board, and a living allowance. Native speakers can provide conversation practice, serve as models for pronunciation, offer additional explanations to students needing them, and provide a wealth of cultural information. Since they are not usually trained to teach, however, they require thorough orientation to the program and its objectives as well as close supervision during their initial classroom experiences.[4]

7.4 STUDENT TEACHERS AND TEACHING INTERNS

Student teachers have finished all or most of their course work and need classroom teaching experience in order to complete the requirements for their bachelor's degree and their teaching credentials. Teaching interns, on the other hand, have already received their diploma and teach two or three classes a day in order to earn certification. While student teachers pay their college or university for supervising their classroom experience, teaching interns receive a small salary from the school where they work. Whether student teachers or teaching interns are available to a particular district depends on the certification procedures of the particular state. In either event, this type of personnel, when properly supervised, can greatly enhance the quality of an individualized program at little or no cost.

Teachers interested in employing precertification personnel should establish contacts with the appropriate professors or administrators at colleges and universities in the region; these university representatives might then visit the school to acquaint themselves with the individualized program and to see how student teachers or interns could be incorporated into it. Some of the duties of these personnel could include marking tests and compositions, preparing teaching and testing materials, creating audio and visual aids, providing individual help and guidance, administering oral and written tests, evaluating individual student progress, presenting cultural information, and leading both small-group and full-class activities. Ultimately, they should be capable of assuming all the teaching and management functions of the certified classroom teacher.[5]

7.5 STUDENT AIDES AND TUTORS

Where student teachers or teaching interns are unavailable, student aides or tutors from within the school system itself can serve as highly valuable adjuncts in an individualized program. Usually, these students are at least one level or one course ahead of the learners they help. While student aides are employed in the classroom to help anyone needing extra attention, tutors usually take responsibility for one or more students whom they meet individually *outside* of class time when both are free. Such teaching arrangements are increasing in popularity because in nearly all cases the students involved profit considerably from the experience.

Tutors and aides may teach during periods when they are not scheduled for classes, or they may volunteer their services before or after school. In some instances, students receive activity credit which qualifies them for membership in language or academic honor societies. If students in a given school have no free periods, then perhaps arrangements can be made to have aiding and tutoring count as a regular foreign-language course. An advantage of giving subject credit to aides and tutors is that the supervisory teacher can meet with these students, give them needed instructions for that particular day or week, and discuss with them problems that may be encountered in class. Student aides might keep a log or diary of their classroom experiences in the foreign language, which they would then submit in order to earn their course credit. They might also be required to pass the oral and written tests of the course before administering them to other students.

The involvement of students in the teaching process is highly recommended when feasible. Not only do the aides and tutors benefit cognitively from teaching; there are also affective rewards of closer relationships with teachers. Students gain a greater sense of belonging, as well as feelings of increased maturity and concern for others when they are responsible for the success of another learner. Based on teachers' recommendations, even average students can become satisfactory aides and should be employed, along with good and outstanding students. If students have already passed the course in which they are to teach, they will need little orientation. Still, teachers need to explain classroom procedures and closely supervise student aides and tutors, especially during the beginning phases of their participation.

The use of aides and tutors must be controlled if the program is to succeed. There are some activities that most student aides should probably not be permitted to carry out. While they may check knowledge of relatively simple activities such as vocabulary items, oral pattern drills, and written exercises—essentially learning steps at taxonomic stages 2 and 3—they should not have the ultimate responsibility for testing and evaluating the students' ability to communicate orally and in writing (Stage 4 behaviors). Their grading of papers must also be limited. While aides can probably mark short-answer tests, they should not have responsibility for compositions or free-response exams. In some cases, students should not have access to the teacher's gradebook. Aside from the question of moral integrity, there is a good chance for human error in the recording process which should therefore be handled only by the teacher, another adult, or, if necessary, a very mature student.

Filing of student papers can be another responsibility of student aides if other clerical help is unavailable, but this should not be their main activity, since it does not relate directly to language learning. Some other areas in which student aides and tutors can function effectively are: explaining simple material to slower students who need extra help or to those who have been absent; checking off vocabulary tests and oral or written drills that have been completed satisfactorily; distributing packets or instruction sheets; handing out written tests from the cabinet; supervising the testing area; collecting test papers; and putting away tapes, cassettes, and visual materials. Highly competent aides may be involved in leading conversation groups, working with accelerated students, correcting pronunciation, and offering additional explanations of difficult material.[6]

7.6 PEER TEACHERS

Peer teaching has also drawn significant favorable comment in professional circles because of positive results in both the cognitive and the affective domains. Peer teachers are students who complete their work more rapidly than their classmates and volunteer to help slower learners rather than proceed to new material. This arrangement is suitable when material for advanced lessons has not yet been prepared, when school policy does not provide for acceleration, or when a student prefers working with a slower-learning friend to going ahead on his own. The responsibilities of peer teachers can include supplementary grammar explanations and oral paired practice of pattern drills and conversation questions. Peers should not normally be allowed to test each other, however. Extra-credit points might be awarded to students who are effective peer teachers.

7.7 SECRETARIAL HELP

Individualized language programs characteristically entail large amounts of clerical work such as typing, filing, and record keeping. Whatever secretarial help can be made available to teachers can greatly ease their burden of preparation and provide additional time for program development and improvement. While more and more schools are providing paid full-time or part-time secretaries to language departments, this practice is still more the exception than the rule. Many teachers will therefore need to find ways of obtaining clerical services at no cost.

One possibility may be parent volunteers from the community who serve several hours a week in the school. Another alternative can be students from business education classes who receive course credit or service credit for helping the foreign-language program. As mentioned above, student aides can assume some light clerical duties, but these should not constitute the major part of their responsibility. Depending on the maturity and the secretarial and linguistic skills of the individual, clerical duties may include: answering correspondence regarding the individualized program; typing learning materials in the foreign language; running off and collating the sheets for learning packets; filing instructional materials and student work; and recording student progress.

7.8 TECHNICAL ASSISTANTS

The need for technical assistance will be determined primarily by the audio-visual equipment the school owns and how it is used. Relatively simple individualized programs that depend primarily on tapes, cassettes, and language masters stored in the classroom can operate successfully merely with teacher supervision supplemented by help from students. Some schools have audio-visual clubs that can provide services such as duplicating tapes, transferring recorded material onto cassettes, and labelling and filing tapes and cassettes. In other schools there are media or materials centers where supplementary audio and visual materials can be prepared on request.

More complex audio-visual arrangements, which include tapes, films, filmstrips, slides, and overhead transparencies for individual student use on a library basis, will naturally require additional staffing of the resource center. Each member of the language department might be assigned to the center for one period each day. Another arrangement is to hire a full-time technician, or perhaps several language majors from nearby colleges or universities for part-time work. The technical assistants can be responsible for maintaining equipment in good working order, establishing filing systems for materials, duplicating audio or visual materials, creating visuals needed by teachers, and ensuring the safe return of materials borrowed by students. Depending on their language backgrounds, they may also be able to offer individual help to students requesting it.

7.9 POSITIVE WORKING RELATIONSHIPS AMONG CLASSROOM PERSONNEL

In a traditionally taught classroom, there is little question as to who gives the orders and who takes them, since the teacher is considerably more mature and more skilled than the students. However, in an individualized classroom staffed by the regular teacher, paraprofessional adults, teachers-in-training, or student aides, the traditional lines of authority may become blurred. In some cases, a paraprofessional may be older than the certified teacher, or a native informant may possess greater linguistic competence than the teacher does. Unless precautionary steps are taken, rivalries may develop that can undermine the program and nullify the benefits of differentiated staffing. Ways of avoiding conflicts are presented below.

7.9.1 *Interviewing Potential Staff Members*

Ideally, teachers should interview all adults who propose to help in the individualized program. This is especially true of paid personnel, though it applies to everyone: native informants, community volunteers, student teachers, teaching interns, secretaries, and technical assistants. The interviewer should evaluate each applicant's foreign-language competence and ask why the applicant wants to work in the individualized program. The philosophy, goals, and teaching methods of the program should be clearly explained in order to determine if the applicant's beliefs are in harmony with them. The duties and responsibilities involved in the position should also be well defined before the person joins the staff. Questions regarding the daily operations of the program should be answered and applicants should have a chance to see what the classroom is like before deciding whether they will feel comfortable as part of it. Though a formal interview may not always prove feasible within the busy schedules of overburdened classroom teachers, they nevertheless may be able to arrange a trial session during which the prospective staff member participates in classroom activities. In the case of student aides, these interview procedures are usually unnecessary. The recommendation of a teacher who is familiar with their classwork as well as the students' own experiences within the individualized program (at least, after its first year of operation) should be sufficient to preclude serious problems.

7.9.2 *Supervising Staff Members*

During the first few days or weeks that paraprofessionals or teachers-in-training spend in the classroom, teachers should endeavor to supervise them directly as much as they can. Any criticisms, however, should be saved for after the class period so as to avoid embarrassing the new staff members in front of students. After this initial period, supervision can become more indirect. Teachers may observe the other ongoing activities in the classroom from the corners of their eyes, even while they themselves are fully engaged in teaching. Or, they can momentarily listen to a teaching activity as they move from one part of the room to another. Teachers should be aware of which students were taught by the other staff members that day, and they could casually ask the students as they leave class (or the next day) whether or not they understood the material presented to them. Another alternative is to test the students—either orally or in writing—over the material that the paraprofessional, native speaker, or teacher-in-training has presented. Suggestions for improvement of the teaching can be made in conference periods held during the school day.

7.9.3 *Avoiding Conflicts of Authority*

Though native informants and student teachers may ultimately carry out the same classroom functions as the certified teachers, the primary authority in classroom situations should rest with the regular teachers, unless they specifically designate another person to assume responsibility. Staff members must understand that they should never contradict the teacher's policies in front of students nor should they openly disagree with the teacher. Differences of opinion should be thoroughly discussed, but this should take place outside of class. Insofar as possible, the teaching and testing procedures as well as classroom management policies of both teachers and their staff members should be uniform. If this is not the case, students will be quick to play one adult against the other. For example, if students think the native speaker gives harder oral tests, they will complain about him or her. Or, if the classroom teacher expressly forbids a certain activity—such as leaving the room very often—and students know that the teaching intern will permit this, they will take advantage of the inconsistency and thereby undermine the teacher's authority. For this reason, all classroom rules, regulations, and procedures must be enforced uniformly by all personnel. Otherwise, serious conflicts of authority may develop.

Conflicts may also arise when classroom teachers possess less linguistic competence than native informants or student teachers. Rather than feel threatened or defensive, these teachers should freely acknowledge to students that sometimes they do not know all the answers and they should encourage students to consult the other teacher. They might also stress how fortunate the class is to have a native speaker who can model pronunciation, help them speak correctly, and present the culture of the foreign country. Privately, teachers may ask the native speaker to list the errors they make and to call them to their attention after class, but not during class. Should the teacher be corrected in front of students, he or she should gracefully acknowledge the error and thank the native for pointing it out.

Another area of potential conflict can involve the grading of students' work. For example, students might complain to the teacher about the evaluation given them by a student teacher, or the reverse may occur. In these circumstances it is extremely important to avoid the direct contradiction of one member of the staff by another. This can be accomplished in two ways. If a simple clerical or computational error has been made, the student should be instructed to discuss the mistake with the person who made it, who will then correct the error if necessary. If the student disputes a subjective evaluation of his or her work, the teacher and the other staff member involved should discuss the paper privately in order to clarify grading criteria and reevaluate the paper. Then, the person who originally assigned the mark should tell the student what action will be taken and explain the reasoning behind it.

7.9.5 *Avoiding Displays of Favoritism*

It is advisable to rotate all teaching personnel among the students, rather than assign a single group to one person. In this way, no students feel deprived of attention from their official teacher, and possible problems with parents are avoided. Another reason for rotating personnel is to enable regular classroom teachers to acquaint themselves with *all* the members of their classes. This is especially important, since the classroom teachers are the ones ultimately responsible for evaluating each student's achievements. When students are asked to form groups for various classroom learning activities, it is advisable to assign a leader *after* the groups have assembled, not before. This procedure precludes the possibility of students choosing to join a group because they like the leader, rather than because they need the activity offered.

An effective management practice is to avoid *all* situations in which students have opportunities to choose between members of the teaching team. Preferences on the part of the learners are almost inevitable, but they should be deemphasized as much as possible so as not to cause feelings of ill will or embarrassment. In some cases, for example, students may choose a student teacher over the regular classroom teacher because they have the impression that the younger person will be less strict with them. Conversely, students may display a preference for the official teacher because he or she may appear clearly more competent than the other personnel. In such cases, the teacher should be alert to the situation and analyze it to make sure there are no serious underlying problems that need to be resolved. If students seem to avoid working with the teacher, this may be due to nothing more serious than the fact that they perceive the teacher as an evaluator, while the student teacher or native paraprofessional is seen as an ally. Regular rotation of teaching and testing duties should largely dispel this impression, though teachers should also make sure that their established policies are carried out with consistency and uniformity by all team members. Careful thought and attention to the dynamics of classroom relationships can promote harmony and cooperation among staff members and can dispel feelings of jealousy or rivalry.

7.10 CAUTION IN STAFFING

A word of caution is in order regarding any use of paraprofessionals as teachers. In many communities both parents' and teachers' organizations oppose this practice on the grounds that teachers are paid to teach and should not be allowed to use untrained and unqualified help in the classroom. This argument has considerable merit, especially in view of the shortage of jobs for certified teachers. Even an outstanding student or native informant can rarely equal the skill of an experienced adult teacher. For this reason, teachers should select personnel carefully, supervise them closely, and limit their teaching activities to auxiliary functions, such as providing additional explanation and practice or checking fairly mechanical oral or written work. Primary teaching functions such as creating materials, presenting new grammar, and testing and evaluating student performance should normally be reserved for certified staff members or closely supervised precertification personnel.

NOTES

[1] A differentiated staff is described in Frank M. Grittner and Fred. H. Laleike, *Individualized Foreign Language Instruction* (Skokie, Ill.: National Textbook Co., 1973), pp. 11–18.

[2] A description of the teaching roles of various staff members is presented in Robert A. Morrey, "Individualization of Foreign Language Instruction Through Differentiated Staffing," *The Modern Language Journal*, vol. 56, no. 8 (December 1972), pp. 483–88.

[3] Amity, Box 118, Del Mar, Calif. 92014.

[4] See also William M. R. Hammelmann and Melvin L. Nielson, "The Native Paraprofessional: Identifying His Role in the Foreign Language Program," *Foreign Language Annals*, vol. 7, no. 3 (March 1974), pp. 346–52.

[5] See also Jean-Pierre Berwald, "Supervising Student Teachers in Individualized Foreign Language Classes," *Modern Language Journal*, vol. 58, no. 3 (March 1974), pp. 91–95.

[6] See also Susan M. Cameron-Bacon, "Using the Student Assistant in Individualized Foreign-Language Instruction," *Modern Language Journal*, vol. 58, no. 3 (March 1974), pp. 353–56.

CHAPTER EIGHT
EQUIPPING AN INDIVIDUALIZED PROGRAM

8.1 GENERAL CONSIDERATIONS

Instructional aids such as tape recorders can serve to free teachers from mechanical drilling so that they can focus on individual learning problems. Films, slides, and transparencies can increase student interest by adding variety and visual appeal to the course. By and large, however, the vast potential of the numerous kinds of audio-visual equipment available today has never been fulfilled on a nationwide scale. All across the country tape recorders stand idle because students refuse to use them; overhead projectors gather dust because interesting visuals are unavailable; video-tape recorders remain locked in storage closets because teachers do not know how to incorporate them into their instructional program; films, filmstrips, and slides are regularly hauled out for viewing as entertainment before vacations but are rarely integrated into the instructional program; foreign-language magazines and newspapers pile up, unread, in large, unwieldy stacks in classroom corners.

A major problem in foreign-language education today is that many teachers and administrators point to the mere existence of expensive machines—even unused machines—as a sign of high quality instruction in their school. This reverence for hardware and relative disregard for the software needed to go with it—interesting tapes, stimulating visuals, ideas for their use by students—has often rendered the equipment itself virtually ineffective in promoting greater subject-matter achievement and more positive feelings toward language learning. Even in schools where audio-visual equipment does constitute an integral and vital part of the overall curriculum, it is still necessary to recognize the inherent limitations of such devices. While films, filmstrips, and slides can present new material in a fresh and appealing format, students receiving the information are essentially passive; some follow-up activity is needed so that students can use the material in a personally meaningful way. Though pictures and other visuals are extremely useful in stimulating conversation, the oral responses students offer are of necessity quite limited. Students often answer what they know their teacher expects, not what they themselves really *want* to say. Visuals are therefore usually more suited to controlled oral and written practice than they are to free communication. Similarly, taped pattern drills necessarily limit students to fixed responses. Though this activity may ultimately facilitate free communication, it should not be confused with it.

The point of this discussion is that behind every machine there must be a person to provide suitable material for it, to guide students in its proper use, and to offer the opportunities for real human communication that are beyond the scope of a mechanical device. Though this chapter will list various types of equipment that may be used in an individualized classroom or learning center, no machine should be considered indispensable. The only indispensable elements in the classroom are the teacher and the students themselves. Furthermore, in deciding whether to invest limited funds in the purchase of certain equipment, it would be well to consider whether there are also creative staff members who can provide the software needed for its effective utilization. One should also consider whether the best long-run investment would be in *human*, rather than nonhuman, resources. For the purposes of this chapter, the term *equipment* will be considered in its broadest sense and will include a wide variety of materials and machines that might conceivably be used in an individualized program. No ideal program is presented, since each school is different in its needs and in available funds. Items are listed roughly from the most essential and inexpensive to those that are less crucial and most costly.[1]

8.2 PAPER AND PAPER PRODUCTS

Individualized programs normally require enormous amounts of paper. If students are to act responsibly while working on their own, they must be given specific written instructions as to what they must do as well as what they *may* do if they choose. Paper products such as folders, index cards, and envelopes are also needed in quantity for organizing and keeping track of student progress and various resource materials.

8.2.1 Dittoing and Stenciling

Learning packet pages may be prepared either on Dittos or stencils. Ditto machines are commonly available at most schools and offer ease of preparation and erasure at fairly low cost. Short-run Dittos can produce roughly 100–200 clear copies of material, while long-run Dittos may offer 200–500 reproductions. Stencils are more costly, harder to prepare and to erase, but can produce about 500–750 legible reproductions.

The duplication method chosen depends on a number of factors. While Dittos may be handwritten or typed, stencils require typing for written material and a special stylus for lines and drawings. During the early experimental phases of an individualized program, when a format for learning packets is still being worked out, less expensive Dittoing is suitable. Once the format has been determined, however, and once the learning materials have proved successful, a large number of stenciled copies can be produced for future classroom use. This practice can lighten the teacher's preparation burden in subsequent years and permit time for additional program development and improvement.

Colored paper for Dittoed and stenciled materials is a convenient and pleasant alternate to the standard white. In addition to giving variety and appeal to the learning materials, the sheets can be systematically color-coded to make them easier to find in filing cabinets or to let teachers know at a glance on what activity students are currently working.

8.2.2 File Folders and Index Cards

In programs that allow students to take tests when they are ready, teachers do not normally hand back exam papers to students. Instead, the papers are often filed in individual student folders, which may be consulted when needed. Large 8½-inch by 11-inch manila file folders are highly suitable for this purpose. They are also useful for filing learning packet sheets, vocabulary lists, extra-credit assignments, conversation sheets, pretests and tests, or any handouts a teacher wants to make available for student use. Manila file folders are also indispensable to teachers who want to organize teaching materials they have gathered from newspapers, magazines, travel agencies, personal travel, and so on.

Index cards have several classroom uses. They may serve as records of what books students have read. They can act as records of what items each student has signed out for home use—such as reading material or equipment—and when the items have been returned. In situations where highly individualized pacing makes using a gradebook impossible, index cards—such as flip cards, designed for business and real estate use—are useful for recording individual student progress.

8.2.3 *Manila Envelopes*

Manila envelopes, with their contents labeled, are very handy for making loose or easily mislaid cultural materials—such as postcards, travel brochures, menus, and so on—accessible to students. They can also be used for storing spelling or vocabulary flashcards as well as games having many pieces.

8.2.4 *Poster Board and Construction Paper*

Though usually found in art departments, poster board or heavy construction paper can serve several purposes in a foreign-language program. These materials are useful for visuals, grammar charts, and flashcards, which either the teacher or students may prepare. They can add a decorative touch to bulletin boards or can serve to chart the progress of individuals in the foreign-language class.

8.3 STORAGE FACILITIES

Since a wide variety of materials is essential to a well-developed program, storage space in an individualized classroom assumes even greater importance than in a traditional one. The storage facilities should allow materials and equipment to be kept neat and orderly, yet permit easy student access to them.

8.3.1 *File Cabinets*

Multiple-drawer file cabinets are indispensable for storing learning packet materials, individual student folders, and alternate forms of written exams. While cabinets with instruction sheets and so on can be open to students at all times, it is usually advisable to lock the test cabinet when it is not in use. If the file cabinets provided are insufficient and funds for additional ones are unavailable, cardboard boxes—perhaps decorated with contact paper—can serve as suitable replacements. When teachers can demonstrate a real need for additional file space, administrators will often agree to provide more cabinets.

8.3.2 *Storage Cabinets*

Many different items need cabinet storage: audio-visual machines, filmstrips, films, cassettes, tape reels, visuals, realia, games, and so on. Some cabinets have partitions designed to accommodate specific items; others provide general storage areas. In determining what the storage needs of a program will be, it is necessary for teachers to consider whether items of similar dimensions are to be stored or whether the materials are varied in size.

If there are large quantities of tapes or filmstrips, for example, specialized storage cabinets might be considered. If miscellaneous items are to be stored, then a general cabinet might be more suitable. When the name or number of each item stored is written on masking tape or paper tags affixed to the shelves, cabinets tend to remain neater, since students and teachers know where to replace the material borrowed.

8.3.3 Shelves

Shelves are needed for the books, magazines, newspapers, and pamphlets used in an individualized program. The type and size of shelves will depend naturally on how much material needs to be accommodated and how much wall space is available. School furniture catalogs offer a wide variety of bookcases, shelves, and open cabinets. If there are no funds to purchase them, perhaps the school's carpenter or students in wood shop classes could make some shelves. Parents in the community may have bookcases or shelving units at home that they are not using and can donate to the school. The old standby of plywood and bricks is another low-cost alternative. Makeshift shelf space can also be created from unused work tables that might be found in other departments or in the school's storerooms.

Library-supply catalogs contain descriptions of equipment designed to keep books, magazines, newspapers, and pamphlets neatly on the shelves. If these are not available to a newly initiated program, standard book ends are workable substitutes. It is important to keep the shelves in good order; if they are sloppy, students will not be eager to use the materials stored on them.

8.3.4 Pegboard

Pegboard and hooks are extremely handy for hanging up earphones when they are not in use. Relatively inexpensive and easily installed, pegboard can be placed near tape, cassette, or record players. It can also be used for hanging envelopes containing teaching materials, as well as frequently used flashcards and visuals.

8.4 AUDIO EQUIPMENT

In the beginning stages of language learning, machines can be helpful in providing students with native pronunciation models and repeated opportunities to practice and master the foreign-language sound system. At advanced levels, machines offer chances to develop skill in understanding authentic samples of foreign-language speech and in gaining greater literary appreciation.

There are at least two basic ways in which audio equipment may be used in an individualized program: either in a centralized lab or learning center, which students use on a library basis, or in a decentralized arrangement where equipment is located in each classroom and is available to students when needed. Machines suitable to both kinds of organization are treated in this section.

8.4.1 Tapes and Cassettes

In recent years cassettes have become increasingly popular, and this trend promises to continue because of several advantages they have over reel-to-reel tapes. Cassettes are durable, there is no need to thread them, and chances for breakage are minimized. When recorded in brief segments of ten minutes or less, they enable students to focus their attention on the particular drills they need. Most major textbook producers offer recorded material both on reel-to-reel tapes and cassettes. When there is opportunity for selection, cassettes are probably more practical.

If students find commercially prepared tapes to be too fast or otherwise too difficult, teachers might consider rerecording the material, adding or lengthening pauses, or making new tapes themselves. An alternative to this extremely time-consuming process is to offer one or more oral presentations of the material to students so as to familiarize them with it before machine practice sessions begin.

8.4.2 Playback Equipment and Tape Recorders

If students are to spend the major portion of their practice time listening to and repeating taped dialog sentences or pattern drills, playback machines are quite adequate for the purpose and are much less expensive than those which also record. Since many students lack the ability to correct their own errors, equipment with recording capability is often no advantage in teaching correct pronunciation. A more efficient approach to the pronunciation problem is to have a staff member work individually with students who need remedial help in this area. In advanced classes, playback equipment is adequate for listening to taped plays, speeches, or cultural materials.

Recording equipment, though, can be potentially useful in conversation courses where students tape oral presentations for teacher evaluation.[2] Also, at all levels of instruction, both oral comprehension and speaking tests can be offered on recording equipment.

An important factor in selecting tape equipment is determining how it will be used. For oral practice in school, fairly heavy machines with high amplification potential are needed. If playback machines are to be taken home for individual student use, then light, inexpensive equipment is also needed.

8.4.3 Jackboxes and Earphones

With a jackbox attachment, from two to eight students can listen to one taped program. A cord connects the jackbox to the tape or cassette player, and students plug their earphones into the jackbox. Earphones can be audioactive to permit students to hear their own pronunciation.

8.4.4 *Audio Flashcards*

In recent years, audio flashcards have become extremely popular for drilling pronunciation, short structural patterns, and sound-symbol relationships. The cards contain short segments of tape, above which are written the words to be played. The student runs the card through the machine to hear the program, which lasts several seconds. An advantage of this technique is its focus on a single item that students can replay as many times as needed. It is also effective in establishing relationships between the pronunciation and the spelling systems of the foreign language. In most cases teachers must prepare their own programs on blank cards, since commercially prepared foreign-language material is generally unavailable. This effort seems worth the trouble, however, since most students enjoy working with the flashcards.

8.4.5 *Record Player and Records*

A record player is useful for playing popular records, either for the whole class or for a group of students who choose to listen to them as an optional activity. Since popular music changes so rapidly, records will not hold their appeal year after year. So, the wear and tear that frequently used records suffer in classroom use is not a major problem. In the case of Christmas or folk music or records of plays or speeches having a lasting appeal and thus a much longer classroom life, it is preferable to transfer the recording to audio tape or cassettes. Records should not, however, be transferred until the teacher receives written permission to do so from the record producing company.

8.4.6 *Repeatcorder*

The Repeatcorder,[3] a relatively new machine on the market, may hold considerable potential for improving listening comprehension and pronunciation ability. It contains one cassette that plays the program and another that simultaneously records from 4 to 90 seconds of it. Whenever teachers or students feel the need to hear a portion of the tape again, they push the repeat button. This action shuts off the program source and activates the recording cassette loop, which replays, as many times as needed, the tape segment immediately preceding. In addition to facilitating oral comprehension of rapidly spoken dialogs, the Repeatcorder can be quite effective in promoting understanding of foreign-language radio broadcasts.

8.4.7 *Short-Wave Radio Receiver*

Foreign-language programs that have been taped from short-wave radio receivers can bring authentic, stimulating, and timely cultural materials into the classroom. They offer an appealing learning alternative for many students, though considerable teacher preparation time is required for taping and editing programs and supplying vocabulary lists and discussion questions, if needed. In some cases the school radio club or a student ham enthusiast may be able to help in preparing programs.

8.4.8 *Tape Duplicator*

If students are to borrow tapes for home practice, or if they can request the ones they need on a library basis from the learning center, several copies of each program must be available. This is particularly true at the beginning level, when most students will start at the same point. Multiple copies may become less essential later on if students settle into different learning paces. In situations where students have deadlines to meet, however, duplicate sets of taped programs at all levels will be necessary. Since tape duplicators are quite expensive, they might be purchased for district-wide use, rather than for one school only. In all cases, of course, written permission must be secured from the publishers before tapes are duplicated.

8.5 VISUAL EQUIPMENT

A visual component is extremely important in an individualized program in order to meet the needs of students whose learning style is primarily eye-oriented. Moreover, the appeal of a wide variety of visual material can greatly stimulate student interest and increase motivation to learn. The term *visual equipment* is used in its broadest sense in this section to include all learning materials and media that students see in the classroom.[4]

8.5.1 *Bulletin Boards*

Bulletin boards are considered unessential by many teachers who, once they put up their travel poster display in September, forget about them until June when they take down the materials, just a little more tattered, yellowed, and faded than before. In an individualized classroom, however, bulletin boards can be an integral part of the instructional program.

Teachers can post permanent announcements and reminders concerning meeting days for conversation groups; report card, unit, or test deadlines (if the program is not a continuous progress one); and dates of full-class presentations such as films, slides, outside speakers, or individual student or group speeches or skits. In this way, there is no longer a need for making the same announcements over and over again. Also, students are encouraged to develop greater self-reliance when they must take responsibility for obtaining necessary information from the bulletin board rather than relying constantly on the teacher's reminders.

Bulletin boards can also be used to display excellent student work, thus giving recognition to outstanding achievement as well as encouraging other students to perform well. Assigning students responsibility for bulletin board displays on a rotating basis is a small-group activity that is appropriate to an individualized classroom. Displays may relate to grammar or culture, or they may depict benefits of foreign-language study.

8.5.2 Blackboard

The blackboard of a traditional classroom can have several uses in an individualized teaching situation. An explanation of new grammar can be put on the board for small groups of students when they are ready for it. Students needing extra practice in spelling or writing can work at the board under the supervision of the teacher or an aide. Students who need extra help or who want to take an oral test can sign their names on the board so that they can be taken care of as soon as the teacher or an aide is free.

8.5.3 Reading Material

A well-developed program provides for the different reading interests of individual students. Though publishers are increasingly making available a sizable number of attractive, simplified readers, other sources should also be considered. Yearly subscriptions to monthly magazines aimed at American language-learners offer an inexpensive means of bringing diversity into the classroom. Magazines from the foreign country provide appealing material both for beginners, who may enjoy merely browsing through them, and for more advanced students, who can understand the articles and advertisements. In addition to the popular picture and news magazines, teachers might also consider ordering special-interest publications dealing with fashion, the home, cooking, cars and auto racing, and sports—especially those that are popular in the foreign country. Mail-order catalogs are also interesting and can serve to teach additional vocabulary words. Actual foreign-language children's books and textbooks used in schools in the foreign country can provide students with useful cultural insights and information.

If the classroom teacher can travel abroad, he or she should try to acquire as much authentic reading material as possible. Alternatively, teachers might request that colleagues or students traveling in a foreign country mail or bring back with them interesting and appealing books or magazines. Another possibility is to establish contact with a teacher of English abroad who would be willing to exchange materials. Funds for such an exchange might be part of the departmental budget. Local airlines, railroads, and travel agencies will provide at no cost considerable information in English about the foreign country; and material in the foreign language can be obtained from local consulates, embassies, tourist offices, or cultural centers established by foreign governments. A letter to overseas chambers of commerce can also yield valuable information. If students write the letters of request, they can learn a worthwhile and meaningful lesson in foreign-language letter writing, including formulas of politeness in salutations and closings.

8.5.4 *Realia*

In order that the foreign language and culture may come alive for students, classroom realia needs to go beyond the postcards and the bus, train, and museum stubs that normally make up the bulk of authentic cultural materials available in classrooms. One under-used and easily available source is labels, wrappings, or packages from imported products sold in the United States, such as food, beverages, clothes, perfume, jewelry, crystal, or porcelain. Foreign-made items displayed in the classroom can serve as props in student-presented skits. These items can also be obtained by writing to companies with overseas branches as well as from tourists returning from trips abroad. Students with relatives or pen pals in the foreign country might also be able to contribute to the classroom's collection of realia. Foreign language road maps, street maps, and tour guide booklets of monuments, hotels, restaurants, campsites and hostels can provide considerable realism in the classroom plus important practical background for students planning foreign travel.

8.5.5 *Flashcards*

Flashcards can be effective teaching aids, especially during the early phases of foreign-language learning. Pairs or small groups of students may use them to drill sound-letter correspondences, vocabulary words, and forms of regular and irregular verbs. The cards may be prepared either by teaching personnel or by the students themselves for extra credit.

8.5.6 *Games*

A well-developed program of individualization should provide enough flexibility to permit students some time to relax from the hectic daily pace of learning new material and passing oral and written tests. A wide variety of games available for student use in the classroom or learning center can supply a welcome break from usual classroom activities. Commercially prepared games that are popular are foreign-language versions of Bingo, Scrabble, and Monopoly, as well as professionally prepared crossword puzzles.[5] A highly productive and relatively unused source of games may be tapped by encouraging students to design grammar- and vocabulary-based games. Students of all ages often display remarkable ingenuity in adapting favorite card games, board games, and television game shows to foreign-language learning activities.

8.5.7 Overhead Projectors and Transparencies

Though originally designed for full-class use, the overhead projector can find a place in an individualized setting as well, provided that the necessary software is available. For example, new grammatical forms can be typed (ideally, on a machine with extra-large letters for better visibility), then permanently transferred by a heat process onto acetate transparencies. Stems and endings, for example, can be distinguished by using different colored marking pens. Though a similar black and white chart might appear in the basic textbook, the transfer of this information to a different medium adds variety and attractiveness to the subject matter and serves to appeal to non-book-oriented students.

Acetate transparencies can also serve to stimulate free conversation. Some commercially prepared materials are available, but the teacher might also consider making transparencies from comic strips and cartoons with the dialog or captions blocked out so that students can supply original ideas. If such visuals are taken from foreign-language magazines, they add a valuable cultural dimension to the lesson. Here too, adding color to the pictures with felt-tipped marking pens can enhance the attractiveness and appeal of the material.

For ease of storage and handling, overhead transparencies can be placed in cardboard frames. These might be filed alphabetically according to subject matter or chronologically according to lesson or unit. Lists of useful vocabulary words could accompany the visuals, particularly those designed for beginning or intermediate students. After two or more students practice with the transparencies, their oral work can serve as the basis for compositions.

8.5.8 Slides, Filmstrips, and Films

Full-class viewing of slides, filmstrips, and films has long been an accepted means of bringing the foreign country and its culture into the classroom. In an individualized classroom, though, students who differ in interests and learning pace will tend to use these media either independently or in small groups. For this reason, teachers might consider acquiring for the classroom or learning center slide, filmstrip, and film projectors designed for individual or small-group use. Since the smaller projectors contain their own screens, the room need not be darkened when they are used, and students can read the accompanying scripts if necessary. After initial viewings the sound track can be eliminated and students can describe orally or in writing the scenes or actions being shown. Alternatively, they may complete worksheets or take written tests over the material presented.

In recent years more and more companies have begun to produce slides and filmstrips with accompanying taped dialogs or descriptions that make them nearly as appealing as more expensive films. The price of this commercial material, though, may preclude its use in many classrooms. In such cases teachers might choose to make their own slides and script. If a trip to the foreign country is not immediately feasible, then a low-budget alternative is to select attractive color pictures from textbooks and, once publishers' permissions have been secured, to photograph them with a camera mounted on a tripod and focused on the open book. Slides made in this manner cost no more than the price of film and development. Students may elect to write and tape a suitable script to accompany homemade slides.

8.5.9 *Movie Cameras and Video-tape Recorders*

In spite of their expense, 8, super 8, and 16 millimeter movie cameras, as well as video recorders, are finding their way into more and more schools. Though far from being indispensable to a successful individualized program, they do offer interesting alternatives for some students if available. Students might create original films or tapes in the foreign language on subjects of interest to them. Skits or dramatizations can be taped and viewed either for individual critiques or purely for the enjoyment of the students themselves and their classmates.

8.5.10 *Time to Create a Variety of Media*

While there is general agreement regarding the motivational importance of visuals, most teachers simply cannot find sufficient time to make audio and visual flashcards, overhead transparencies, and slides as well as gather cultural realia for student use. In some fortunate districts, media specialists can help in creating some of these materials, but such aid is by far the exception rather than the rule. Logically, commercial firms are best equipped to create alternative media that may permit greater individualization of the courses they produce. Perhaps research into student learning preferences will lead to greater public demand for materials suited to a variety of learning modes, which companies may then attempt to satisfy. Until that time, however, teachers need to create whatever materials they can, knowing that a fully individualized multimedia course will not result overnight, but rather from their accumulated efforts over a period of several years. Whenever feasible, students should be involved in creating supplementary materials.

8.6 CLASSROOM FURNISHINGS

Special furniture for an individualized classroom or learning center is considered last in this chapter. Successfully individualized classes depend least on special furnishings that differ markedly from standard equipment available in most classrooms. Still, certain items that facilitate individualization may be of interest for schools where sufficient funds are available.[6]

8.6.1 *Tables and Chairs*

Trapezoidal tables, which can seat three students or can be combined into hexagons or rectangles seating six, are popular in many individualized classrooms, since they facilitate small-group work and take up less space than several individual student desks moved together into a circle. Saving space can be important, especially in standard-sized rooms, because a well-developed individualized course requires a considerable amount of extra room for storage of equipment, materials, and supplies. Chairs equipped with racks for students' books can help avoid unnecessary and distracting clutter on the worktables.

8.6.2 *Study Carrels*

Individual carrels, which provide students with some privacy while studying, have become increasingly popular additions to some classrooms and, more often, to learning centers. Carrels help students to learn on their own by cutting down distractions from other on-going activities. While some carrels are "dry," consisting simply of two walls and a desk top, other models are "wet," and include electrical outlets for learning machines such as individual slide or filmstrip viewers, cassette players, and—in some cases—computer terminals.

8.6.3 *Room Dividers*

Room dividers may be useful in providing differentiated work areas within one classroom. Some of these areas might include corners for quiet study, conversation, grammar instruction, pattern drilling, browsing through magazines and newspapers, listening to records or tapes, taking oral or written tests, playing games, working with realia, or viewing slides, films, or filmstrips. An advantage of movable room dividers is their flexibility and the ease with which they may be shifted as teaching needs change. A low-cost substitute for commercially produced room dividers can be constructed by hinging plywood boards at right angles to each other. Dividers made from pegboard can also serve for hanging worksheets, vocabulary or verb flashcards, and other learning materials. Homemade dividers can be made more attractive by painting or covering them with decorative adhesive paper.

8.6.4 *Acoustic Engineering*

Depending upon the structural materials used in building the classroom, the noise made by several students talking at once can result in no problem or in a major one. In some cases, the most workable and cheapest solution is to have students sit closer to each other and lower their voices. When groups of larger than 25 meet in acoustically poor surroundings, however, additional remedies need to be found. Sound-absorbing panels can be installed on ceilings and room dividers, and carpeting can be laid on the floor. Though expensive, these procedures are effective.

8.6.5 Sofas and Easy Chairs

In some classrooms an air of informality is established by providing sofas and easy chairs, usually donated by members of the community. These furnishings provide a more relaxing setting for conversation practice and for browsing through foreign-language publications. For younger students, cushions or rugs on the floor may serve the same purpose.

NOTES

[1] Two recent reviews of the status of audio-visual equipment in foreign-language teachings are Charles P. Richardson "Teachers, Students, and Media as Co-agents in Learning," in Dale L. Lange and Charles J. James, eds., *The ACTFL Review of Foreign Language Education*, vol. 4 (Skokie, Ill.: National Textbook Co., 1972), pp. 295–320; and Harry Reinert, "Extending the Teacher," in Gilbert A. Jarvis, ed., *The ACTFL Review of Foreign Language Education*, vol. 6 (Skokie, Ill.: National Textbook Co., 1975).

[2] See "Advanced French Conversation," in F. William D. Love and Lucille J. Honig, *Options and Perspectives: A Sourcebook of Innovative Foreign Language Programs in Action, K-12* (New York: Modern Language Association of America, 1973), pp. 259–61; also described in Michael Agatstein, "Individualization of Language Learning Through the Cassette Recorder," *Journal of the National Association of Language Laboratory Directors*, vol. 6, no. 2 (December 1971), pp. 27–32.

[3] The Repeatcorder is manufactured by Canon U.S.A., Inc., 10 Nevada Drive, Lake Success, Long Island, N.Y. 11040.

[4] Photos of an individualized program with a highly developed visual component can be found in Gerald E. Logan, *Individualized Foreign Language Learning: An Organic Process* (Rowley, Mass.: Newbury House Publishers, 1973), pp. 111–18.

[5] A well-known commercial distributor of foreign-language games is Gessler Publishing Co., 131 East 23rd St., New York, N.Y. 10010. Other sources may be located by visiting exhibition booths at local, regional, and national language conventions and by consulting advertisements in professional journals.

[6] Descriptions of several ways of arranging an individualized classroom as well as two diagrams are found in June K. Phillips, "Individualization and Personalization," in Gilbert A. Jarvis, ed., *The ACTFL Review of Foreign Language Education*, vol. 5 (Skokie, Ill.: National Textbook Co., 1974), pp. 240–41.

CHAPTER NINE
MAKING THE TRANSITION TO INDIVIDUALIZED INSTRUCTION

9.1 GENERAL CONSIDERATIONS

A decision to individualize instruction made on Friday at 3 P.M. cannot be implemented at 9 A.M. the following Monday. In preparation for this far-reaching change in classroom structure, teachers need to devote a considerable amount of time—perhaps a summer, an entire academic year, or even more—to thinking out details of planning and implementation. A newly designed program of individualized instruction will have better chances for success if it is preceded by a period of thorough preparation and gradual transition from full-class to open-class instruction. Teachers need to acquire considerable background information, and they need to develop new styles of instruction that work well for them. A period of unofficial experimentation on a limited basis can furnish the experience necessary for designing an effective program. The important transitional process will be examined in this chapter.

9.2 ACQUIRING KNOWLEDGE

A good first step in acquiring knowledge about individualization is to read widely—both in the fields of foreign-language teaching and in the area of general educational philosophy and psychology. Recently published books and current professional journals can provide excellent sources of background information and concrete suggestions. Some useful publications are listed in the footnoted end-of-chapter references throughout this book.[1]

9.2.1 *Professional Meetings and Workshops*

Professional meetings at the local, regional, and national levels can also prove helpful. In view of considerable professional interest in individualizing instruction, many meetings are being devoted to this topic, and conference speakers are contributing important insights into the how's and why's of this approach to teaching. Workshops sponsored by AAT chapters, by state departments of education, and by colleges and universities offer guidance in how to individualize and how to prepare needed materials. Listings of workshops may be found in newsletters published by state departments of foreign-language education, in professional journals, and in catalogs of local colleges and universities.

9.2.2 *Classroom Observation*

Observation of individualized classes—whether in foreign language or not—can prove to be a profitable experience. No oral or written descriptions can begin to convey what an individualized classroom is really like. Reciprocal visits between teachers initiating new programs, plus exchanges of insights, ideas, and techniques, can be powerful sources of professional growth and development.

9.2.3 *Discussions with Colleagues*

Colleagues need to get together to exchange ideas on individualization. This might occur during regularly scheduled department meetings, during afternoon or summer workshops, on the phone after school, or during the few minutes between classes. Though longer meetings are preferable, a considerable amount of planning can be accomplished by dedicated professionals with only limited amounts of time at their disposal. What is most important is that teachers work in teams of at least two. Individualizing instruction is a complicated process that has only recently entered the educational spotlight. Until concrete data regarding methods of implementing this approach are gathered, there is bound to be some degree of trial and error in experimenting with it. At such times, it is useful, comforting, and necessary to have an understanding, supportive colleague with whom to discuss why certain activities did not turn out as planned and how they might be improved.

9.3 FINDING TIME

Time to plan, time to write, time to think—time seems to be a major obstacle to successful individualization. There never seems to be enough of it, yet enormous amounts are wasted every day. Basically, however, when there is a strong commitment to a goal, the time needed to reach it can always be found. With proper planning, time can become a teacher's slave, not his master. Some suggestions are offered here for using limited time resources more efficiently.

9.3.1 *Establishing Time Priorities*

No one should expect a program of individualization to spring up overnight. The period of transition in only one level may well take a year. Spreading out the work over several months is one way of dealing with limited time. A list of priorities in descending order of importance can guide the teacher's decisions about what needs to be done first. For example, it is difficult to individualize the rate of instruction unless students know what is expected of them. So, writing performance objectives and learning activities must be given high priority. Handing out complete learning packets at the start of each unit is convenient but may be impossible for the beginning teacher who is barely able to remain a few days ahead of the students. In this case, the pages of the packet could be distributed as they are prepared. Collating unit pages, then, is a low priority item.

The following exercise in establishing priorities is a list of tasks that must be accomplished in order to individualize learning rates. Number them from one to ten in descending order of importance; that is, number 1 is the most important task, number 10 the least important.

_____ Creating taped listening tests
_____ Producing alternate forms of written tests for retesting
_____ Establishing unit performance objectives
_____ Putting dialogs and pattern drills on cassettes
_____ Producing written explanations of new grammar
_____ Creating visual materials such as slides or overhead transparencies
_____ Setting up a library of supplementary reading materials
_____ Creating checklists of student progress
_____ Writing learning activities that lead to mastery of objectives
_____ Assembling learning packets

No "right" answers can be offered here. Several items might even share equal priority. What teachers choose to accomplish first depends on materials already on hand as well as on personal interests and talents. The essential matter is to establish a list of priorities that are valid in one's own school situation.

9.3.2 *Sharing Preparation Responsibilities*

Another time-saving device is the sharing of responsibilities for preparation with one or more colleagues. Several types of sharing are possible: A team of teachers adapting one level may split the work by having one member write learning packets and the other prepare oral and written exercises and tests. A third person (if there is one) might be responsible for tapes, while a fourth could handle the preparation of visuals. If two teachers are both involved in teaching two different preparations—Levels II and III, for example—then one teacher can assume entire responsibility for preparing Level II for both his colleague and himself, while the other does the same with Level III. Cutting the number of daily preparations reduces considerably the burden of starting to individualize.

When mini-courses are the focus of individualization, perhaps each member of the department teaching a particular language may take the responsibility of designing one of the courses to be offered. The results of this group effort can then be pooled. If an entire language department consists of only one or two people, or if each teacher is in charge of a different language, team-planning with a student teacher might be considered a workable alternative. If this too proves impossible, the teachers will need to accept the reality that progress toward individualization in their school will, of necessity, be slower than they might desire.

9.3.3 *Limiting the Scope of the Work*

Lack of sufficient time can be compensated for by limiting the scope of the project to what can realistically be accomplished within given limits. If all levels cannot be individualized at once, perhaps *one* level can. If even an entire level seems like too formidable an undertaking, perhaps several units can be adapted. In looking over the number of units making up a given level, teachers often find that one or more units may be omitted with no detrimental effect on the learners, provided that vocabulary and structure items are included with subsequent material. Dropping out less essential units assumes prime importance when teaching for 80 percent or greater mastery. Since the vast majority of curricula are too overloaded to permit most learners to master all the material presented, some judicious omissions are in order. Careful scrutiny of the contents of the beginning levels can reveal that, except for topics concerning pronouns, verb tenses, adjective agreement, and word order, most other grammatical topics can be taught informally as vocabulary items.

The scope of the project can also be limited by choosing to work in only one of the four areas of individualization—objectives of learning, pace of learning, method of learning, or content of learning. The area chosen would in large part depend on the teacher's particular interests, the language and age-level of students for whom the program is intended, and availability of resources in the particular school situation.

Some teachers have limited the scope of their initial efforts by individualizing only one of their classes—the most cooperative one, or the most intelligent, or the most mature, or the smallest, or the one they most enjoy working with for any number of reasons. This cautious approach is wise because it greatly enhances the teacher's chances of succeeding. Initial success is vitally important, since it can serve as a solid foundation for future experimentation and further successes.

9.3.4 Participating in Workshops

Participating in regional or local workshops is one practical way of finding the time to prepare for individualization. Several types of workshop formats, each with its advantages and disadvantages, merit examination.

Regional workshops sponsored by state language associations or by individual universities offer the participant opportunities to profit from the expertise of one or more professionally recognized consultants. Participants also enjoy the chance to exchange ideas and shoptalk with teachers from other schools. A limitation of such workshops is that they tend to be brief— lasting from a couple of days to a couple of weeks. Since they normally occur during school vacations and on weekends, they may conflict with the family responsibilities of some teachers. While these workshops can offer a solid background in theory, they often do not last long enough to solve the individual teacher's problems, nor do they permit development of materials for an entire level. Nevertheless, a regional workshop is a good place to start developing an individualized program. Ideally, any costs involved should be paid by the school district. This is most likely to occur when administrators initiate the impetus for change or when they back individual teacher efforts.

A local summer workshop of several weeks or more offers distinct advantages. Teachers are more relaxed, there are no student distractions, and it is easier for several colleagues to plan for an entire level. The workshop focuses on the particular philosophy and problems of implementation in the local district. A broader perspective might be introduced by inviting an outside consultant—preferably a full-time language teacher—who has successfully individualized his or her own classes. The cost involved in setting up such a workshop makes it a luxury for schools with tight budgets. In order to gain the most from a summer workshop, it is advisable that participants come to it with some background—either in terms of some classroom experimentation or of extensive reading in the fields of individualizing and humanizing instruction. In fact, an optimum time for a summer workshop might be *after* the first year or the first semester of experimentation, rather than before. In this way, teachers can have a better idea of what problems need to be solved and what additional work needs to be done.

An in-service workshop held right after school or even during the school day is a desirable alternative when financial resources are limited. Teachers working on materials for individualization could meet once a week to compare notes, discuss their progress, and set common goals. Or, teachers interested in individualizing might be assigned a common curriculum development period instead of study hall or corridor duty. If possible, teachers working to individualize instruction might have their teaching loads reduced. An advantage of in-service workshops during the school day is that as soon as new materials are created, they may be tested out in the classroom and revised according to how well they work. Furthermore, the necessity of preparing a lesson for the next day acts as a powerful stimulus to creativity. The immediate feedback provided by students and colleagues serves to improve the quality of what is produced.

9.4 GAINING SUPPORT

In addition to lack of time, lack of support often presents itself as a barrier to individualizing instruction. The support being withheld may be moral as well as financial. Ways of gaining support for this innovation are considered in this section.

9.4.1 *Moral Support*

Lack of interest on the part of colleagues, supervisors, and administrators in a teacher's efforts to individualize can be demoralizing. Teachers who spend long hours at home working on innovative programs want to share their experience with others. They want to talk about their failures and their successes, their fears and their ideals. Even more disheartening than lack of interest is the active attempt by colleagues to sabotage their programs through gossip and negative criticism.

One way of dealing with this situation is to attempt to gain support by discussing one's reasons for individualizing. Or, once a program is working well, colleagues might be invited to observe some classes and perhaps help teach them. Even if only one colleague responds with interest or enthusiasm, that person can provide some needed moral support and feedback. Visitors from other schools can also serve this purpose, provided that the program is ready to be observed. Viewing one's own program through the eyes of outsiders demands courage, but it is extremely useful in pointing out areas where improvement is needed. Supportive colleagues may also be found at professional meetings.

Teachers who wish to gain support for individualization—or at least minimize hostile criticism of their efforts—need to be especially tactful with conservative colleagues. Nothing they say or do should imply that their methods are superior to their colleagues'. They should in no way suggest that individualization is the only way or the best way to teach a foreign language—even if in their enthusiasm they believe this to be true. They should recognize that outstanding teaching took place before the advent of individualized instruction and that it is a teaching style that may not be suited to all teachers. An attitude of respect and tolerance toward more traditional colleagues is instrumental in promoting cooperative teaching efforts and departmental harmony.

9.4.2 *Financial Support*

Inadequate budgetary allotments for individualized foreign-language programs are physical manifestations of lack of philosophical support in one's school. What is not valued is not funded. Therefore, teachers wishing to gain financial support for a workshop, for new equipment, or for resource personnel need to show their administrators that their programs are worthwhile. In an era of accountability, this value must be proved in terms of concrete statistics, rather than abstract rhetoric. When asking for additional funds, teachers stand a better chance of having their requests approved if they can point to objective accomplishments.

Have enrollments for the coming year increased?
Has the failure rate gone down?
Do outside observers give the program high ratings?
Has the teacher already proved himself or herself capable of implementing a viable program?
Is the teacher's program being used by others in the school?
Are the students' grades mostly B's or better?
Do supervisory evaluations warrant support of the program?
In what specific ways can the requested workshop (or equipment or resource personnel) improve the quality of the program?

In view of the need for concrete justification of additional funding, it is probably a good idea to wait until the end of the first year of experimentation before making requests. (This is much less of a problem, of course, in school districts where the impetus for change comes from administrators, rather than from classroom teachers.) Even when local budget conditions seem to rule out funding attempts, teachers should nevertheless file their requests—and keep triplicates to file in subsequent years. Times change, and what may seem experimentally far-out one year may well become part of the educational mainstream the next. At any rate, teachers stand at worst to lose a little time, while their programs of individualization can only gain from the attempt.

9.4.3 *Supportive Equipment and Personnel*

Some teachers feel that they cannot begin to individualize because certain resources are lacking: cassette players, octagonal tables, file cabinets, various projectors, teaching aides, or clerical aides. In comparison to the problems discussed so far, lack of time and lack of support, this third area poses far less of an obstacle to individualization than is generally supposed. Successful programs have been initiated that draw on nothing more than a basic textbook and teacher creativity and cost no more than the paper used. In essence, the imaginative, intelligent, and dedicated teacher is the only indispensable classroom resource. Without a competent teacher to structure and guide learning activities, even the most modern, ultra-equipped classroom will fail to bring about greater foreign-language skill.

9.4.4 *Supportive Publicity*

An effective means of developing support—both moral and financial—for a newly created program of individualization is to publicize the accomplishments of the teachers and students involved. Once the program is fairly well established, the teacher and the department chairman or supervisor should seek ways of letting other people know about it. One publicity vehicle could be the bulletin or newsletter published by the local parent-teacher's organization. If the school employs a public relations director, a brief note or phone call to that person can bring favorable publicity. Local or community newspapers should also be contacted when there are newsworthy items to report. Such items may include: foreign-language fairs, winners of local or national language contests, interviews with students and teachers involved in individualized programs, professional activities of innovative teachers, descriptions of new equipment or techniques employed in foreign-language classes, a tour of the media or learning center, student trips abroad, interviews with paraprofessionals who supplement the efforts of the regular teaching staff, tape or letter exchanges between local and foreign students, and so on. The list is limited only by the imagination of the classroom teacher and his or her resourcefulness in using public relations techniques to gain administrative and community support for the program. In an era of shrinking enrollments and staff and budgetary cutbacks, the often neglected public relations aspects of foreign-language teaching must no longer be ignored.[2]

9.5 DECIDING WHERE TO BEGIN

The choice of possible ways in which to begin individualizing instruction can seem overwhelming: by introducing learning packets, by adding to the staff, by starting multimedia programs, or by instituting new grouping and grading policies. There can be no one right answer for all teachers because facilities, administrative policies, and amounts of financial support vary widely among schools. Perhaps the best answer for individual teachers is to start where they feel most comfortable or in the area that most interests them or that presents the path of least resistance.[3] The starting point may also be determined by the goals established for the program: facilitating continuous progress, meeting different interest needs, offering choice of learning modes, developing student responsibility and initiative, promoting oral fluency, and so on. While all these goals are desirable and are not mutually exclusive, the teacher preparation time required to realize each one is so great that some priorities must normally be set. Some consequences of selecting various starting points are considered in the following paragraphs.

9.5.1 *Beginning with Learning Packets*

Many teachers decide to begin individualizing by writing learning packets, study guides, or check-off lists for students to follow. This step is instrumental in facilitating individualization of learning rates either via continuous progress or flexible pacing (as described in Chapter Six). A drawback, though, in starting with packets is that they will most likely be based on the format of the full-class teaching situation. In some cases, this may mean that oral activities are subordinated to pencil and paper work, with a resulting loss of speaking practice. In addition, since the writing of learning packets is time consuming, there may be a tendency, at least initially, to create them for one course—perhaps a four-skills, college-preparatory sequence—rather than for courses that aim at satisfying different interests or learning styles. Another possible drawback to beginning with learning packets is that unless considerable material has been prepared in advance, or unless the learning pace is flexible rather than continuous, many teachers will find it extremely difficult to stay ahead of the most advanced students. Problems may then result from students having to wait for new material, and negative feelings may be created because the teacher could not deliver what was promised.

9.5.2 *Beginning with Small-Group Work*

Introducing small-group work into the standard lesson is an excellent alternative to beginning with learning packets. Though the vertical progress dimension may be quite limited, small-group work offers opportunities for horizontal enrichment through alternative learning activities and, most important, promotes speaking practice. Group work is a low-risk, essentially conservative first step that requires little or no administrative support. Within the framework of full-class instruction, the teacher can arrange to set aside ten or fifteen minutes for pattern practice in pairs or for small-group conversation based on new material. (Specific techniques are discussed in Part Three of this book.) As students become used to indirect teacher supervision, greater amounts of class time can be devoted to small-group work; if students do not work well together, the amount of time can be decreased, or supervision increased, until a working relationship evolves that is appropriate to the particular class.

When both the teacher and the students have become accustomed to small-group oral activities and the necessary materials have been created, the next step toward individualization may follow: learning packets can be designed that incorporate conversation activities. An advantage of this approach is that the vital oral skills are not neglected in the process of individualization. Group work activities can provide a needed transition for both teachers and students from full-class learning to independent study activities. The small-group approach is also suitable to programs whose major goals include affective learning: developing better self-images in learners, helping students clarify the values they hold, and promoting tolerance, understanding, and real communication in the classroom.

9.5.3 *Establishing a Multimedia Curriculum*

The goal of individualizing learning rates may also take second place to the objective of developing alternative methods of learning. This approach may be suitable in situations where there are high failure rates in language courses because many learners require audio or visual alternatives to the single textbook being used. Younger learners, in particular, can benefit from attractive and colorful visuals, a variety of films, filmstrips, and slides, as well as cassettes and language masters. In schools where there is considerable philosophical and financial support for this approach and where teachers themselves are interested in multiplying student learning choices, this can be a highly rewarding first step.

9.5.4 *Employing Paraprofessionals*

Though paraprofessionals can make important contributions to a program's success, it is unlikely that most teachers, operating without special funds or grants, will be able to employ native speakers, college language majors, or secretarial help during the first year of individualization. Most administrators want an experimental program to prove its effectiveness before they invest additional funds in it. In view of this, teachers may want to plan a course that can operate effectively with unpaid student aides. If this proves successful, then perhaps additional help can be provided in subsequent years. Methods of working with minimal or no outside help are discussed in Chapter Twelve.

9.5.5 *Changing School Grouping and Grading Policies*

A change from lockstepped grouping and grading toward nongraded, heterogeneous classes and a system of awarding fractional credit as each unit of learning is completed is a vital prerequisite to a fully developed individualized program. The decision to institute greater flexibility in this area is primarily an administrative one. Principals and school boards, however, are hesitant to institute such changes unless they feel that a majority of their teachers strongly favor more liberal policies. Otherwise, bitter teacher-administrator confrontations may result from imposing change from above.

Ideally, the desire to change should originate with classroom teachers who make their wishes known via established channels of communication. In view of this, most individualized programs may have to operate initially within a rigid system of grouping and grading, and compromises will have to be made. Once some success has been experienced, however, there is a greater chance that more flexibility may be introduced in placing students and in awarding credit.

9.5.6 *Developing Mini-Courses*

Once students have acquired a basic working knowledge of the most important grammatical structures of the foreign language, they are ready for mini-courses. Offered either at the intermediate or advanced levels, these courses may be instrumental in catering to diverse student interests. Teachers wishing to individualize instruction beyond the elementary level may well choose mini-courses as a worthwhile starting point.

9.5.7 *Interdisciplinary Studies*

With increased recognition that the ultimate goal of foreign-language instruction need not necessarily be specialized literary studies, there has been growing interest in teaching other subject areas—such as history, art, and science—in the foreign language. Teachers who possess competence in other subjects, or who can work closely with a colleague in another department, might consider creating an interdisciplinary course as the first step toward individualization.

9.5.8 *Choosing Which Class to Individualize*

A healthily conservative approach is to select only one class for individualization. By limiting experimentation, teachers can be more confident of their ability to prepare adequately and can thereby increase their chances for success. Conversely, if the new techniques do not work well, the "damage" to students is minimized.

The class or classes chosen for initial experiments can be determined by a number of considerations. Teachers interested in individualizing learning rates may select lower-level classes; those interested in developing mini-courses may begin with intermediate or advanced students. If a multimedia approach is chosen as a starting point, either beginning or intermediate classes would be appropriate choices. A teacher's decision may be influenced by problems facing the language department. If high failure and drop-out rates in "required" first and second courses are major sources of concern, the teacher might begin by creating learning alternatives for those levels: multimedia presentations, instructional packets that facilitate individual pacing, or development of noncollege preparatory courses. In schools with high attrition at intermediate or advanced levels, mini-courses appealing to expressed student interests provide a worthwhile place to begin. In cases where teachers feel that any of their classes could benefit equally from individualization, they can determine which one is the smallest, or the most intelligent, or the most cooperative, or the easiest to manage; they should then elect the alternative that maximizes their chances for success. Once encouraged by this success, they can expand their efforts to include other classes.

If the teacher starts individualizing at the top of the language sequence, he or she will not have the same students for follow-up activities during the next year. Despite this disadvantage, however, some teachers still prefer this approach because advanced classes are usually smaller and students tend not to present the motivation and discipline problems sometimes found at elementary or intermediate levels. Other teachers might decide to begin individualization from the beginning of the language sequence, problems and all, so that each year a new level of instruction may be individualized, with at least some of the same students participating.

NOTES

[1] An extremely useful guide to pre-service and in-service training that also offers suggestions for self-training is Warren C. Born, ed., *Toward Student-Centered Foreign-Language Programs*. Reports of the Working Committees of the Northeast Conference on the Teaching of Foreign Languages. (New York: Modern Language Association Materials Center, 1974), pp. 15–72.

[2] For additional information on this topic see Anita Monsees and Dona B. Reeves, "Public Awareness," in Gilbert A. Jarvis, ed., *The ACTFL Review of Foreign Language Education*, vol. 6 (Skokie, Ill.: National Textbook Co., 1974); Alan Garfinkel, "The Public Image of Foreign Language Instruction, 1972–1973," *Modern Language Journal*, vol. 58, no. 3 (March 1974), pp. 108–12; and Born, 1974 (see note 1), pp. 12–27.

[3] An interesting method for charting this path objectively is presented in Leon A. Jakobovits, "Initiating Change: The EBTAMobile Trip," in Ronald L. Gougher, ed., *Individualization of Instruction in Foreign Languages: A Practical Guide* (Philadelphia: Center for Curriculum Development, 1972), pp. 46–48.

CHAPTER TEN
ORIENTATION

10.1 GENERAL CONSIDERATIONS

For most people in the 1970s, individualized instruction is a new experience. Therefore, a well thought out program of orientation is essential for everyone involved: teachers, students, administrators, guidance counselors, and parents. The rationale of the program, its major characteristics, and how it will operate need to be explained clearly. The importance of this communication cannot be overemphasized. Specific information offered at the start of a program of individualization can prevent serious misunderstandings that might block its effective implementation.

10.2 ORIENTING DEPARTMENT MEMBERS

If the impetus for individualized instruction originates from administrators or department chairmen, these people can arrange for orientation sessions for members of the foreign-language department. Meetings may be scheduled after school is over, on weekends, or during regularly scheduled workshops held during the course of the school day. While the desirability of individualizing instruction may be stressed, it is inadvisable, as well as impractical, to impose this teaching style on all department members. During the initial stages of developing the new program, support, encouragement, and practical help can be offered to the teachers who demonstrate interest in experimenting with the new approach. Favorable results can then stimulate other teachers to join in the process of innovation. If the department chairman is among the first to individualize, he or she can provide a valuable model for others to follow, especially if teachers are encouraged to visit the chairman's classes and share his or her knowledge and experience.

10.3 ORIENTING ONESELF

A classroom teacher's initial orientation may occur through reading professional literature, attending conferences and meetings, and participating in workshops at the national, state, local, or district levels, as has been mentioned. In the final analysis, however, a teacher's orientation is ultimately accomplished in his or her own classroom. Here the teacher is essentially alone and unsupervised. Though in many respects even experienced educators may again feel like beginners, the support commonly offered to new teachers during their first year of instruction may not be available to them. This is particularly true if the teacher is the first in the department to individualize. While it is helpful to profit from the support and advice of a colleague or department chairman, it is up to teachers themselves to design programs and class formats that work for both their students and themselves.

Inevitably, a certain amount of trial and error will be involved as the teacher experiments with different techniques. What has been recommended in a book or at a conference or even by a colleague may not work well in the teacher's particular situation. The only way to find out, though, is through practical classroom application. Most teachers, understandably, would prefer that all learning activities proceed successfully. In this respect, tried-and-true methods of full-class instruction hold infinitely more appeal than untested techniques for individualization. However, if teachers choose to limit themselves only to what they know and are sure of, they needlessly close off new opportunities for self-understanding and continued professional growth. Even should the worst occur, with none of the techniques of individualization working well in the classroom, the teacher has at least discovered more about his or her preferred teaching style.

When initiating an individualized style of instruction, teachers should maintain a pragmatic attitude: if one technique falls short of expectations, perhaps certain modifications will make it work better; or perhaps the technique is totally unsuitable and should be completely abandoned. This becomes less difficult if teachers have not committed themselves too early to a rigid classroom format. They might in fact announce to students that they are experimenting with several approaches to teaching in order to help the students learn more effectively. Some techniques, they may explain, will be more effective than others and will be repeated; others that work less well will be eliminated. If students know they should expect changes during the course of the year, and if changes are announced in advance, they will be less resistant and hostile when the changes occur. This will be particularly true if student opinion is solicited at frequent intervals by written questionnaires. (Program evaluation is discussed in detail in Chapter Fourteen.) Students who understand that their teacher is sincerely trying to help them tend to be tolerant and supportive of his or her efforts.

It is helpful to make policies self-limiting. For example, the teacher may say that the new methods will be used only for the next topic or unit, which may last a week or more. Then, in case the experience proves less than satisfactory, it can end automatically and with a minimum of embarrassment to the teacher. New policies, aimed at correcting the deficiencies experienced, may be instituted for the next unit, or the class can return to former ways of learning and the teacher can try a new experiment with a different group of students.

An extremely high degree of teacher organization is also essential to successful experimentation. The teacher must be prepared at all times. Dittoed or stenciled handouts must be ready when students need them. Test papers and compositions need to be graded and returned promptly. All announced policies regarding testing and grading should be carried out as described—at least within the time limit set. And even if the teacher no longer uses a lesson plan, nevertheless it is still important to have a clear idea of what activities should go on during the class period, and the teacher should communicate this information to students. Though individualized instruction involves appealing to individual interests and learning styles, teachers will invite chaos and ultimate failure if they ask students what they want to do or what they feel like learning. A more effective approach is to present students with several alternatives and ask them to choose among them, perhaps with an option of suggesting an original activity or assignment subject to the teacher's approval. Most students are quite content to choose among several suggestions; few beginners are capable of creating their own assignments, although this skill can be developed in an individualized program.

Perhaps the most important idea to keep in mind is that successful teachers are not the ones who never make mistakes; successful teachers are the ones who never *repeat* their mistakes. All teachers—including highly experienced ones—can make errors in judgment when trying a new technique for the first time. This can occur in traditionally taught classes as well as in individualized situations. Making errors is quite human and pardonable. Failing to learn from mistakes, if still human, is less pardonable. If both teachers and supervisors can come to view experimental efforts primarily as learning experiences, there will be less hesitancy to improve instruction through innovative techniques.

10.4 ORIENTING STUDENTS

Once a workable format for individualization has been created, methods for orienting incoming students can be worked out. Some teachers may prefer to teach traditionally for the first few months in order to acquaint themselves with their classes before individualizing; others may feel sufficiently experienced to initiate the new techniques right away. In either case, certain information communicated to students during orientation sessions can greatly facilitate the transition to an individualized style of learning.

10.4.1 *Locating Needed Material*

First of all, it is useful to tell students where they can find the materials they will need. This may include the location of learning packets; records, tapes, cassettes, and language master cards; supplementary readers; magazines and newspapers; and films, filmstrips, slides, and overhead transparencies. They need to know what equipment they must use in school (tape or cassette recorder, language master, phonograph, or any type of projector) and what equipment may be signed out for home use. Students should be familiar with the materials available in the classroom as well as those they may use in the library, resource center, or language lab (depending on which of these exist in a particular school).

10.4.2 *Describing How the Program Will Operate*

There should be some description of what activities students may normally expect in the classroom: full group presentations, small conversation groups, practice in pairs, or independent study. If certain days are designated as full-class days, or if certain assigned groups are scheduled to meet on certain days, this too should be announced. The type of testing, oral or written or both, should be described, as well as the frequency of testing students may expect. If the class is to operate within fixed deadlines, students must know this. If there are no rigid deadlines, the criteria for determining a "normal" or satisfactory rate of speed need to be established and explained. The teacher must also say whether students are to test when ready or whether there are fixed dates by which they must have passed certain tests. In addition, students should know if they are expected to do homework and, if so, approximately how much time they should average per evening. They should also be told what criteria will be used in determining their grades. If retests and extra-credit assignments are available, students should be so informed. (Grading systems are discussed in Chapter Thirteen.)

Though some classroom teachers may be very enthusiastic about individualization and may consider it much better than other methods of instruction, they should take care not to "oversell" the program to students. If very high expectations are created, disappointments may easily result if students find that the new program requires considerable effort and hard work on their part. Instead of saying that the program will be "better" than previous ways of learning, teachers may stress the fact that students who *want* to learn will have many opportunities to succeed. They may point out the various aids to learning available to the students, such as additional personnel, audio-visual equipment, resource or media centers, and so on. If glittering promises are avoided, satisfaction with individualization can develop gradually as students experience success under the new system.

10.4.3 *Communicating Classroom Regulations*

Classroom rules should be communicated so that students clearly know what they may and may not do. Holt* makes a convincing argument for stating rules negatively—in terms of what the teacher will not tolerate—rather than in terms of what students are free to do. In practice, the "do not's" will be relatively few in number; except for these, the students may safely assume that other activities are permissible. In effect, this practice grants students greater freedom than no rules at all, a policy that cannot stand up to imaginative testing by students. Furthermore, a firm set of limitations reduces the student anxiety that may result when existing policies are not made clear.

Some classroom rules are dictated by general school regulations; others are specific to the teacher. It is especially important that teachers make known to students their own particular preferences and quirks. Class rules might relate to the following areas: absence, tardiness, and cutting; whether written homework may be done in class; whether studying for another class is permitted; ways in which unstructured time may or may not be used; how students are to take oral and written tests; from whom students may seek extra help; make-up policies for short- and long-term absences; gum chewing and hair combing (if important); coming to class with books, paper, and writing implements; and so on.

10.4.4 *Explaining the Teacher's Philosophy*

Teachers may also want to present their philosophy of teaching and learning. If students have never before experienced individualized instruction, teachers can explain their reasons for conducting the class in the manner they have described. In doing so, certain terms should be avoided. Teachers should not promise "freedom" when all they really mean is that they are offering more than one learning choice. Teachers should not tell students that they will learn at their own rate if, in reality, they must cover a minimum amount of material in each marking period. Many students become quite upset when informed that they must learn "on their own." If their past experience has been that, even with the teacher's help, foreign-language learning has been

---

* John Holt, *Freedom and Beyond* (New York: Dell Publishing Co., 1972), pp. 18–19.

difficult, the elimination of this major area of support can be quite alarming and can even result in active student efforts to sabotage the program. What a teacher might say instead is that students may choose how to learn: from the teacher, from an aide, from a written or taped explanation, or from the textbook.

10.4.5 Training Students to Work with Packets

A common error in the initial stages of programs of individualization is to hand out the learning packet and expect students to begin working right away according to the instructions. Even if the objectives and learning steps are indeed crystal clear (they may not be, if it is the first packet), some students will balk at reading them. If students complain that they "don't know what to do," or that they "don't understand the instructions," the teacher may offer to read and explain the instructions to those needing it. To facilitate student understanding, the instructions in the first few packets can be written in English. When the students are ready, the teacher may write the instructions in the foreign language, then read and translate them. After this has occurred several times, the teacher may ask if it is necessary to continue doing so. More often than not, students will elect to read the packet by themselves, with fewer and fewer requesting oral explanations.

10.4.6 Preparing Orientation Booklets

Teachers who have sufficient time may choose to prepare in advance orientation booklets containing the information about the course that students need to know. An advantage of this approach is that if students are absent or if they forget what has been explained, they can always refer back to the booklet. Written orientation material is also a useful reference for supervisors, administrators, counselors, and parents. One drawback to consider is that during the initial phases of an individualized program, many of the established rules may have to be changed if they do not work out as planned. If rules are unwritten, there is less commitment to them, and it is easier to institute new policies if this becomes necessary. Once a program has been tested and has proved effective, however, orientation packets can expedite considerably the process of training students to work more independently. A sample of topics for orientation materials appears in Appendix D.

10.5 ORIENTING AIDES AND PARAPROFESSIONALS

It is important that student aides, native speakers, and clerical personnel understand clearly what their responsibilities will be. Ideally, orientation sessions should take place prior to the beginning of the school year and before the start of each day's classes. This is particularly important during the first year of individualization, when new staff members and students are not yet familiar with procedures for taking attendance, testing, filing materials, leading conversation groups, and offering individual help. It is advisable that teachers closely supervise student aides and paraprofessionals during the first few months of instruction to make sure that the program is being implemented as it should be. If formal orientation sessions cannot be scheduled, teachers should at least spend a few minutes before class explaining the procedures to be followed that day. During the second year of operation, this problem assumes far less importance, since both the teacher and most of the additional personnel are more experienced.

Before staff members assume any teaching responsibility in the classroom, they should first have a chance to observe the teacher or another experienced person perform the desired activity. The classroom teacher should make sure that paraprofessionals or teachers in training clearly understand what they are expected to do. At times, more than one explanation may be needed for something that appears quite simple to the experienced teacher but is quite complex or confusing to a newcomer to the classroom. The classroom teacher should also be sure that new staff members can find their way around the building and can also locate all necessary materials both in and outside the classroom. This can prevent the embarrassment for staff members of not being able to answer a simple request by a student.

10.6 ORIENTING SUPERVISORS AND ADMINISTRATORS

If the impetus for individualization originates from an administrative decision, the responsibility of teachers to administrators is primarily one of communicating their progress, rather than actual orientation. If, on the other hand, the program results from the initiative of teachers, some kind of orientation report should be made to their superiors. The nature of this report will vary according to the educational philosophy operating in the school and the personalities of the people working there, as well as according to the specific nature of the program to be implemented.

In conservative school districts where parents and administrators value neatness, quiet, orderliness, and discipline above all else, the teacher may anticipate some opposition to allowing students to walk around the classroom, meet in small groups, and go to the library or lab at will. There may also be objections from colleagues in neighboring classrooms if the students become too noisy. In many institutions, students are not allowed to pass freely from room to room, and teachers are responsible at all times for knowing exactly where their students are. Under these circumstances, the prime responsibility of innovative teachers is to abide by school regulations. Teachers may, however, explain to their immediate supervisor or to their principal what they are trying to accomplish and secure permission for some limited activities that will not interfere with other classes in the school.

As long as the individualized program functions within established school policies for grouping students, covering the curriculum, and reporting grades, administrative tolerance, rather than active support, is of basic importance. However, once teachers contemplate a more radical program, they must work closely with and gain the approval of their superiors. They need administrative backing if they contemplate eliminating failing grades, awarding credit as units are mastered, or allowing slow learners additional time for mastery. Cooperation between administrators and teachers is essential if alternate courses are to be created, if additional staff or equipment is required for the program, or if class scheduling needs modification. Should continuous progress instruction be considered, it would be necessary to ascertain whether the teacher of the next level will be capable of accommodating students who are at different places in the course.

10.7 ORIENTING GUIDANCE COUNSELORS

Innovations approved for the program must be communicated to the guidance office. Counselors are frequently in a position to hear complaints from students or parents. For this reason, it is vitally important that they know what is going on and that they be able to explain the rationale for individualizing instruction. Since counselors are often instrumental in students' decisions regarding whether or not to pursue foreign-language study, support from guidance personnel is conducive to maintaining and increasing foreign-language enrollments. In situations where students may choose from among two or more alternative courses—perhaps a traditional four-skills curriculum and a conversation sequence—counselors can help students choose the one that most closely meets their objectives and needs. If department catalogs describe courses that students may choose, several copies should be sent to guidance counselors along with any other explanatory material that counselors might find helpful.

10.8 ORIENTING PARENTS

The type of orientation offered to parents will depend in large measure on the nature of the individualized program and on the educational values held by members of the community. In districts where parents place considerable importance on learning, pride themselves in being open to innovation, and traditionally favor experimentation and change, teachers will find considerable support for individualization. At parents' nights, open school programs, or at PTA meetings, teachers should communicate to parents the distinctive features of their programs: peer teaching, development of learner initiative, nongrading, self-pacing, elective courses, and so on.

In conservative communities, teachers may have to play down certain aspects of their programs. Parents may resent the use of student aides or paraprofessionals. Teachers, they reason, are paid to teach; they should do their jobs, not give them to people who are unqualified. Parents may also feel that children learn best from teachers, not from other students who know almost as little as they do. There may also be objections to offering students a choice of learning activities. Parents may believe that students do not know what they should study; they need the teacher to tell them what to do. In situations like these, teachers should stress the fact that they constantly supervise the whole program and assure quality instruction through frequent oral and written testing. If students have trouble with a topic, teachers are available to offer additional explanations and individual help. Teachers can stress the ways in which they "make" students learn—packets listing learning steps, frequent checking of individual progress, a variety of learning media that students "must" use, regularly assigned homework, and so on. Without deception or misrepresentation, an astute teacher can allay parental misgivings about individualization by emphasizing course requirements and provisions for student accountability.

In the event that radical changes are to be inaugurated—such as those that affect traditional grouping and grading policies—parents may be informed via special meetings or by letters to their homes. These measures are particularly important if parental cooperation is solicited in assuring satisfactory individual progress or if explanation of newly adopted report card procedures is needed. Parents might also choose in advance of the school year whether they want their children enrolled in individualized or traditional classes.

CHAPTER ELEVEN
HUMANIZING RELATIONSHIPS BETWEEN TEACHERS AND STUDENTS

11.1 GENERAL CONSIDERATIONS

A teacher cannot make students learn. He or she can only make them *want* to learn. It is well known that highly motivated students can learn in spite of less than ideal equipment and materials and even less than ideal teaching. Since years of inquiry and research into methodology have so far failed to yield techniques that have proved widely applicable and highly effective in enabling the majority of American students to communicate in a foreign language, perhaps another approach should be adopted. Rather than limiting investigation to *how* students learn, it might also be useful to ask *why* they learn. Teachers who are aware of the motivational needs of their students may then devise ways of structuring the classroom so that the chances of meeting these needs may be increased.

In this chapter suggestions are offered for dealing with students in ways that may serve to promote their desire to learn. Certain basic assumptions underlie these proposals: Students need and want to succeed in school. They respond more favorably to Theory-Y type management (as discussed in Chapter Three), in which rewards, rather than punishments, encourage motivation. They need to be treated with fairness and respect; their dignity as human beings must not be violated. Students perform better in a classroom environment characterized by trust, caring, and cooperation.

Theory-Y management principles assume even greater importance in an individualized classroom than in a teacher-centered situation. Once the constraints of direct teacher supervision are lifted during part or all of the class period, student *willingness* to cooperate becomes all-important. Unless there is voluntary compliance with established rules of classroom behavior, an individualized program may well become unmanageable.

11.2 PROMOTING SYNERGY

Synergy has been defined as

> the social-institutional arrangements which fuse selfishness and unselfishness by transcending their oppositeness and polarity so that the dichotomy between selfishness and altruism is resolved and transcended...[1]

An example of synergy given by Maslow[2] is the graduated income tax. Under this system, the more a person succeeds in enriching himself, the greater the sum of money he pays to the government. In this instance, the good of the individual and the good of society are identical. The polarity that may be thought to exist between the needs of the individual and the needs of others has been fused and transcended. Maslow points out that synergy operates most successfully in societies where conditions are good, that is, where there is an abundance of goods and services for all members of the society, where there is no want, deprivation, or lack of basic necessities for life.[3]

11.2.1 *Encouraging Subject-Matter Success*

A classroom based on sound management principles can be structured to promote synergy. Appropriate regulations can eliminate the polarity of teacher versus students and can fuse their seemingly opposite interests into common goals, which both work to achieve. One such goal can be success in mastering the subject matter. Students who earn good grades feel proud of their achievements and themselves. They more willingly carry out the tasks assigned to them. Teachers whose students achieve the course objectives are similarly rewarded. They feel genuine pride in their students' success as well as in their own teaching ability. Hostilities need no longer exist between teachers who believe that all students are "lazy" and are "trying to get away with something" and students who believe that the teacher is "out to get them" or "enjoys giving low grades."

Teachers who hope to make subject-matter success a mutual goal for their students and themselves should communicate their intention. They may tell students that they want to give high grades because high grades can prove that they are effective teachers. They may say that there is no limit on the number of good grades they give and that writing A or B on report cards costs them no more time or effort or expense than writing C, D, or F, though they would *prefer* giving the better grades. Teachers can also outline the procedures they will institute in order to help students succeed: performance objectives; pretests; retests; additional teaching personnel; written and taped explanations; individual conferences; individually prescribed instruction; choice of objectives, materials, and learning style; and so on. At the same time, they can make clear that good grades are not gifts; they are evaluations merited by the quality of the students' work.

11.2.2 *Encouraging Affective Success*

Another goal that teachers and students may share is that of getting along well together. No one enjoys daily arguments, conflicts, tensions, insults, threats, and the like. In view of the large amount of time teachers and students must spend together, it makes sense that both parties should want relationships that are at least harmonious and anxiety-free. Ideally, these relationships should be characterized by understanding, support, tolerance, cooperation, caring, respect, and enjoyment.

Teachers may communicate this mutually desirable goal not so much by what they say as by what they do. In their everyday dealings with students, teachers' actions should demonstrate the behaviors that promote a positive class atmosphere. It may be trite to quote the Golden Rule—"Do unto others as you would have others do unto you"—but the fact that this rule is so often forgotten in the classroom suggests that it merits repetition here. Teachers who treat their students with respect, acceptance, and understanding are likely to evoke these behaviors on the part of their students. Teachers may also show their concern for developing and maintaining positive feelings toward language learning by soliciting student reactions through class meetings, "rap sessions," and questionnaires. This topic will be further developed in Chapter Fourteen, which deals with program evaluation.

11.3 IMPROVING COMMUNICATION BETWEEN TEACHERS AND STUDENTS

Teachers often teach in the way they themselves were taught. In many cases this means that a teacher's natural methods for maintaining attention and discipline will tend to be negative, punitive, and authoritative. Flanders' work in interaction analysis has shown that direct means of control are less effective than indirect methods involving praise, clarifying and using pupils' ideas, and asking questions.⁴ Teachers who wish to increase their classroom effectiveness may move toward achieving this goal by adopting new ways of relating to students. What can matter most is not *what* they say but *how* they say it. This section will deal with some effective ways of handling common classroom situations.⁵

11.3.1 Criticize the Behavior, Not the Individual

When students behave in an unacceptable or unsatisfactory manner, the teacher's criticism should focus on the particular situation, not on the general nature of the learner's character. For example, here are two possible ways of responding to a student who neglected to skip lines on a composition after having been told specifically to do so: 1) "Don't you ever listen to directions? How many times must I tell you the same things over and over? Are you deaf?" 2) "Could you please recopy this paper and skip lines? I can't grade it unless I have room for corrections." The second response invites cooperation; the first one invites hostility and resistance.

11.3.2 When Angry, Use "I" Messages

Many teachers feel guilty when they are angry and try to hide or deny their feelings. The realities and daily demands of the teaching situation, however, make some anger or frustration inevitable. When teachers are irritated, they should try to express their authentic feelings in acceptable ways, rather than cover them up. Instead of pretending to be calm or telling students what they really think of them when they are rowdy, teachers should use an "I" message to convey their reactions. Rather than saying, "You act like a bunch of wild animals," they may say, "I am very annoyed that you are so loud. I can't even hear myself think."

11.3.3 Grant in Fantasy What Cannot Be Granted in Reality

At times students in an individualized classroom demand more attention than they actually need or more than the teacher is able to give them at a particular moment. "Leave me alone" or "I can't talk to you now" are less effective responses than granting in fantasy what cannot be granted in reality by saying: "I wish I could talk to you now, but I'm afraid I can't."

11.3.4 Accept Students' Feelings Instead of Denying Them

Though language learning can be very difficult for some students, well-meaning teachers may tell learners who are having trouble, "But this is so easy. You shouldn't have any problems with it." In effect, this statement denies the feelings students are actually experiencing and tells them they should instead have other feelings. Students would feel more assured if their teacher said to them, "I know this is hard. I had trouble with it too when I was a student. But I am here to help you learn it." A statement like this lets students know that they are normal; that the difficulty they encounter is legitimate; and that the teacher understands and accepts them as they are.

11.3.5 Avoid Verbal Overkill

When a student commits a fairly minor offense, such as forgetting to bring his book to class, teachers should give the behavior no more importance than it justly deserves. They may simply lend the student a book, ask him to share one with a friend, or, if the forgetfulness occurs repeatedly, have him do without the book that day, since this deprivation is no more than the natural consequence of his actions. An inappropriate response would be to launch into a lengthy tirade regarding the necessity of always being prepared for class, a history of the student's failure to perform a number of other requirements, and an enumeration of the various punishments to be imposed if the undesirable behavior continues. Such verbal overkill magnifies the seriousness of a relatively minor infraction. In effect, student misbehavior is being rewarded through increased attention, when the opposite should occur: Misbehavior should result in minimum attention, while compliance should bring considerable notice from the teacher.

11.3.6 Avoid Escalation and Confrontation

Another way in which relatively minor classroom incidents become major areas of teacher-student conflict is by unnecessary escalation and confrontation. A student passes a note, or forgets his homework, or fails to pay attention to an explanation. The teacher criticizes the student personally and imposes a punishment far harsher than what the situation demands. The student is asked to leave the room, or write a note of apology, or is sent to the disciplinary office. At this point, the student feels that the teacher does not like him. He must also maintain his dignity before his peers, who are anxious to see what will happen next. The teacher too feels his or her dignity is at stake. If he or she backs down, there is the possibility of losing the respect of the class for the rest of the year. Nobody can benefit from such a confrontation; its only result is increased hostility, animosity, and mistrust between teachers and students. There is no good way out of major confrontations. The best policy is to prevent their occurring in the first place. Disagreements between students and teachers should be handled privately, not in front of other students whose presence provokes undue ego involvement and consequent escalation.

11.3.7 Use Descriptions or Questions Instead of Commands

Commands increase student defiance, since they infringe upon the students' desire for autonomy. Less resistance is met when teachers describe the situation that needs correction, or when they ask a question. A less effective means of dealing with students who, for instance, are not working in groups as they should would be to say: "Now you stop talking right away and get to work. This fooling around must end." An alternative communication that should arouse less hostility is a simple description: "I don't see you practicing your drills"; or a question: "Are you practicing your drills?"

11.3.8 Use Body Language Instead of Verbal Language

When students are engaged in different activities, the teacher who is busy helping one group may find it difficult to manage the others. In this situation, body language can be very useful to convey necessary information. Eye control—letting a group of students know the teacher sees what they are doing—is a highly effective means of maintaining discipline without interrupting ongoing activities. Or, a teacher may be in the process of making important announcements when several students come in late. She does not want to stop what she is doing, yet she wants to show obvious disapproval of the tardiness. She may shake her head slightly as she watches the students take their places. No further verbal comment is needed. Or, a teacher who is working with an individual may indicate by snapping her fingers that she disapproves of the behavior of some students who are not performing the activities required of them.

11.3.9 Use Humor Instead of Rebukes

Younger students who are not yet used to the free movement allowed in individualized classes may start fighting. Teachers who want to stop fights without getting involved with the details of how and why a fight started may humor the participants with: "Stop loving each other so much," or (turning to the smaller student) "I don't want you bullying him." If the comment is made in the foreign language, this tactic is even more effective.

11.3.10 Solicit Student Commitment to Class Rules

If certain students chronically disrupt normal class activities, the teacher should take them aside and explain that he will not tolerate their behavior because they are preventing him from teaching and classmates from learning. He may offer them a choice: either they show by their behavior that they are willing to abide by the rules of the class, or they can no longer be part of the class—that is, they must sit alone, in a corner, in the hall, or in the disciplinary office. If improvement does not result, the punishments invoked are based on student choice, not on arbitrary teacher authority.

11.3.11 Be a Real Person

> As Ginott states:[6]
>
> A teacher cannot be artificial and effective. Nothing defeats him more than phoniness. No one can pretend respect and care without being detected. Skill divorced from genuineness is soon unmasked.

Though the types of responses described in this section may be foreign to a teacher's repertoire of classroom behaviors, they can be learned. Human beings can change themselves—if they genuinely want to. Adopting the ways of communication described above does not make the teacher a "phony." Though certain methods of expression may not at first be spontaneous, they can become so through practice as well as by adapting the messages to suit one's own personality and classroom situation. A teacher's real desire to improve his rapport with his students can prevent artificiality. Presumably, teachers who have taken the trouble to learn a foreign language can also teach themselves to use their native language more effectively and thereby change their behavior as well.

11.4 HUMANIZING AND PERSONALIZING INSTRUCTION

A major advantage of an open classroom style of teaching is that it facilitates the individualization and personalization of instruction to an extent impossible to achieve in a teacher-centered situation. Some of the ways this may be accomplished are illustrated in this section.

11.4.1 *Individualized Learning Prescriptions*

Individualization permits teachers to prescribe learning activities according to individual needs. For example, a student may have considerable trouble producing the sound /r/ in the foreign language despite having practiced with tapes. The teacher can spend a few minutes explaining to him how the sound is produced and write out words and sentences containing it. The student repeats after the teacher and practices the material outside of class. He reports the next day to the teacher for further evaluation. Another student's composition may show that she forgets to make her subjects and verbs agree. The teacher explains how to make corrections and assigns her a written drill that stresses the needed agreement. Finally, two students may have written an original dialog that is imaginative but fails to employ the correct forms of the irregular present tense. The teacher produces a list of the verbs that have been taught and asks the students to check off the ones they have trouble remembering. Then the teacher proposes a deal: If they memorize the conjugations of the difficult verbs and write them out without error, she will award them extra-credit points.

11.4.2 *Extra Help in Class*

Individualization also permits offering extra help in class, rather than after school. For example, a student may be unable to write an exercise on object pronouns because she does not understand what the questions mean, is not sure which pronouns to use or where to place them, and has trouble forming comprehensible sentences in the foreign language. The teacher asks a highly competent student aide, student teacher, or paraprofessional to do the exercise orally with her. After this help the student should be able to complete it herself and check her written answers with the key. A second student may report to the teacher for an oral test unprepared. He forgets the meaning of key words in the questions, and his answers are halting. The teacher asks him to practice some more with a friend and to take the oral test again when he is ready. At times, extra help may be needed by a student because of an extended absence from school. If feasible, the teacher may send learning materials to the student's home so that he may keep up with schoolwork to some extent. Upon his return to school, the teacher can offer any explanations needed and can provide for oral practice sessions.

11.4.3 *Guidance in Specific Skill Areas*

11.4.3a ORAL COMPREHENSION

Teachers can use an open classroom to guide students in skill areas where they experience difficulty. For those having trouble with oral comprehension, the teacher may suggest that an aide help by playing tapes, which he or she stops at intervals to check for student understanding. In addition, the teacher may arrange for these students to take oral tests in a special way: they may write out each question asked as well as their answer to it. Then they read their answer to the teacher. The teacher may use this method with students who he suspects have trouble remembering a sequence of foreign-language words.

11.4.3b VOCABULARY

Students may also encounter difficulty, particularly at intermediate levels, when asked to memorize lists of new vocabulary words. In such instances the teacher may ask an aide or a peer teacher to drill students individually, thus supplying the discipline they may lack when working alone. Another approach involves training students in how to learn. The teacher directs students to cross off the vocabulary list all the words they already know. Then they test themselves on each word and mark those they miss. After studying the words they do not know, they once again test themselves and mark a second time the words they still do not remember. They continue this process, studying only the words marked until they learn the entire list. An advantage of this procedure is that the number of unknown words normally decreases each time students go through the list, and, ultimately, the words most difficult to remember are easily identified, since they have a greater number of checks.

11.4.3c SPEAKING

An important way to help learners develop speaking skill is to have brief conversations with individuals during class. By encouraging students to express themselves freely—mistakes and all—and especially by *listening* attentively, teachers can help students build the self-confidence they need to speak the foreign language. An advantage of speaking with individuals—as opposed to conversations involving, theoretically, the entire class—is the personal quality of the dialog that adds realism and meaning to it.

11.4.3d READING

When students have trouble passing multiple choice reading tests, the teacher may ask them to translate the test material. Often, she will find that the students do not know many common words, mainly abstract ones like prepositions, negations, adverbs, and interrogative words. They therefore tend to skip over what they do not understand. Having identified a cause of lack of comprehension, the teacher may write out a list of these key words, which the students are asked to memorize. She also stresses the importance of reading every word for an accurate interpretation of the text and suggests that students use their index fingers to guide their eyes along each line of print. This practice should help them focus on each sentence element.

Another reading problem may result, particularly at the intermediate level, from an entirely different cause. Inquiry into the reading strategies of different students may reveal that some individuals are over zealous in trying to understand every new word in the text and therefore read too slowly to complete their assignments. The teacher may explain to these students that one goal of the year's course is to develop rapid reading skills that stress overall comprehension more than an understanding of every single detail. Overly careful readers may be assured that they can get along quite well without knowing the exact meaning of each word. The teacher should then show individuals how they may guess intelligently at words they do not know.

11.4.3e WRITING

Many foreign-language learners have difficulty writing compositions. Some students' work is nearly incomprehensible because they tend to leave out key words like verbs and prepositions. During individual conferences the teacher may translate each student's composition into English to demonstrate how hard it is to understand when words are missing. She may suggest that before handing in the next composition they read it aloud and, if necessary, translate it into English word by word to see if it makes sense.

Some otherwise successful learners have trouble with compositions because they try to write in the foreign language with the same degree of complexity that they use in their native language. As a result, structures, which are cast according to English patterns, are often stilted, and many of the words, found in the dictionary, are inappropriate. The teacher may urge these learners to simplify their ideas and to draft compositions in the foreign language, not in English. If they do not know how to say exactly what they want to, they should choose to say something similar, but less complicated, that *can* be expressed. The teacher may also show students how to use the abbreviations in a dictionary entry to help them choose the appropriate word from among those listed.

11.4.4 *Support and Encouragement*

Foreign-language instruction is humanized and personalized when teachers provide support and encouragement during their personal contacts with students.

For example, when a new student arrives in the middle of the year, he may feel strange and alone in the new school. The teacher may ask him what textbook was used in the former school and make sure that the changeover to the new book will not be difficult. The teacher can encourage the newcomer to ask for help whenever he has a learning problem and can introduce him to a group of students who can orient him for that day and provide help if needed. Teachers may also offer encouragement to students who do not have sufficient confidence in their abilities. Likewise, teachers may suggest that capable students accelerate their rate of progress, or, if this does not appeal to them, they may serve as peer teachers in the classroom. Or, teachers can provide needed assurance to students when they experience frustration or disappointment in language learning.

Conversations in the foreign language between the teacher and students can assume a highly personal nature. They may concern articles of clothing or jewelry, weekend plans, current school activities, and so on. During these personal encounters teachers may discover areas of students' interests—hockey, stamp collecting, ham radios, medicine, horses, and so on—that may possibly be incorporated into the course work. At times, teachers may inadvertently discover certain out-of-class influences on student achievement—after-school jobs, illness at home, or other personal problems. Though teachers are not equipped to deal with these matters, their knowledge may help them to be more understanding with students in class.

11.4.5 *Provision for Individual Needs, Interests, and Learning Styles*

Teachers in an individualized classroom may attempt to provide for the individual needs, interests, and learning styles of various members of the class. Some students may have trouble meeting the writing requirements of a four-skills, college preparatory, first-level course. They do well in pronunciation and speaking, but have considerable trouble spelling and expressing their thoughts in writing. In such cases the teacher may substitute additional oral assignments for some of the written ones. At the intermediate or advanced levels, many students may look forward to reading novels, but others might prefer short stories, poetry, drama, or perhaps none of these. A wide range of available teaching materials can facilitate individualization according to student interests. Alternatively, in a culture course, students may choose to report on areas of personal interest—cuisine, music, current events, art, and so on.

For some students grammar explanations that involve abstract terminology are confusing. Their learning style demands concreteness. A teacher can respond to these needs by avoiding unnecessary abstractions. Instead of referring to "object pronouns," the teacher may simply say, "him," "to him," and so on. Students will provide verb forms more readily if the stimulus is, for example, "we," rather than "first person plural." Hand gestures may be used to indicate present, past, and future verb tenses. Instead of constantly repeating word-order rules, students may learn syntax by playing a game in which each word of a foreign-language sentence is written on a different card. The players must arrange and rearrange the cards until the sentence is syntactically acceptable.

Some students do not enjoy practicing with *recorded* drills because they find the tapes too fast and the pauses too short, or because they lose their place in the book and do not understand what is said. Such students may prefer to work instead with audio-flashcards. Moving each card through the language master machine can hold their attention, since the words heard are written right on the cards. The cards may be replayed as needed to ensure comprehension.

NOTES

[1] Abraham H. Maslow, *Eupsychian Management: A Journal* (Homewood, Ill.: Dow Jones Irwin, 1965), p. 103.

[2] *Ibid.*, p. 91.

[3] *Ibid.*, p. 96.

[4] N. A. Flanders, *Teacher Influence, Pupil Attitudes, and Achievement.* Co-Operative Research Monograph No. 12, OE-25040. (Washington, D.C.: U.S. Department of Health, Education, and Welfare, Office of Education, 1965.)

[5] This section is based on ideas in Haim G. Ginott, *Teacher and Child* (New York: The Macmillan Company, 1972).

[6] *Ibid.*, p. 121.

CHAPTER TWELVE
OVERCOMING COMMON MANAGEMENT PROBLEMS

12.1 GENERAL CONSIDERATIONS

A newly initiated program of individualized instruction that does not encounter some problems during the early phases of its development is indeed a rarity. Most teachers can expect at least a few experiences to fall short of the ideal situation envisioned. Rather than serving as sources of discouragement, these less than perfect results should function as stimuli for analyzing the problems and devising appropriate solutions. Some of the difficulties most commonly encountered in managing newly individualized classes are presented in this chapter. Possible causes of the problems are considered and various solutions proposed. The discussion, however, is by no means definitive. Conditions vary so widely among individual teachers, classes, and schools that it is impossible to guarantee that the proposals made here will be universally applicable and successful. It is hoped, rather, that teachers will take encouragement from knowing that the difficulties they may experience are not unique, and that the ideas presented here can be used as points of departure for the development of solutions appropriate to one's own situation.

12.2 HEAVY TEACHER PREPARATION

Many teachers find that the change to individualization results in an overwhelming burden of preparation. They are soon buried beneath what seems to be an unsurmountable load of paperwork: Packets for the fastest students must be written ahead of time, test papers need correction, alternate exams have to be duplicated. In addition, audio and visual materials must be arranged for easy student access, and supplementary reading or cultural assignments must be prepared. In the face of these problems several time-saving procedures are open to teachers.

12.2.1 *Limiting the Scope of Individualization*

If the teacher cannot cope with the amount of preparation needed for his original plan of individualization, he might have to relinquish, temporarily, some of its features. During the first year, it may be impossible to allow students to accelerate, particularly if the teacher cannot prepare adequately for the most rapid learners. Instead, the fastest students might elect extra-credit work or could serve as tutors to classmates. Then, the next year, after the packets and supporting materials have been written, students may be permitted to advance at their own pace.

Providing a fully individualized, multimedia program may also prove impossible in the initial phases. Teachers may have to choose among the materials they create: either cassettes or overhead transparencies; either language masters or vocabulary flashcards; either supplementary basic readers or additional cultural materials; either written explanations of grammar or taped explanations; either alternate forms of the same test or original material to stimulate free oral communication. Actually, the teacher may never be faced with the precise choices mentioned here; however, this list may serve as a model for one he may prepare. Such a list should include all the various areas of preparation he anticipates. Each item is assigned a number according to the importance attached to it; items with the highest priority can be selected for implementation during the first year, while those with lower priority must await attention during subsequent years.

12.2.2 *Shortening Written Materials*

A workable means of easing the burden of preparing alternate forms of written tests is to make them as short as possible. There is nothing sacrosanct about ten-, twenty-, or twenty-five-item tests. In most cases, a teacher can ascertain whether or not students have learned an irregular verb or have understood a reading selection, for example, by administering a test of five, six, or seven items. If the exams are simply graded on a pass or fail basis, with a specified maximum number of errors permitted in order to pass, the teacher can be freed from writing and correcting the much longer tests, which are tied, unnecessarily, to a grading system of 60, 70, 80, 90, or 100. She is also freed from time-consuming mathematical calculations of students' grades.

Other materials that can also be shortened are the instruction sheets of the learning packets. Once students become used to the format of the course and are familiar with the performance objectives for each unit, there is little need for the teacher to continue specifying in detail the purpose of each assignment, the desired behaviors, how the students will be tested, and the minimum criteria for passing. The lengthy descriptiveness of the early packets can give way to a more concise checklist format. An example of how a lengthy packet may be shortened is given in Appendix B.

12.2.3 *Enlisting Help*

An overburdened teacher should investigate ways of obtaining help either from students or colleagues. Students might volunteer to run off stencils or Dittos; they can put instructional materials in folders and help file students' test papers; they might run errands to and from the duplicating machines, the learning center, the language lab, or the audio-visual room. Asking students to grade papers, however, is not recommended. Most students lack sufficient skill to grade accurately. Furthermore, since the teacher who wants to help with individual learning problems needs to know the achievement level of his students on each test, having students grade papers defeats this purpose. If necessary, though, students might be trusted to record the grades the teacher has assigned. Nevertheless, the teacher must still check to see that the grades are reported correctly.

Help can come too from a colleague in the language department. Two teachers might agree to divide the preparation duties for the level they are both teaching. Or, two teachers assigned the same two levels might split them so that each person takes charge of only one of the preparations and produces materials for both to use. Cooperation can also take place less formally with exchanges of ideas, techniques, and suggestions for improvement.

12.2.4 *Developing Efficient Grading Procedures*

A simple grading system that enables teachers to evaluate student performance rapidly can greatly help teachers in coping with the burden of preparation during the first year of individualization. Instead of listing in the gradebook every single drill and exercise the students have completed successfully, teachers can limit themselves to recording the results of only major oral and written tests. Students are not permitted to take these tests until they present their packet checklists with signatures showing that they have performed satisfactorily on the preceding learning steps, thus assuring the teacher that all assignments prior to the tests have been completed.

Marking papers "pass" or "fail" can reduce considerably the time and effort required to add up grades and then average them. If each assignment a student has passed is assigned a certain small number of points, perhaps five or ten, then the teacher can merely count up the points earned and translate them into number or letter grades.

12.3 EFFICIENT STUDENT USE OF CLASS TIME

Many teachers who enthusiastically adopt an individualized instructional style are soon disappointed to find the students wasting considerable amounts of time in class. In part, this problem may be one of overly high teacher expectations. Though students should, ideally, spend the entire class period on their assignments, this is not the case in many instances. Five or ten minutes are often wasted either when students are settling down to work or, at the end of the period, after students feel they have completed their work for that day. This is normal and not particularly serious. After all, in traditional, teacher-centered classrooms comparable amounts of time can be wasted in distributing papers, waiting for students to finish tests, or maintaining student attention or discipline—concerns that rarely trouble teachers of individualized classes. In situations where greater amounts of wasted time make this problem more serious—particularly when deadlines for minimum performance must be met—the concerned teacher may consider applying any of the following suggested procedures.

12.3.1 *Establishing Appropriate Deadlines*

A major cause of students' wasting time in class is the lack of well-defined and appropriate deadlines for completing classwork. While well-motivated learners do not require precise time-schedules, their less well motivated classmates do require this structure. Deadlines set for a grading period, for example, may not be sufficiently limited for the needs of many learners. Similarly, unit deadlines stretching over a period of three or four weeks may also be too broad to encourage students to use their time efficiently in class. Some teachers may find that weekly—or even daily—deadlines may be required at the beginning of a program of individualization, at least until students become used to the greater freedom allowed them and begin to assume more responsibility for their assignments.

At times, particularly during the early phases of individualization, the deadlines set may be too long or too short in terms of the amount of work students must complete. While appropriate deadlines often result after a year of trial and error, a useful guideline in establishing them can be this one: The teacher may estimate how many days it would take to teach and test the material in a full-class situation. Then, one or two days may be added to this figure to allow slower learners to keep up with the pace. If the teacher contemplates oral testing of individuals or groups of students, she should calculate how much time this will take and add an appropriate number of class periods to the basic full-class pace in order to accommodate this activity.

12.3.2 Limiting the Amount of Free Time in Class

Students with forty to fifty minutes at their disposal often feel that they can waste half of it talking to their friends and still complete what is required of them. This attitude is far less prevalent when students have only twenty to thirty minutes for their work. If necessary, a teacher may plan to use roughly the first half of the class period for full-group grammar or cultural presentations, or for small-group conversation activities in which all students must participate. Then, during the second part of the period, students engage in individual or paired practice and testing. By thus reducing the amount of free time allowed students, the teacher may ensure their using it more efficiently. This approach is particularly applicable to a flexibly paced style of individualization where minimum amounts of material must be covered within a given amount of time. In a continuous progress situation, however, wasting time may be less of a concern, since credit is withheld from students if they do not perform satisfactorily.

12.3.3 Training Students Not to Wait

Sometimes when students are asked why they are not working, they may answer, often with considerable frustration, that they have nothing else to do because they must wait to be tested orally, or that they are waiting for their papers to be marked. In such situations, teachers must examine their testing and grading procedures to be sure that they are realistic and appropriate in their classrooms. (Methods of accomplishing this are suggested in Chapter Thirteen.) If the procedures being used are satisfactory, the teacher needs to adopt another approach. He must train students not to wait. If they cannot have the attention they want precisely at the moment they want it, they should choose another activity in the meantime. For example, students waiting their turn for an oral test may practice the material in pairs or in small groups led by aides. Students who have finished ahead of time and are waiting for an oral explanation of new grammar might be advised to read it in the book or ask the help of a more advanced student. Instead of having students wait for their test grades before continuing, they can be advised to assume that they have passed and proceed accordingly. As soon as the test papers are marked, the teacher will show them to the students. If a tape recorder, cassette player, or audio flash-card reader is not available at the time a student needs it, he can choose to work on another learning step for the time being. If students are taught to be flexible in completing their assigned learning steps, the amount of time lost in waiting can be held to a minimum.

12.3.4 Providing Alternative Activities

In some cases, students waste time when they have finished the activities required of them and either cannot or do not want to begin new material. This may occur especially on Fridays or on the days preceding school vacations. Forcing students to keep busy at one of these times—especially if they have worked diligently up to that point—makes little sense and promotes unnecessary friction. What a teacher may do instead is provide students with activities that, though perhaps not directly related to the required course work, nevertheless promote foreign-language learning. They can play vocabulary, grammar, or culture games. They might be encouraged to have a conversation with a friend—something they want to do anyway—but entirely in the foreign language. They might choose to browse through foreign-language magazines—either those from abroad or American publications written for students. Information from these materials can serve as the basis for extra-credit projects. Students might listen to the latest popular songs on a phonograph. Or, they could use class time to find a book from the classroom or department library or for writing a letter to a pen pal. If the teacher establishes a firm classroom rule that "Everyone must always do *something* related to foreign-language learning," and if sufficient alternatives are provided, most students will engage in fruitful activities most of the time.

12.3.5 *Providing Adequate Structure*

A common error of teachers beginning to individualize is not providing adequate structure. For example, though students should eventually take the responsibility for determining what they must study or write outside of class, they probably will not be able to do so at the beginning of the year. Therefore, the teacher should assign homework. He should state clearly what assignments must be done by the next day or the next week. As students become more accustomed to the class routine, he may ask instead, "What are some of the things you might do tonight?" A chorus of student voices should come up with several suggestions. By the beginning of the second semester these announcements should become unnecessary.

Some individualized programs run into initial problems because they provide students with too much choice. Students who have been trained to follow their teacher's directions to the letter will experience difficulty adjusting to a situation in which they are told to pick their mode of learning, or select which drills they will do, or choose an extra-credit assignment. As Holt points out,* a wide range of choices can produce anxiety in adult learners, and even more so in children. He suggests that only two or three options be presented to students at first. These can be gradually expanded as students become used to making choices. A teacher who notices indecision in certain students may tell them to engage in a specific activity because he thinks they "need it." This may or may not be the case, especially at the start of the term when the teacher is not fully acquainted with his students, but it does temporarily relieve them from the anxiety of choosing and makes them feel that the teacher cares about them. On subsequent occasions, the teacher may suggest that these students try new or different activities. Once they have tried out

---

* John Holt, *Freedom and Beyond* (New York: Dell Publishing Co., 1972).

several of the learning choices offered, most will know which they prefer and will make selections accordingly.

Though nongraded continuous progress instruction that encourages students to master the material at their own rate may be the ideal of a fully developed program, individualized classrooms will have to work within deadlines if the grading system in the school does not allow for awarding fractional credit (sometimes called variable credit) as each unit is completed. In any event, most students need some type of deadline in order to set an appropriate learning pace for themselves.

12.4 STUDENTS' DEMANDS FOR ATTENTION

When too many students want the same activity at the same time, it may be impossible for the teacher and the aides, if any, to take care of all the requests promptly. This situation, which frustrates student progress, can seriously impair the effectiveness of the individualized program and should be remedied as soon as the cause is discovered.

12.4.1 *Examining the Structure of the Learning Packet*

Sometimes excessive student demands for attention may be inherent in the nature of the learning packet. For example, it may be impossible to carry out all the oral and written checking called for in the packet. In this case, several alternative solutions may be implemented: reducing the number of check steps, providing more class time for checking, increasing the number of student aides, or shortening the amount of time spent with each individual. The appropriate balance of activities must be worked out by trial and error until the teacher comes up with a manageable format, given the number of students in her class, their ability levels, and the personnel available to provide help.

12.4.2 *Advoiding Last-Minute Work*

Heavy demands for attention may also result when, in programs with specific deadlines, students wait until the very last day to submit their work or take all their required tests. This may result in impossible demands on the teacher's time. The problem may be approached in several ways. First of all, the teacher can establish more frequent deadlines—perhaps weekly ones—until students become accustomed to taking responsibility for pacing themselves. In this way an overly large amount of work is not permitted to accumulate. Each deadline, though, should be generous; that is, one or two extra days should be allowed beyond the minimum number students normally require. For example, if most students need a minimum of four days to master a certain grammatical topic, pileups become inevitable on the last day of the four-day period. If six days are provided, however, testing may be spread out over the fourth, fifth, and sixth days, thereby avoiding the last-minute rush.

Students must be encouraged, however, to work ahead of generous deadlines; otherwise the same problem will recur. Some reward should be offered so that finishing early becomes more attractive than waiting for the final day. First of all, the teacher might explain that if students test ahead of the deadline and do not pass, they will still have one or two more days on which to take retests. If they wait for the final day, they will have to retest after school or during a lunch or free period—which is far less appealing to them. This logic, though, does not work with students who optimistically—and often wrongly—believe that they can pass on their first try. Other motivations must be supplied. A teacher might announce that students who pass their tests ahead of time are eligible to become aides. They can tutor students needing help and, perhaps, earn extra credit for it. This arrangement holds considerable appeal for students who like the prestige of helping others and enjoy feeling responsible for them. It can also be instrumental in building feelings of self-confidence that, in turn, can lead to improved performance. A different reward is permitting students who have completed their assignments to play foreign-language card games or Scrabble or Monopoly. Speaking credit can be awarded if they use the foreign language. Here too, the time "lost" playing is compensated for by more positive feelings toward language learning, which may in turn result in better achievement. A list of commonly used game expressions and their French equivalents is provided in Appendix D.

If the suggestions above are not feasible because of a particular class situation, still another approach can be used. The teacher can simply tell the class that if everyone waits until the last minute, he will not be able to accommodate them all, the purposes of the individualization will be defeated, and the program will be abandoned. He might ask for their cooperation in scheduling themselves for tests over a period of several days. This can work well with mature students and in heterogeneously grouped classes where there are wide differences in ability and in learning rates.

12.5 EFFICIENT USE OF THE TEACHER'S TIME

Unless a teacher manages the time in class well and carefully plans the activities to be carried out, she may find the experiences in an individual classroom somewhat less than completely satisfying. Common problems result from students demanding too much individual attention, from excessive checking and testing, and from inadequate delegation of some instructional activities.

12.5.1 *Coping with Excessive Demands for Individual Attention*

Once in a while individual students demand so much attention from the teacher that she has little time left to spend with other individuals needing help. One method of approaching the problem is to encourage students to work with a friend or a classroom aide. If they nevertheless insist on monopolizing attention, the teacher will have to explain that her time is, unfortunately, limited, and she simply cannot offer the amount of attention desired without neglecting others in the class.

12.5.2 Avoiding Excessive Checking and Testing

Teachers who envision themselves conferring frequently with students and offering guidance for individual learning problems become sorely disappointed when the need to check student progress results in their virtual imprisonment behind their desks. They rightfully resent their almost exclusive role as checkers and testers. Surely, they think, this has little to do with the humanization and personalization that individualized instruction is supposed to encourage. In such instances the problem may be that the learning packet calls for too much checking in relationship to the time made available for it in class. Another possibility is that there may not be enough help in the classroom. If aides cannot be obtained, the teacher might ask a student to volunteer, perhaps just for that day, to help in giving out test papers or checking off simple assignments such as pattern drills and written exercises. A teacher who must conduct most of his classes without aides needs to modify his program accordingly. He may have to limit the amount of checking, reduce the length of oral and written tests, or substitute oral tests in groups for individual checking.

Teachers should also bear in mind which classroom activities only they can handle and which should be delegated to other teaching personnel. For example, some of the more mechanical aspects of foreign-language learning, such as oral pattern practice, correction of written exercises, and simple vocabulary drills, can be managed by aides or by the students themselves if answer keys are provided. This can permit teachers to devote themselves to more demanding activities that require their special expertise: discussing test results with students, making individualized learning prescriptions, and offering additional explanations when needed.

12.6 PROBLEMS RESULTING FROM STUDENT MISJUDGMENTS

The provision of choice is basic to the individualization of instruction. In theory, at least, allowing students to choose activities, materials, and learning style serves to meet their individual needs and promotes higher subject matter achievement. In practice, however, this theory has yet to be proved. So far, most individualized programs have reported gains primarily in the affective domain; in some programs there have even been losses in subject-matter achievement. What happens in many cases is that students make poor choices: They hurriedly check off their own learning activities and present themselves too soon for tests that they cannot pass. They elect to do the written steps in class, then neglect the oral practice they need. They skip all steps marked "optional." They select objectives that are inappropriate for them or content themselves with working below their ability.

After completing an individualized unit of instruction the teacher may find herself making rules and imposing limitations that contradict her philosophic ideals. She may have to require certain activities of all students. She may ask students to complete oral steps before attempting the written ones. She may eliminate a considerable amount of student self-checking. She may forbid certain members of the class to work together. If students are as yet unable to choose wisely, this is a responsible course of action that the teacher must take.

Perhaps the best way of solving problems such as these is to take steps to avoid their occurrence in the first place. In starting an individualized program, teachers should limit the amount of choice available to the students. Once students prove that they can act responsibly, the choices offered them can be broadened. It is much easier to liberalize a classroom in progressive steps than it is to withdraw certain options once they have been in effect.

12.7 NEATNESS AND ORDER

The problem of maintaining neatness and order in learning materials is greater in an individualized classroom than in a traditional one. When students have access to a wide variety of books and magazines, tapes, pictures and visuals, cultural realia, and audio and visual equipment, materials will almost inevitably be mislaid unless necessary precautions are taken. One solution to the problem is creating a learning center to house materials that all students in language classes may use. The center could be staffed by paraprofessionals in charge of signing materials in and out and placing all items where they belong. For many schools, however, space and budgetary limitations preclude establishing such a center. In these situations materials will, of necessity, be housed within each classroom. Despite the less formal nature of this arrangement, material and equipment can be kept in an orderly manner if the teacher takes some necessary management steps.

Assuming that adequate storage facilities are available in the classroom (as discussed in Chapter Eight) teachers may, as part of their student orientation program, stress the importance of replacing materials neatly in the same way they were found. Labels on both equipment and storage facilities that clearly indicate where items belong can help students keep the classroom neat and orderly. Teachers may also solicit student cooperation by pointing out that unless materials are put back where they belong, they will no longer be available for student use. In classrooms where large amounts of materials are in heavy daily use, teachers may, as a matter of course, set aside the last five minutes for clean-up. Alternatively, they may appoint student monitors on a permanent or rotating basis to make sure that everything is put away. In spite of these provisions, teachers may still have to do some straightening up from time to time. This should be a last resort, however, after other courses of action have been employed; it should not be a daily responsibility. As much as possible of teachers' valuable and limited time should be spent in activities related more directly to the improvement of student achievements in foreign-language learning.

12.8 STUDENT DISSATISFACTION WITH INDIVIDUALIZATION

Perhaps the most serious management problems involve student dissatisfaction with individualized instruction. If, after the first unit or two, most students are not generally content with the way the class is run, the teacher will lack the cooperation needed for a successful program. Common student complaints may be: "I never know what to do," "I don't understand what is going on," "I waste too much time in class and can't get my work done," "I don't have enough self-discipline to work on my own," or "I like the *teacher* to explain the material, not ... (the aide, the tape, the written explanation sheet, the book, and so on)."

Comments such as these reveal that there is insufficient structure for at least some of the students. To correct this, the teacher may have to provide greater control and less freedom in the classroom. He may conduct more full-group presentations, read the packet instructions to those needing it, or write out daily assignments for students to do both in class and at home. He may have to bring in additional teaching personnel and designate specific testing days on which everyone—ready or not—must take a test. While this may be disappointing or disconcerting, it is useless to conduct a class in a manner antithetical to the learning style of most students. This topic will be treated further in Chapter Fourteen.

CHAPTER THIRTEEN
TESTING, GRADING, AND RECORD KEEPING

13.1 GENERAL CONSIDERATIONS

Testing assumes a central role in an individualized program. If students spend some or most of their time engaging in activities that are not directly supervised, the teacher must have some means of checking their work and ensuring quality performance. Testing when ready, an option offered in many individualized classrooms, can pose problems to the teacher accustomed to administering a single test to all students at the same time. An advantage of individualization over conventional full-class teaching is that it permits a greater amount of oral testing. This too, however, can create management difficulties if the teacher has not developed procedures for handling tests of speaking ability. Suggestions for managing testing, grading, and record keeping are offered in this chapter.

13.2 GUIDELINES FOR TEST CONSTRUCTION

Well-constructed tests can greatly enhance the effectiveness of an individualized program.

Properly administered, tests can provide not only measurement of students' progress but also diagnoses of their learning problems. This can serve as the basis for individualized help and guidance. Some guidelines for test construction are presented in this section.

13.2.1 *Tests Should Be Short*

Since frequent checking is essential to a well-run individualized classroom, it is vital that all tests be as short as possible. Otherwise, students may complain that they spend most of their time taking tests rather than learning. This complaint is particularly true of students who must take several tests before they finally pass. Short tests also facilitate immediate correction in class and reduce the time teachers or aides must spend discussing students' work. In determining test length, teachers might write out how many different points the test is to cover and then make a random selection from them. For example, students may study twenty-five vocabulary words but be tested on only five. They may practice answering ten oral questions but respond to just three on the test. Student knowledge of grammatical patterns may be checked by presenting them with one sentence from each drill. An entire dialog may be assigned for spelling practice but only a sentence or two selected for dictation. Similarly, required compositions should be short, with an upper word limit of perhaps fifty words in beginning levels.

13.2.2 *Tests Should Be Criterion-Referenced*

Student performance will improve if the precise nature of the test is clearly spelled out. The teacher should provide students with information they need in order to direct their study efforts toward the type of test they will have. In addition to providing sample test questions, the teacher may also indicate exactly what material will be covered. For example, the students might be provided with the vocabulary lists or verb charts on which the test will be based. They should also know how many items there will be and the maximum number of errors permitted for a passing grade.

13.2.3 *Tests Should Be Easy to Grade*

Grading criteria that focus on several performance aspects or involve complicated or extensive mathematical calculations must be avoided. Otherwise, assigning grades will become so laborious and time-consuming that the teacher will be unable to carry out the frequent testing needed in an individualized class. For example, a test on reading a dialog aloud that provides for different ratings—based on the student's fluency, his pronunciation, his intonation, and his ability to make appropriate liaisons—does not lend itself to rapid grading. What might be done instead is to evaluate the student's performance simply as "pass" or "fail," depending on whether his overall performance is satisfactory or not. Alternatively, only one aspect of performance—perhaps pronunciation—might be evaluated at one time. A written test requiring that nouns be replaced by two object pronouns will cause grading problems if separate point values are assigned to the correct uses of each pronoun and still others to their appropriate placement in the sentence. It is much easier to allow a predetermined maximum number of errors of any type in order to pass.

The grading of compositions also needs simplification. Rather than counting the number of errors made or assigning grades according to subjective criteria, teachers of beginning classes might grade as "pass" all compositions that are comprehensible. Grammar errors are marked, but students receive credit only after they have corrected their mistakes. At intermediate or advanced levels, students may be allowed no more than a maximum number of elementary errors in order to receive credit for the assignment. Evaluating compositions may also be speeded by using correction symbols and abbreviations. A sample list of those that students can use for reference is provided in Appendix D.

An advantage of "pass" or "fail" evaluation is that it may be used easily with tests containing only the minimum number of items needed to test a particular topic. It frees teachers from slavery to tests of ten or twenty items whose length is attributable far more to arithmetic convenience than to any real measurement necessity. A "pass" or "fail" grade contingent upon a student's ability to make himself understood in the foreign language, rather than on a specific number of errors, can facilitate testing for communicative competence instead of solely for grammatical accuracy. It can also enable teachers to require higher standards of performance from capable students while at the same time permitting them to accept responses from less able learners who are putting forth considerable effort. Teachers need only vary to some degree whether they "understand" students' answers.

13.2.4   *Tests Should Be Suited to the Students Taking Them*

An ideal of individualized instruction is to suit the different learning styles and course objectives of the students enrolled. Unfortunately, there are virtually no reliable scientific data available regarding the nature of these differences or ways of diagnosing them. Until research efforts yield the needed information, teachers will have to rely on their classroom perceptions, native intuition, and common-sense judgments. Some possible considerations in this area are offered here.

If student goals include a strong desire to communicate in the foreign language, oral or written exams requiring full-sentence responses are more appropriate than fill-in-the-blank type questions. While creative, imaginative students may enjoy relatively unstructured assignments that allow them to show originality, less proficient students may prefer more clearly defined assignments that involve memory work or adaptation of existing models.

Alternate forms of grammar and reading tests can be prepared for students who perform better orally and for those who excel in written testing. Some students may respond better to visual cues than they do to verbal or written ones. Insofar as possible and practical, students may be permitted to choose the type of tests they take.

13.2.5 *Students Should Have Opportunities to Retest*

If relatively high passing standards are set, students normally unaccustomed to achieving them may need several opportunities to reach the required performance level. Alternate forms of oral and written tests can be instrumental in helping students reach the mastery standard. Retesting enables the teacher to diagnose the errors of individual students and reteach them the particular skills or information the test shows they still lack. It is important that no penalty be attached to retests so that students are not discouraged from taking them. A goal of individualized instruction is to maximize learning, not to penalize students who may need more time to master a topic. The paper work involved in retesting may be made manageable by shortening tests to the minimum number of items needed to show the student's mastery of a topic.

The question arises whether a retest should be the same as the original test or different from it. This depends on the goal of the assignment. If the aim is to assimilate certain facts—such as irregular verb forms or cultural information—there is no problem in offering students the same test until they pass it. However, if the goal is to develop skill in using information in new situations, retests should present the new material in restructured contexts.

The number of times students may retest also poses a question; no clearcut answers can be offered, since the policy chosen must depend on a highly variable number of factors: the teacher's philosophy, school administrative procedures, and the nature of the student and the course in question. Unlimited retesting may be workable in situations where there are no deadlines and students advance purely at the rate of speed they themselves determine. Where some deadlines must be imposed in order to ensure minimum rates of progress, a total of three or four tests, if they are brief, has proved manageable.

What may be most exciting about retesting is its affective dimension. Being given several chances to pass a test shows students that the teacher wants to help them succeed and raises their morale. Furthermore, when students are required to perform at high levels of accuracy, and when they actually achieve standards that previously they may have considered impossible, their whole self-image as language learners changes. They come to think of themselves as more competent and more capable of assimilating new information. They realize that their success results from their own efforts, not from some teacher's whim or from blind guessing on a test. Students feel good when they know a subject matter, and they feel especially good when they know they know. This added confidence that may result from retesting can considerably enhance student performance in a foreign-language course.

13.3 ADMINISTERING WRITTEN TESTS

Written tests have long been used to evaluate student achievement in grammar, vocabulary, spelling, reading, and, in some instances, oral comprehension. Though a well-managed individualized classroom presupposes the trustworthiness of students, it would be naive not to establish procedures to guarantee the integrity of the tests. The classroom teacher has the obligation to reduce the temptation to cheat as well as to minimize the opportunities students may have to do so. These considerations take on added importance when students are permitted to take tests when they are ready, or if testing goes on at the same time as other classroom activities. Copying answers from a book or from a classmate, or giving information to students who have not yet passed the test, can be minimized if appropriate measures are taken beforehand, and if the testing situation is properly structured.

13.3.1 *Discouraging Cheating*

It may be more realistic to speak of "discouraging" cheating rather than "eliminating" it entirely. Conceivably, there may be at least a small amount of cheating under any system of classroom organization, full-class or individualized; teachers can never know with absolute certainty the extent of cheating in their classes. What they *can* do, though, is take action to make cheating unnecessary as well as difficult to accomplish. A reasonable goal might be to ensure that incidents of cheating are sufficiently rare so that report card grades are not affected.

Since cheating often results from anxiety about chances for success, teachers should take measures to reduce the pressure students feel. Performance objectives that specify what must be done in order to pass, lists of the verbs or vocabulary words that may appear on the test, and homework exercises resembling the test format may all serve to accomplish this purpose. Opportunities for retesting can also decrease student fears of failing. If appropriate, teachers may offer a general explanation *during the test* to students who request one. Or, they may explain unfamiliar vocabulary words that are not focal points of the test. A motto might be, "Ask *me*, not your friends. *I'll* help you." The trust built up in this manner greatly enhances the quality of classroom relationships. Students come to understand that the teacher's primary purpose is to help them learn, not to give them low grades. Help, of course, must be kept within limits. If a student flatly asks to be told an answer on the test, the teacher should simply refuse, saying that the student is responsible for knowing it. Students, though, should at least not be afraid of asking the teacher about something they do not understand. This can be important if, as can easily occur, test items are ambiguous, illegible, or include information that has inadvertently not been taught or not taught thoroughly.

13.3.2 *Establishing a Testing Area*

Students taking written tests should be subject to some supervision, even if it consists of no more than the corner of the teacher's eye. Supervision is facilitated if a testing area in the classroom is established—preferably one that the teacher can see easily from her desk or from wherever she normally works. At the beginning of the year students may be instructed that written tests may be taken only within this specific area and nowhere else in the classroom. Once students enter the testing area they should remove their books or notes from the desk or table; no talking is permitted. After they have finished their test they should hand it to the teacher or an aide or place it in the appropriate folder or "in" box and then leave the testing area.

13.3.3 *Creating an Efficient Filing System*

Test security is maintained when there is a clearly established and well-organized system for processing and filing student papers. It is a good idea to keep all tests in a file cabinet that can be locked when not in use. File folders must be clearly labeled with the title of each test and its unit or packet number so that the teacher or teacher's aides can hand out the material rapidly. If one or more alternate forms of a test have been prepared, all forms can be used—if necessary—during one testing session. This procedure serves to discourage copying, which is more prevalent than memorizing test questions and passing them to friends.

Once papers have been completed, the teacher may grade them in class, if time permits, or they can be filed in the folder for that particular class and graded and recorded as soon afterwards as possible. Ideally, students should be informed no later than the next day about how they performed. The teacher should show students their papers—in the testing area—and offer additional help to those who did not pass. Once students have seen their tests, the papers can be marked with a check or circle to indicate this. Then they may be filed in another drawer containing alphabetized folders of each student's work. Individual file folders for students are important. Since testing-when-ready makes it inadvisable to allow students to keep their test papers (lest they pass them to friends who have not yet taken the test), the folders permit students, or parents, to examine previous work if they wish. This file is also useful for checking the teacher's grade record. In a system where different tests are submitted at different times, it is not unusual for errors to occur in recording grades, particularly when aides help with the recording. In case of doubt about whether or not a student has passed a certain test, the individual's folder provides a ready and indisputable answer. If the drawer with individual folders cannot be locked, it should be designated "off limits" to students.

13.4 ADMINISTERING ORAL TESTS

Oral testing can be a significant element in developing oral comprehension and speaking ability. In some cases, it can free teachers from some of the burden of correcting written work. An advantage of oral tests is that correction can be immediate; a disadvantage is that if not properly handled they can be overly time-consuming and ultimately unmanageable. Whether or not oral testing works well depends on a number of factors that teachers should consider while planning the course.

13.4.1 *Styles of Oral Testing*

The highest quality test situation involves individual examination of each student by the teacher or by using tapes. This is feasible when class sizes are small or when sufficient teaching personnel and tape recorders are available to accommodate all the students. If individual testing proves unworkable, a teacher with minimal equipment or no supplementary teaching help might try group testing. Here, the teacher examines from four to eight students during one session, posing one, two, or three questions to each based on the lesson taught. He passes those who have performed well and asks students who need more practice to attend a later test session. Another possibility for teachers who lack classroom help and adequate tape facilities is to conduct one teaching session in which the new lesson is presented. After the students have practiced, they present themselves in a group and are tested on the same material they have studied. A highly informal method of oral checking is for the teacher to walk around the class and listen to students as they practice with tapes or with friends. Though this technique falls short of actual testing, the teacher nevertheless can gain a general impression of individual oral proficiency, which may be used as the basis for prescribing further learning activities.

13.4.2 *Expediting Teacher-Administered Tests*

Even in situations where adequate help is available for oral testing, it is nevertheless important that the process move forward rapidly, so that sufficient time is provided for other teaching activities. One means of accomplishing this is to have students who want to be tested sign up at the blackboard. This prevents loss of time when the teacher needs to determine how many students want to be tested, and how much time should be allowed for this activity. It also reduces student frustration caused when the teacher, perhaps busy with another activity, is unaware that students are ready for tests. Signing up for tests may be especially important to shy or nonaggressive students, who may not receive the attention they need simply because they do not demand it as insistently as their classmates do. It also gives students an idea of when their turn will come up so that they can engage in productive activities in the meantime.

Another way of expediting oral tests is to make them as brief as possible, so that they consist of, perhaps, only one, two, or three items. In oral testing, the development of good pronunciation habits, fluency, and oral comprehension is more important than meticulously checking each new vocabulary word or grammatical form, tasks that can be accomplished more efficiently on written tests. Since considerable student hesitation in answering can lengthen testing time unreasonably, a rule establishing a time limit might be adopted: Though thinking out an answer is encouraged, the teacher cannot wait more than five or ten seconds for a response. If more time than that is needed, students should practice more and sign up again for the test. There might also be a limitation on the number of times a teacher will repeat a test question—perhaps no more than two or three times for beginning students or those not accustomed to being tested orally.

If the need to expedite testing is especially urgent, time can be saved by having two students at a time report for oral testing. Once the first student has finished, the second one is ready for his test, and another student joins him to wait his turn. This procedure eliminates the time lost waiting for students to walk from their seat to the test area.

13.4.3 *Types of Oral Tests*

The nature of oral test questions will vary, naturally, with the course level and ability of the students, as well as with the teacher's objectives. Some sample test types are presented here; further treatment of speaking skills may be found in Chapter Sixteen.

Oral tests can consist of pattern drills, sentences to pronounce, or questions on new grammar or vocabulary. Students might also be asked to summarize a textbook reading selection or a library book they have read. Or, they might speak freely in an interview situation, which can give the teacher an impression of over-all communication ability. Group skits or individual oral presentations to the class based, perhaps, on grammatical, literary, or cultural material also constitute a type of oral test.

If the test material closely resembles what students have practiced (taxonomic Stage 2), the testing will proceed fairly rapidly. If, however, the items consist of recombinations of familiar elements (taxonomic Stage 3), more time should be allowed for testing. Though this latter type of test takes longer, it provides the opportunity to develop student oral comprehension in a natural manner.

Tests that must be administered by paraprofessionals or by the teacher have the disadvantage of tying up classroom personnel for considerable periods of time. Taped tests, however, also pose problems. Recording and filing the tapes requires considerable out-of-class preparation; so does evaluating them, while correction and grading of teacher-administered oral tests is immediate. Also, questions on a teacher-administered test can be changed quite often, if necessary; recording alternate test forms, however, is more time-consuming. Ultimately, a fully individualized continuous progress program will require a large number of taped tests so that teaching personnel can be freed to give individual help and guidance. Until these tests are created, however, teacher-administered questions can constitute a workable method of oral evaluation.

13.5 ESTABLISHING A GRADING SYSTEM

A well-designed, carefully thought out grading system can contribute significantly to improved subject-matter achievement. It is important that students clearly understand the criteria that will be used to determine their marks. If grading appears capricious or seems to depend on the teacher's preferences for certain learners, students will attach less importance to performing well on written or oral evaluations. Though details of a grading system will vary in individual situations, certain broad approaches will be suggested here, which may be modified to suit local requirements.

13.5.1 *Continuous Progress Grading and Record Keeping*

A prime necessity of continuous progress instruction is being able to know at any given moment at what point in the course each student is working. Conventional gradebooks become unwieldy when wide differences in progress rates exist within one class, or when students are working on different courses. This problem may be remedied by keeping an alphabetized looseleaf notebook containing a page for each student enrolled. The page lists the student's name, the course title (if the class is nongraded), the particular unit number, and the assignments it contains. As each assignment is completed, the teacher checks it off or initials it. Once a unit is finished, the page is placed alphabetically in an evaluation notebook and a new unit page is inserted in the daily work notebook. When report card grades or progress reports must be sent home, the teacher need only consult the notebooks to determine the quality of a student's work and evaluate his rate of progress.

A widely accepted practice in individualized programs is to assign only A or B grades. Students demonstrate "mastery" (usually 80 percent accuracy or better) of completed assignments in order to earn a B. Those desiring an A elect additional assignments and sometimes must demonstrate higher levels of mastery on required work. Eliminating "bad" grades—those below B—exerts positive motivational influence by holding out to students the chance for success. Students realize that the teacher is there to help them achieve the "good" grades, which are the only ones he offers.

Many programs that allow students to proceed at their own pace nevertheless establish a basic and perhaps very minimal number of units that a student must complete in order to remain in the course. When a student falls below this rate of progress, the teacher may confer with him and perhaps also with parents and guidance counselors. If it is determined that the course is too difficult, the student may withdraw from it, or perhaps, if practical, elect a different language course more suitable to his interests and abilities.[1, 2]

13.5.2   *Grading within Deadlines*

In schools where the administration will not authorize continuous progress instruction, or where all members of one department do not agree to adopt this teaching style, individualization will have to proceed within unit or assignment deadlines. In these cases, other procedures must be worked out.

Though a minimum amount of material must be covered by all students, the grading system can be humanized. For example, the course content may be cut to a minimum so that students have time to learn well what is presented to them. Some dialogs or reading selections in the text may not be worth spending time on. Certain less essential grammar topics that have proven extremely difficult and complex in past years may be taught only for recognition rather than for active production. Some advanced grammar topics, such as present participles, past infinitives, and causative constructions, in French, for example, can be taught as vocabulary items rather than being accorded the amount of attention normally devoted to teaching major areas, such as new verb tenses.

Even though reasonable and perhaps even generous deadlines have been established, there may be some students who are still unable to complete their work on time. In this instance, a system of two deadlines may be established: in-class and out-of-class deadlines. Students who have not passed their tests by the expiration of the in-class deadline have the option of making up the work during the following week or two outside of class—during a free period or after school. During this time, however, new material will, of necessity, be presented in class.

As with the continuous progress system, all students who demonstrate mastery of the required work receive grades of B. Those who, in addition, elect additional assignments may earn A's. One of these extra-credit options may consist of speaking the foreign language to the teacher or to friends during the class. The teacher gauges the students' oral ability and awards appropriate extra credit. If some students do not complete all the requirements by the report card deadlines, the teacher may have to assign grades lower than B. Another alternative might be to report an "incomplete" grade, though this practice may not be permitted in some conservative schools.

13.5.3   *Grade Contracts*

A grade contract is an agreement between a teacher and a student that states that completion of a specified number of assignments within a certain length of time will result in the student's earning a predetermined grade. Contracts enjoyed considerable popularity in the 1920s and are experiencing renewed interest in the 1970s.³ Though problems of implementation may limit their applicability, they can be effective in selected learning situations.

A major advantage of the process of drawing up a contract is that it promotes meaningful teacher-student communication about the objectives and requirements of a course. Active student involvement in the creation of the learning contract results in personalization of instruction as well as greater student commitment to learning. Grade contracts can thus serve as a means for gearing course content to the needs and interests of those enrolled.

These ideals, however, cannot be achieved in all classrooms. First of all, there is a basic flaw in the contract concept. Teachers and students are not peers engaging freely in professional or industrial types of contract negotiation. The constraints of curriculum and school policies, as well as differences of age and status, severely limit the areas for negotiation between students and teachers. This may be particularly true in beginning and intermediate courses that consist of a well-defined sequence of material, all of which must be learned. In situations where alternatives do exist in the early levels of language learning, there may not be sufficient time for the teacher to meet individually or in small groups with students to negotiate contracts and, if necessary, renegotiate them. Therefore, in the initial phases of instruction, contracting may be limited to students' selecting extra-credit assignments either from a teacher-prepared list or suggesting original activities or projects that interest them. In beginning courses, student-elected assignments may constitute 10 to 20 percent of the grade, with required work totalling 80 to 90 percent. In intermediate classes student electives may constitute much higher percentages of the course work.⁴

Grade contracts may be best suited to advanced courses. Once students possess a basic command of the language and its structures, both they and their teacher can exercise considerable latitude in determining the nature of the course. This is particularly true when class sizes are small and numerous opportunities are provided for teacher-student conferences. Success has been reported with grade contracts in an advanced French class.⁵

13.5.4 *Student Self-Grading*

Self-grading according to predetermined criteria can increase students' feelings of responsibility for their own success. In advanced literature or civilization courses students can evaluate the papers or tests they write according to criteria the teacher has proposed (or that teacher and students have agreed upon beforehand). Or, students may submit to the teacher the report card grade they believe they deserve based upon the work they have submitted, their participation in class, and any subjective factors they feel may be relevant. In case of discrepancies between student and teacher evaluations, a conference can be held to resolve them. Though self-grading has not been widely practiced nor commonly discussed in the professional literature, teachers who have instituted some system of self-evaluation in their classes have found that by and large the great majority of students agree with their teacher's evaluation of the quality of their work; a sizable number, however, grade themselves too low, while only a very small percentage ask for grades higher than the teacher feels they deserve. In these last two instances, either the teacher's evaluation is ultimately accepted after the conference or a compromise grade is agreed upon. The experience of many teachers with self-grading has been that it promotes greater communication and increased respect between the students and themselves.

Self-grading, though, need not be limited to mature, advanced students. Even in beginning non–continuous-progress courses, a highly structured system of self-grading can increase students' feelings of control over the evaluation of their work. This in turn can motivate them to higher quality performance. One such system might work as follows: At the beginning of the grading period, students receive a list of the tests they will be required to pass in order to earn a grade of B, along with extra-credit activities that they may elect to raise their grades. Each test and assignment is worth a specified number of points, and as each is completed students record their total on a form provided for that purpose. At any time in the course, the students know how many points they need for the grade they desire and the total they have earned so far. Before the teacher assigns report card grades, students submit their own grading forms on which they have written the grade they deserve. This system is convenient if parents or guidance counselors ask how a particular student is doing. It also serves as a check of the teacher's accuracy and can help teachers avoid errors in reporting. Students who are encouraged to grade themselves show greater responsibility in asking for extra help and in making up their work. A sample of a self-grading form for students is presented in Appendix E.

NOTES

[1] A useful discussion of this topic may be found in Gerald E. Logan, *Individualized Foreign Language Learning: An Organic Approach* (Rowley, Mass.: Newbury House Publishers, 1973), pp. 87–93.

[2] Another system of grading is described in Will Robert Teetor, "Grading and Awarding Credit on a 'Humane' and Sensible Basis: The Ithaca Experience," in Ronald L. Gougher, ed., *Individualization of Instruction in Foreign Languages: A Practical Guide* (Chicago: Rand-McNally Publishers, 1972), pp. 149–65.

[3] A detailed account of the rise, fall, and rise of grade contracts is presented in John F. Bockman and Valerie M. Bockman, "Contracts versus the Commitment Process," *Foreign Language Annals,* vol. 6, no. 3 (March 1973), pp. 359–66.

[4] Further discussion of this topic may be found in John F. Bockman, "The Process of Contracting," in Howard B. Altman and Robert L. Politzer, eds., *Individualizing Foreign Language Instruction: The Proceedings of the Stanford Conference* (Rowley, Mass.: Newbury House Publishers, 1971), pp. 119–24.

[5] Joan H. Bornscheuer, "The Grade Contract and the Language Class," *Foreign Language Annals*, vol. 6, no. 3 (March 1973), pp. 367–70.

CHAPTER FOURTEEN
PROGRAM EVALUATION

14.1 GENERAL CONSIDERATIONS

Evaluation of an individualized program is a key to its further development and improvement. Teachers need to know which aspects of the teaching situation are satisfactory and which may call for revision. The extent to which a program is individualized is another factor that should be evaluated. Primary sources of such evaluative data are the teachers involved and the students themselves, though supervisors and administrative personnel may also contribute important information. Data may be obtained through daily observations as well as by formal questionnaires.

14.2 FEEDBACK FROM STUDENTS

From the time an individualized program is initiated, a teacher should be aware of students' reactions to it. The most immediate way of obtaining data is simply by observing how students act in the classroom every day. More information may be gathered by devoting some class time for discussion and evaluation of the new teaching method. Formal written questionnaires are also effective in gauging student reactions to individualized instruction.

14.2.1 Observation of Students

Though managing several different ongoing activities is quite detailed and demanding, a teacher should nevertheless be constantly aware of what is happening in every part of the classroom. Even when working with one student or with a small group, an effective teacher must know in general what every member of the class is doing. Observations of students can offer teachers valuable information on how well individualization is working in their classrooms. Are all students engaged in language-related activities? Do they seem to know what is expected of them, or are they sitting aimlessly waiting for instructions? If some students are not using their time wisely, what are the causes? Have instructions been communicated clearly? Do students understand the various learning activity options available to them? Could some students benefit from closer supervision by the teacher? Is the class sufficiently structured so that students are in some way held accountable for their oral and written work?

Rate of learning is another factor that should be monitored. Is each student progressing at a pace that may be considered satisfactory for him? If some students are slower than others, can they be helped by additional tutoring? Are the fastest students learning the material thoroughly, or might they benefit from slowing down somewhat? A teacher should be aware of which students might profit from peer teachers and should form pairs when appropriate. If a sizable number of students are progressing more slowly than they should, the teacher should consider what the reasons may be. Are the students really mastering the material and therefore needing more time than they did when they were treating it superficially? Are students spending a sufficient amount of time doing homework? Would more frequent dealines provide some students with the structure they may need?

In the fairly relaxed atmosphere of an individualized classroom, students display a wide range of reactions and emotions; observation of these can be quite helpful to teachers trying to determine the effectiveness of instruction. Do most of the students look interested and involved in the learning activities? Do any students look frustrated or angry because they cannot receive the explanation or oral test they need at the time they want it? Are any students neglected because they are too timid to seek the help they require? Are some overly aggressive students monopolizing the time of the teacher and the teacher's aides? Do students generally cooperate and help each other, or do they compete for attention and for the use of classroom equipment? Could students who are isolated be integrated to a greater extent with their classmates?

14.2.2 *Discussion with Students*

The problems or areas of concern a teacher may have identified through daily observations can serve as the basis for discussion with students. An important advantage of individualized instruction is that it greatly facilitates this type of informal communication. It is easy for a teacher to sit down next to a student or a group of students and to say that she sees they are not working or that they look confused and to ask how she might help. Or a teacher can ask class members individually if they understand what is required of them, if they feel they have enough attention, or if they are encountering any problems that need to be solved.

At times a teacher may wish to discuss with the entire class a problem that affects all its members. For instance, supplies and materials may not be put away correctly, or equipment may be misused or abused. The teacher can present the problem to the class and ask for possible solutions. The full class may participate in an oral evaluation of the individualized program, but certain controls should be instituted to ensure that the discussion is a positive experience for both teacher and students. One drawback to this form of evaluation is that it can become dominated by a vocal minority of dissatisfied students, with the students who are content with the new system remaining silent. To prevent this, the teacher may ask that each member of the class, in turn, express his or her feelings in positive, concrete terms. The students should avoid negative statements and broad generalities that are not backed up with specific examples. Students must speak only for themselves, not for others in the class. The teacher should accept the reactions respectfully and without defensive rejoinders. She should thank the students for their comments and say that they will be taken into consideration in her planning. At the next class session, after the teacher has had a chance to reflect on what students have said, she may announce which suggestions have been accepted and may explain why other requested changes cannot be made.

14.3 QUESTIONNAIRES FOR STUDENT EVALUATIONS

When time does not permit evaluative discussions, or when teacher-student relationships are not sufficiently open and trusting, an alternative procedure can be the use of questionnaires to solicit students' reactions to the individualized program. A questionnaire may be administered after only a week or two, or after a month, of classes. Items may concern any area where a teacher feels he needs more information in order to make the program more successful. Some areas might be: suitability of learning pace; whether sufficient help is available at all times; degree of student interest in learning a foreign language; attitudes of students toward the individualized method of instruction, and reasons for the attitudes expressed; clarity of instructions and explanations; reactions to the grading system; student responses to the text and to audio-visual equipment used; particular needs or interests that the student may want the foreign language class to meet; and general suggestions for improving classroom instruction and increasing learning.

Short-answer items are preferable to a general essay question. They are effective for focusing student attention on the areas of inquiry and require less effort to answer. Short-answer items are also easier to score, if statistical evaluations of the program are desired. A teacher might, however, supplement short-answer questions by a request that the students add any further comments they wish on topics not included in the questionnaire.

Several types of items are suitable for questionnaires dealing with program evaluation. Students may indicate their reactions to various aspects of the course by rating their attitudes as very negative, negative, neutral, positive, and very positive. Given a list of various learning activities, they may rank them in order of their preferences. Students may be asked to list the three things they like most about the course and the three things they like least. Unfinished statements about the course ("I think foreign language class is ...") can be completed by students in a few words. Direct questions ("What do you hope to learn this year?") are also useful.

In most cases students should respond anonymously so that they may answer truthfully and not be concerned with how their answers may affect their grades or their teacher's opinion of them. Students should complete the questionnaires independently, without comparing their responses with what their friends have written. Ideally, the teacher should encourage students to be frank but nevertheless tactful and considerate. After having read the questionnaires and perhaps tabulating them, the teacher may report some or all of the results to the class, also telling them what action he intends to take. A sample questionnaire is included in Appendix E.

A word of caution and one of encouragement: It is extremely difficult—especially in a newly initiated program—to obtain overwhelmingly positive answers to questionnaires. It is very hard—if not impossible—to satisfy all the students all the time. Maslow's statement to this effect, made in regard to the industrial situation seems equally apropos in the classroom:*

> Human beings will always complain. There is no Garden of Eden, there is no paradise, there is no heaven except for a passing moment or two. Whatever satisfactions are given to human beings, it is inconceivable that they should be perfectly content with these.... We should, according to motivation theory, never expect a cessation of complaints; we should expect only that these complaints will get to be higher and higher complaints.... This is in accordance in principle with what I have written about human motivation being never-ending and simply proceeding to higher and higher levels all the time as conditions improve.

* Abraham H. Maslow, *The Farther Reaches of Human Nature* (New York: Viking Press, 1971), p. 242.

In view of what Maslow says about human nature, perhaps it is realistic for teachers to content themselves with noticeable improvements in their classrooms as a result of individualization rather than to expect a utopian situation that can never materialize. It may also be fruitful to analyze the nature of students' complaints. If students consider the teacher's disciplinary procedures unfair or inconsistent, they are unconsciously demonstrating their need for safety. If they are dissatisfied with low grades, their self-esteem needs are threatened. If they want more individual help and attention, they may be seeking to satisfy their love and belongingness needs. If they consider the study of foreign language boring and irrelevant, they may be expressing a desire to fulfill their needs for self-actualization. While ideally teachers would want no dissatisfaction among their students, they may nevertheless find some consolation if the majority of their students' complaints relate to the higher levels of the basic needs hierarchy (love and belongingness and self-actualization) rather than to the lower ones.

14.4 EVALUATION OF THE INDIVIDUALIZED CURRICULUM

It is important to keep in mind that individualization is not an end in itself. It is but a means to the end of enabling students to enjoy communicating in a foreign language. Therefore, in evaluating the extent to which a program is individualized, a high degree of individualization does not in itself mean that the program is successful. Effectiveness must be determined by measures of student achievement and student course evaluations. Similarly, a program with a moderate degree of flexibility is not necessarily inferior in quality to one with an extensive range of learning options. The basic question to ask is not, "How can we individualize further?" Rather, it should be, *"In our school* will a larger number of learning choices promote student achievement and lead to greater appreciation of foreign-language study?"

14.4.1 *Determining Type and Extent of Learning Choices Offered*

As has been stated in Chapters One and Six, there are four dimensions of classroom instruction that may be individualized by providing for various choices. They are objectives of learning, rate of learning, method of learning, and content of learning. Since the various types of individualization are most appropriate at different levels of instruction, it is useful for a teacher or administrator to determine the suitability of the types of individualization being carried out. The following evaluation form, when adapted to local needs, may be helpful in this respect. Each statement is intended to be rated on a scale from one to five according to the amount of choice available to students: 1—no choice; 2—little choice; 3—some choice; 4—considerable choice; and 5—extensive choice.

    1. *Individualization of objectives:* Students choose learning objectives from among several possibilities.

2. *Individualization of rate:* Students determine their rate of learning within broad deadlines (weekly, monthly, unit, quarterly).
3. *Individualization of method:* Students choose how they will learn from among several possibilities: teacher, aides, peers, text, audio and video materials.
4. *Individualization of content:* Students choose what the content of the course will be.

In a traditional teacher-centered course all four of these areas would be evaluated 1 (no choice). An independent studies course might rate 5 (extensive choice) in objectives, rate, and mode. The course content may or may not be individualized depending on the level. A fully developed continuous-progress and multimedia course would earn 5's in rate and mode. Lower-level courses, though, may display less flexibility in objectives and content than upper-level courses. A newly initiated program operating within a conservative school may score 2 or 3 (little or some choice) on objectives, rate, mode, and content. Mini-courses would rate 5's for extensive choice of course content but might evidence little or no choice in the other areas, particularly if they are at an advanced level. Again, it should be stressed that a program need not earn 5's on all dimensions of individualization to be effective. Rather, it is more important that the areas most relevant to particular levels of instruction (as explained in Chapter Six) be structured in order to permit learning choices.

14.4.2 *Determining the Quality of Classroom Management*

A different type of evaluation has to do with the quality of management in an individualized classroom. A well-run class displays a satisfactory balance between the need for student freedom and choice and the need for a structure that assures a steady rate of learning. Some areas for evaluation of beginning or intermediate courses are suggested below. Each item may be rated by the teacher or his supervisor along a five-point scale as follows: 1—rarely; 2—occasionally; 3—often; 4—usually; 5—always.

1. Written performance objectives clearly communicate to students what is expected of them.
2. Students' work is checked frequently, both orally and in writing.
3. Students must display mastery of subject matter in order to pass.
4. Test results are discussed with individual students as necessary.
5. Recommendations of learning activities are made according to the results of oral and written evaluations.
6. Within broad deadlines, students may test when they are ready.
7. Students may retest without penalty.
8. Folders containing the students' work are kept for reference during conferences with students or parents.
9. Students take responsibility for keeping track of their grades and rate of progress in the course.

10. Students are free to go to the library or learning center during the class period.
11. Students form groups based on common learning needs.
12. Peer teaching takes place in the classroom.
13. Different teaching strategies are used according to individual student needs.
14. Students use a variety of audio and visual aids and equipment.
15. All learning materials are kept in a neat, orderly manner so that students may obtain them easily.
16. A variety of reading materials is available to students either in the classroom or in the library or learning center.
17. Students receive the help or test they need without unreasonable delay.
18. All students engage in activities that relate directly or indirectly to foreign-language learning.
19. The amount of foreign language used by teacher and students is commensurate with the level of instruction.

The preceding list is intended to be suggestive rather than definitive. Many items can be replaced and others added in accordance with the conditions in various teaching situations. Ratings of 4 and 5 may be typical of well-developed programs that have been in operation for several years and enjoy considerable administrative support. Ratings of 3, though, may be considered very satisfactory for newly initiated programs or those that must function within the structure of a traditionally organized school.

PART THREE
TEACHING CONSIDERATIONS

CHAPTER FIFTEEN
TECHNIQUES OF INDIVDUIALIZATION I: PRONUNCIATION, SPELLING, VOCABULARY, GRAMMAR

15.1 GENERAL CONSIDERATION FOR PART THREE

The three final chapters that follow present some ways of adapting traditional teaching techniques for use in an individualized classroom as well as methods uniquely suited to facilitate this type of instruction. Readers desiring a more comprehensive and general treatment of foreign-language teaching methods are encouraged to consult the sources listed at the end of this chapter.[1,2,3]

15.2 PRONUNCIATION

Learning to pronounce the foreign language correctly belongs, primarily, in the curriculum of the first level of instruction. Since beginning students demonstrate highly divergent aptitudes for mimicry, these differences must be accounted for in an individualized program. While some students pick up the foreign pronunciation effortlessly, others require a considerable degree of structure and guidance from their teacher. These diverse needs must be met by the teaching methods employed in the classroom.

15.2.1 *Full-Class Teacher Presentation and Oral Testing*

For part of the class period the teacher models the new material and elicits choral and individual responses. During the second part of the class, students form pairs to practice the material presented, while the teacher (and aides, if any) circulates to listen and offer individual help. When students feel ready to pass an oral check of the material, they raise their hands or sign up on the blackboard. Students who fail to pass the first check need additional practice time before retesting (with no penalty). Students who pass early may offer help to their classmates or may be freed to work on extra-credit assignments, such as writing dialogs, reading supplementary books, or learning more about the foreign culture.

15.2.2 *Tapes and Cassettes*

After the teacher has modeled the new material, students go to tape recorders, cassette players, or language masters for additional practice. Up to six or eight students can be accommodated at one tape or cassette player if a jackbox is plugged into the program source and individual earphones are plugged into the jackbox. Cassettes are preferable to reel-to-reel tapes because they are relatively indestructible, and they facilitate considerably finding the right starting place. An orderly, accessible storage cabinet where tapes or cassettes are clearly identified can promote student responsibility in using the material and can free the teacher for offering individual help and guidance in other areas.

Another means of liberating the teacher for more creative classroom activities is the use of tapes—or, preferably, cassettes—for oral testing. When he is ready, the student identifies himself, records his answers according to directions, and hands in the taped test for future evaluation. Teachers interested in using this technique should carefully weigh its consequences. Grading oral tests outside of class is quite time-consuming, and teachers need to be sure they have sufficient time for evaluation. A drawback to testing on tape is that correction and feedback cannot be as immediate as when oral tests are taken "live" with the teacher. Even if not regularly used for oral testing, playback tape equipment is nevertheless helpful in that it lets students listen to themselves and evaluate their efforts. If possible, this evaluation should be done with a teacher present, since many students are incapable of hearing and correcting their own mistakes. Another advantage of playback tape machines and recorders is that many students who are not particularly interested in language learning are extremely enthusiastic about using electronic equipment. By providing for this individual learning preference, teachers can promote better student performance in the course.

15.2.3 *Programed Materials*

Pronunciation is a natural area for programing. It is a well-defined body of information with discernible right and wrong responses. Programed pronunciation materials exist in several languages; their use is especially suited to highly motivated and mature students. Because of the considerable degree of independence and maturity needed, their use can be particularly effective for high-school students pursuing a second foreign language or with college-level students.[4]

15.3 SPELLING

Spelling comes quite easily to some foreign-language learners and quite painfully to others. Teachers need to develop techniques that take into account these wide ranges of natural ability—even in so-called homogeneously grouped classes.

15.3.1 *Dictation and Individual Help*

The teacher or her aide reads the new spelling material to the class. This may consist of dialog sentences taken from the text or, preferably, variations on them. Two or more good students write the material on the board for all to see, while the teacher and her aide(s) circulate among the students to help them correct their work and offer individual explanations when needed.

15.3.2 *Remedial Help*

Students who have failed a spelling test are invited to join an extra-help group, which will prepare them to pass the retest. Students who have passed the test may proceed to other activities such as moving to the next activity in the unit, looking through foreign-language periodicals for new vocabulary words, making a culture scrapbook, or writing dialog variations. In forming remedial groups to drill on sound-letter correspondences, it is extremely important for teachers to stress the positive aspect of it ("I want to help you pass") rather than its negative side ("You're dumb because you didn't get it the first time"). Students are sensitive to grouping and it is likely that some members of the remedial group will consider themselves too unintelligent to spell accurately. Since negative self-images will promote failure, a sensitive teacher will let students know they are not disliked just because they need a little more time and help.

15.3.4 Choice of Tests

Two sorts of spelling tests might be offered: one that contains the exact material presented in the book and another that is a recombination of it. Since memorization is much easier than transfer, students who have difficulty spelling will be encouraged by the fact that they know exactly what material will be on the test, while students who find language learning easy can be offered the intellectual challenge—and the reward of a higher grade or extra credit—of being tested on a dialog or narrative variation.

15.3.5 Tapes and Cassettes

If students can look at written versions of the material they are practicing orally, this can help them in the formation of sound-letter correspondences. Spelling tests and dictation material may also be recorded so that students may take their tests when they are ready.

15.4 VOCABULARY

A student's knowledge of foreign language vocabulary words needs to be both active and passive. Students should use high frequency words in original sentences. They should also be able to understand the meaning of less commonly used words. This dual approach is reflected in the techniques suggested below.

15.4.1 Oral Vocabulary Sentences

Students receive lists of the new vocabulary words for which they will be actively responsible. Definitions of the words are supplied either in English or in the foreign language, or their meanings are made clear through pictures. Students pair off to practice memorizing the new words and forming original oral sentences of at least five words in which the new words are used correctly. The teacher and aides circulate among the pairs to offer help when needed. When ready, each student signs up on the board for an oral test in which he must supply an original foreign-language sentence for each word presented to him by the teacher or an aide either in English or in the foreign language. At the first level, from five to ten new words per day is a reasonable number to learn. This may be increased to ten to twenty per day for second level students. An oral test on three words is usually a sufficient check. Sentences should be graded solely on comprehensibility—not on precise grammatical accuracy. This procedure can be instrumental in developing correct syntactical habits as well as oral fluency during the early levels of foreign-language learning. Students who cannot produce satisfactory sentences may retest. This same technique might be employed for written vocabulary sentences, but an oral approach reduces the teacher's load of paperwork. On the other hand, lack of aides in the classroom might make oral testing impractical. In such instances, a testing chain could be established. The teacher tests the first five students who, in turn, test their classmates while the teacher supervises. Though students who have had to prove themselves to their teacher are not likely to allow friends to slide through—particularly when retest opportunities are available—this testing style may be less desirable in some cases than having someone who is not a class member administer the tests.

15.4.2 Vocabulary-based Compositions

This activity may be required, or it may be an optional assignment for students who finish their basic work ahead of the others. Students choose five to ten words from their vocabulary list and weave them into a dialog or a narrative of forty to seventy-five words, or from five to ten sentences. Once corrected, these may be presented orally to the class, or they may be posted on the bulletin board for others to read. Short assignments offer the advantages of appealing to students and of decreasing the time a teacher spends correcting papers.

15.4.3 Vocabulary Building Assignment

Students who learn more rapidly can use their extra time to look through foreign-language magazines and newspapers available in the classroom. They can cut out new words they are curious to learn from headlines and advertisements they see, along with pictures illustrating them. The cutout materials could be assembled into a scrapbook submitted for extra credit. The cultural dimension is an important aspect of this first-level assignment.

15.4.4 Supplementary Reading Vocabulary Lists

As part of their outside reading assignments, students keep vocabulary lists of new words they encounter and would like to learn. A minimum of one to five words per page may be required. Students present their lists to the teacher or aide, who pronounces the foreign-language word and asks for an English meaning. This is essentially a test of passive vocabulary recognition, a skill needed for reading. Brighter students can elect an active test (for additional credit) in which they must supply the foreign-language equivalents for English words read to them. In view of the diversity of material students may read and the differences in new vocabulary words they may choose to learn, administering this test orally is far less complicated than administering it in writing.

If an entire class is assigned the same outside reading book, vocabulary lists can be provided to facilitate their reading. If the list is quite lengthy, the important words to be included on the oral test can be starred. An advantage of oral tests over written ones is that each test is new; information about which words are on the test cannot leak out, as might be the case if the tests were written. Here too, a form of chain testing can be practical in classes without aides. Students sign up on the board to take the test. The first one tests the second, the second in turn tests the third, and so on. Testing can occur in the vicinity of the teacher so that it can be supervised to an extent. This activity is suited to the second and third levels, when vocabulary building, as well as the teaching of new grammar, becomes a major focus of instruction.

15.4.5 *Overhead Projector*

Groups of three to six students gather around a projected transparency containing pictures of the new vocabulary words or series of actions. Each student in turn makes up a question based on one of the pictures which other members of the group must answer. Or students may work on a story to explain the activities they see. A more structured use of the overhead projector can involve giving students written questions based on each visual as well as a key with semicomplete answers. If possible, each group should be supervised by a teacher or an aide. This activity is especially appropriate for teaching concrete vocabulary words occurring in level one and early in level two.[5]

15.5 GRAMMAR

Individualizing the teaching of grammar entails varying not only the rate but also the method of presentation. At the higher levels, some variation in content can also occur.

15.5.1 *Oral Explanation by the Teacher*

Many students want grammar explained to them personally by their teacher. This is the way they have been accustomed to learning; they have been successful at it, and they do not want to change. An advantage of oral in-person explanation is that the teacher can see immediately whether students understand, or whether they need additional explanations. A disadvantage is that it can be time-consuming and can severely limit the teacher's availability for individual conferences. It is practical, though, in flexibly paced classes when most students are working on the same lesson with variations of perhaps only a few days between the fastest and slowest learners. Oral explanation is recommended during the first level and also for the first phase of transition to individualization when students are not yet accustomed to learning on their own.

The amount of grammar presented at one time should be limited so that the explanation does not last more than ten or fifteen minutes—the maximum attention span of most beginning students for this activity. Students who feel they have understood move on to the next learning step. Those who would like to hear the explanation again are invited to remain with the teacher. Attention is usually good even though material is being repeated because students have *elected* to attend the group, and they realize that their teacher cares about meeting their individual needs.

15.5.2   *Oral Explanation by Aides*

In cases where students have been absent on the day of the grammar presentation or did not thoroughly understand it the first time, a teaching aide might be assigned to further explain it. So that learning does not suffer from the teacher's absence, the aide should be briefed in advance as to how the explanation should be carried out. This could occur during the teacher's preparation period, during the few minutes between classes, or at the very start of the period as students needing the explanation form their group. Briefing is less of a problem if the aide is an adult or student teacher or a student who has heard the presentation the day before. Many, though not all, students are quite adept at explaining grammar clearly, particularly on a one-to-one basis. Teachers may discover which student aides to trust with grammar explanations by direct supervision or by asking students afterwards whether they understood the aide's explanation. Teachers who have taught student aides in prior years can also judge how much responsibility to allow them.

15.5.3   *Written Explanations*

Written explanations of grammar may be those in conventional textbooks; they may be teacher-prepared; or they may be programed. In general, written explanations can offer the possibility of liberating the teacher for more personal contact with individual students. They are also instrumental when implementing a system of continuous progress, in which students proceed through a course at their own rate. If students in a single classroom are working on three or four different units, the teacher cannot easily find the time to give oral grammar explanations when needed. Students will need to assume greater responsibility for learning new grammar on their own. This crucial area of student responsibility must be closely examined by teachers contemplating wide variations of learning rates within one classroom.

15.5.4   *Textbook Explanations*

Many textbook explanations seem to have been written for teachers, not for students. They tend to be highly abstract and unnecessarily complicated, presenting both general rules and numerous exceptions simultaneously. In reading the explanations in the basic textbook, the teacher should consider which students would be comfortable learning from it: only the brightest learners, most average and above average students, or all the students in the course. If the textbook seems unsuitable for all but a minority of gifted students and cannot be changed, teachers should consider assigning explanations from other grammar books available in the classroom; or they might want to write their own materials.

15.5.5 Teacher-prepared Explanations

Teacher-prepared materials offer the advantage of being tailor-made to suit a particular group of students whom the writer knows and understands very well. A limitation of this practice is that not all teachers are either qualified or inclined to write their own explanations. A second drawback is the enormous amount of time needed to write truly excellent materials—especially those incorporating visuals. Most teachers beginning to individualize instruction simply do not have sufficient time for such demanding preparation. Several workable alternatives present themselves in this situation. If the teachers planning to individualize operate as a team, the writing responsibility can either be divided among them or else performed by the person most able or most interested in creating the grammar explanations. If a teacher is working alone, she may have to forgo her goal of continuous progress during her first year of individualization and remain content with offering one basic learning rate coupled with numerous options for enrichment activities. Then during the second year she may further develop her initial efforts, perhaps through a local or regional workshop. Before attempting this major project, however, she should be reasonably sure that a significant number of her students will possess the intelligence, maturity, and inclination to learn grammar via written explanations.

15.5.6 Taped Explanations

Another method of presenting grammar is to record the explanation on tapes or cassettes. Students who have been absent or those who want to hear the teacher's explanation more than once can listen to the tapes as needed. If teachers do not have sufficient time after classes in order to prepare this material, they may set up recorders in their classroom and tape the grammar presentations made to students. (Special recorders that pick up only the major program source and screen out extraneous background noises are invaluable for this purpose.) Programs that are successful are filed so that they may be reused subsequently.

15.5.7 Programed Explanations

Widespread, large-scale use of programed instructional materials is a fairly recent development in foreign-language teaching. Many programs—particularly those relying on the use of computers—are still experimental, and additional data need to be assembled before conclusions can be drawn as to the suitability of this approach. Even assuming that teachers have at their disposal a program that has already been tested and proved effective, they must nevertheless consider whether this approach is appropriate to all students enrolled in their courses. Certainly, a good measure of student independence and maturity is needed if this teaching style is to be successful. Perhaps the programed materials should constitute only one of the options offered in the course, with other more conventional learning methods also available.

NOTES

[1] Edward D. Allen and Rebecca M. Valette, *Modern Language Classroom Techniques: A Handbook* (New York: Harcourt Brace Jovanovich, 1972).

[2] Kenneth Chastain, *The Development of Modern Language Skills: Theory to Practice* (Philadelphia: Center for Curriculum Development, 1971).

[3] Wilga M. Rivers, *Teaching Foreign Language Skills* (Chicago: University of Chicago Press, 1968).

[4] One programed course in French pronunciation is offered by Wible Language Institute, 24 South Eighth Street, Allentown, Pa. 18105.

[5] Excellent ideas for using an overhead projector that can be adapted for individualized classrooms are offered in Thomas P. Carter, "The Imaginative Use of Projected Visuals," *Foreign Language Annals*, vol. 7, no. 3 (March 1974), pp. 314–24.

CHAPTER SIXTEEN
TECHNIQUES OF INDIVIDUALIZATION II: LISTENING, SPEAKING, READING, WRITING

16.1 LISTENING COMPREHENSION

Ability to understand foreign-language utterances can be developed directly, through drills designed to improve listening comprehension, and indirectly, through conversations. Both these approaches are treated in this section.

16.1.1 *Aural Drills*

In a flexibly paced classroom, listening comprehension drills (found in the instructor's manuals of many textbooks and also in many tape programs) can be administered to the entire class during the first part of the period. Some teachers like to administer them early in the grammar unit; others find that students perform with greater success if they listen to the drills after they have mastered the grammar topic. Teachers should try both approaches to see which works best in their particular situations.

In a continuous progress classroom, aural comprehension drills, of necessity, must be available on tape or on cassettes. If the commercially prepared material is too rapid for most learners, the teacher is faced with the task of either rerecording it or having aides read the texts at a slower speed when needed. If students listen to taped comprehension drills on their own, there must be some kind of check on their work: the signature of an aide or language lab assistant, written answers on a worksheet, or listening tests based on the material practiced.

If no listening comprehension drills accompany the basic text being used, the teachers can adapt suitable materials from a different book or can write their own. Should these alternatives prove impractical during the first year of individualization, teachers might consider teaching listening comprehension informally, through conversation.

16.1.2 *Personal Interaction*

Every time the teacher uses the foreign language to give directions, make explanations, answer individual questions, or simply to talk informally, he indirectly develops listening comprehension skills in students. This development will occur even when the focus of the activity is quite different, such as classroom management, grammar explanation, or personal communication with students. An advantage of developing this skill through classroom communication, as well as through conventional pattern practice drills, is that students pay better attention when they need or want to hear a message that relates to them. Drills, of necessity, are abstract and normally irrelevant. On the other hand, foreign-language communication with a teacher, an aide, or with peers is inherently much more interesting, since it can be highly personalized. Specific methods for developing listening comprehension informally are included in the next section on speaking. It is recommended that both the direct and indirect approaches mentioned be employed when possible, because they are essentially complementary.

16.2 SPEAKING

Ability to speak the foreign language being studied is considered by many to be the most useful, and therefore the most important, skill. A major problem in an individualized classroom is making sure that learners use the foreign language among themselves when they are freed from the teacher's direct supervision.

16.2.1 *Pattern Practice in Pairs*

After learning to pronounce the foreign language, the next step in developing oral fluency is the performance of pattern practice drills. After initially presenting the new drills to the full class, the teacher instructs students to practice them in pairs: One partner cues, the other responds; then roles are reversed. During this time, the teacher may work with those students most in need of help. If the textbook does not supply answers, keys may be distributed for difficult drills. A follow-up activity to help maintain teacher control over pair drilling is to administer oral tests on the material. Each student supplies one response from each pattern practiced. The test may be given individually or in groups of three to five.

16.2.2 Tapes, Cassettes, or Language Masters

Students who possess the maturity and responsibility to work independently can develop oral fluency through practice drilling with tapes, cassettes, or language masters. Quality control can be maintained by requiring students to pass short oral tests on the material administered by an aide. Another control is to require that the oral test on the drills be signed in the learning packet before the student is permitted to continue to the next step.

16.2.3 Questions and Answers in Small Groups

If students are to express their own ideas orally in the foreign language, classroom activities must go beyond mere drillwork; students need to spend considerable time talking to each other. During the early stages of language study, student conversations will, of necessity, be fairly controlled. This structure can gradually give way to freer communication as speaking ability increases.

For decades teachers have traditionally used conversation questions in full-class situations in order to promote speaking activity. This material can be adapted for use in small groups of from four to eight by distributing the questions and answer keys to the students. An advantage of this approach is that group work provides greater student involvement and more individual practice. Several people can speak at once, rather than just one at a time as with full-class teaching. A limitation of this method, however, is that many student responses can go uncorrected. This can be alleviated to some extent by placing someone in charge of each group—either the teacher, an aide, or an exceptionally competent member of the class. If this does not entirely solve the problem, it is useful to note that even in the full-class situation many answers go uncorrected—because students are not afforded sufficient opportunities to respond in the first place. Certainly, student silence should not be equated with ability to speak accurately. Besides, group work offers the advantage of encouraging spontaneity by freeing students from the fear of making mistakes and being corrected in front of the whole class. If some errors do remain unnoticed, at least students gain in terms of self-confidence and oral fluency. Once the ability to communicate clearly has been developed, correction of errors can always follow.

Several types of material lend themselves well to use in small conversation groups. Among them are questions and answers based on grammar, vocabulary, dialogs, or reading selections with the new structure or new words underlined to call student attention to them. There may also be grammar-related incomplete statements, such as, "I am happiest when ... ," "I will be punished if I ... ," or "Today I feel ... because ... ." If group members answer each of the questions in turn, they are not only practicing how to speak the foreign language, they are also sharing their feelings with others. This serves to humanize the classroom and to make language learning more relevant to personal needs. Since dealing with emotions is a sensitive area, students should not be forced to respond to questions they do not care to answer.[1]

Most currently popular textbooks are long on drills and relatively short on free-response exercises. Teachers may therefore find it necessary to write their own supplementary conversation materials. In view of their effectiveness in developing oral fluency, such supplementary materials are well worth the time and effort spent on preparing them. In setting up a program of individualized instruction, teachers should assign a very high priority to the preparation of these materials, higher than that assigned to the preparation of drills. Some sample conversation materials, both cognitive and affective, are included in Appendix C.

If, after the initial presentation of conversation materials, students practice answering without using their sheets, they are developing listening comprehension and speaking ability at the same time. Oral comprehension is also developed if oral tests are based on the original practice materials but are not identical to them. When students know they must make an oral response to a question or statement, they tend to listen very closely. Over a period of time, this will greatly increase their listening comprehension skills.

16.2.4 *Directed Dialogs*

In preference to or in addition to lists of discrete conversation stimuli, some teachers have successfully used directed dialogs with small groups. Though this exercise limits the variety of student responses, controlled conversations offer the advantage of compelling students to use new structures and vocabulary words. Self-correction with a key or by student aides is relatively simple, since answers will usually be more or less predictable. The absence of self-expression in this controlled exercise is compensated for by the fact that student answers are in the context of a situation that may have greater inherent interest than disconnected statements or questions. Many textbooks contain directed dialogs, which a creative teacher can supplement as needed. The most methodical application of this technique so far is in German.[2]

16.2.5 *Role Playing*

Students who do not like exposing their personal interests and feelings often enjoy role playing. Here they use the foreign language to communicate but can protect their privacy by pretending they are someone else—a family member, a friend, a teacher, and so on. This activity is structured by dividing the class into groups of from four to eight and distributing sheets on which ideas for role play are written. Each group leader (the teacher, aide, or class member) reads the story line and asks students to choose roles. If students are hesitant, one strong student can be assigned a role and can in turn choose a friend to act with her. Alternatively, if students are very reluctant to talk, or if the group is very large, two or three people may be assigned to one role, with conferences allowed. Another possibility is to have the group leader play a role during the first few times the class performs this activity. Later on this becomes unnecessary.

Role playing is suitable, with modifications, for levels one through four. During the first level, the situations can be modifications of those encountered in textbook dialogs and narratives. This will minimize problems beginners experience with structure and vocabulary. At more advanced levels situations can be freer. The most interesting ones—and those which students most enjoy acting out—involve conflict and persuasion: family members argue over what television program to watch or which movie to see; a youngster tries to persuade his parents to allow him to use the family car or to take an overnight trip with friends; a student tries to talk her teacher into giving her a better grade; a girl tries to talk her way out of a date with someone she does not like. A simple way of obtaining good ideas is to explain to students the type of material needed and ask them to write at home several ideas for skits they would enjoy doing. The teacher can then prepare instruction sheets in the foreign language based on the best suggestions. Appendix C includes a list of ideas solicited in this manner that were used successfully toward the end of the year in level-two classes.

Role playing should be informal, relaxed, and just for fun, so that students are encouraged to participate wholeheartedly and spontaneously. It is best not to grade participants. Group leaders may prompt when necessary (perhaps by whispering) to keep the dialog going, or may supply a needed word, but corrections and interruptions should be kept to a minimum. The goal of this activity is comprehensible free communication, not strict grammatical accuracy, which can be developed in oral and written drills. Students may role play just for their own group, or they may choose to repeat an especially enjoyable skit for the whole class. In any event, the activity can be repeated several times during the school year and is especially useful for bringing together classes whose members are working at widely varying rates.

16.2.6 *Films and Video Tapes*

Students at the intermediate or advanced level often enjoy preparing tape or film programs to be viewed in other classrooms or at a language day assembly. Skits, dramatizations of stories, or programs of songs or folk dances can be video-taped as part of a class project or a mini-course assignment. Students may elect to film a topic of interest to them and create an original sound track in the foreign language. Opportunities to be creative stimulate student motivation at advanced levels.

16.2.7 *Informal Conversation*

Speaking the foreign language in controlled or semicontrolled situations is a necessary goal, but not a final one. Ultimately, learners should be able to use the foreign language to fulfill their own real needs. Moreover, they should *want* to do this. This affective dimension is crucial. Often learners possess the vocabulary and structure they need to express their thoughts, but still choose to use the native language. The teacher's task, then, is twofold: first, to teach students *how* to say what they need to; then to encourage them to *want* to use what they already know. The problem of promoting free self-expression not only between teacher and students but also between students themselves is especially acute in an individualized classroom. If students who are free to work on their own converse with each other in English, some of the benefits of a full-class lesson taught entirely in the foreign language are lost. Also, unless students use the foreign language for matters they consider important—who phoned them last night, how they will spend the weekend, what grade they got on their math test—language learning will be considered irrelevant by them and their motivation to learn it will dwindle. There are several things teachers might do to show students that they can and should use the foreign language for personal self-expression, as described in the following sections.

16.2.8 *Lists of Useful Expressions*

For much of the first year or semester, students will not yet be able to express themselves freely, and a large part of their class time will be spent in structured or semistructured oral activities. Still, learners must be impressed from the start with the idea that they can use the foreign language to satisfy certain really felt needs. The teacher hands out to students the foreign-language equivalents of the most commonly used classroom expressions: Did I pass my test? May I leave the room? I didn't do my homework; and so on. The list may also be posted on the bulletin board as a reminder. (A student can volunteer to letter it if the teacher is too busy.) The class rule is that every time a student needs to use an expression on the list, he must say it in the foreign language—or else he will not get what he wants. As the year progresses, the list can be expanded and modified according to classroom needs. If the list is given for the first time beyond the first level, students may be required to memorize it and take their first oral test of the year on it. As a variation, if at times language games are played in class (such as Scrabble, Bingo, Monopoly, and so on), students may be provided with the expressions they will need (such as, "It's my turn," and so on) to play the game in the foreign language. Suggestions for what may be included in these lists appear in Appendix D.

16.2.9 Free Conversation Time

As soon as students are able to express themselves even minimally, they should be allowed a certain amount of time in class during which they may say anything they want to anyone they want—as long as they say it in the foreign language. Five to ten minutes is a good amount of time for beginners. It can be extended as student speaking ability improves. After fifteen minutes, though, most students—other than the brightest ones—run out of things to say. After their first few experiences with free conversation, however, students are often surprised to see how much they are indeed able to say. Building this self-confidence is an essential first step toward liberated use of the foreign language.

During conversation practice, the teacher and aides should circulate to provide vocabulary help if requested but should avoid listening to student conversations that seem to be of a personal nature. The teacher's role is mainly supportive—he is there to help—rather than judgmental. Correcting grammar errors while students are struggling to express themselves tends to inhibit their further attempts at free communication. This activity is suitable for using up the last few odd minutes of the period, but it should not be used exclusively at the end of class or students may consider it merely a time-filler, rather than one of the major goals of the course. When used at the beginning of the period, free conversation is a suitable warm-up activity.

After students have begun to communicate successfully with each other, the teacher can build upon the activity by praising them and telling them—preferably in the foreign language—that they have considerable ability and should consider using their skills outside of class. Perhaps they can use the foreign language as a code with friends or brothers and sisters, so that others will not understand what they are saying. This idea of secrecy and exclusivity has considerable appeal for junior-high-school students and even for older ones. A good follow-up is to ask, from time to time, who has spoken the foreign language outside of class.

16.2.10 Evaluation of Free Speaking

Many students will not perform an activity unless it is graded. This is unfortunate but often true of learners who are not intrinsically motivated by a love of the foreign language and culture. Students who consider grades important will tend to perform if the criteria for evaluation are clearly stated on grading forms distributed to them. Though a teacher's estimate of speaking ability may be highly subjective, he can nevertheless communicate to students in writing what factors will be important to him in arriving at his conclusions: amount of daily free use of the foreign-language with the teacher, aides, and peers; quality of foreign-language communication; and individual effort. (An example of the grading criteria used by one Level-Two teacher will be found in Appendix E.) Each time students perform in one of the stated categories, they secure, at the end of the class, the signature of the teacher or an aide who has heard them using the foreign language. Students' charts are collected at the end of each marking period, and extra points can be awarded for speaking skill. Though signing the oral credit sheets is time consuming, this practice is well worth the five minutes needed at the end of class, since it can definitely exert a positive effect on developing liberated self-expression in the classroom.

16.2.11 *Friendly Persuasion*

For students who do not respond to direct tactics—admonitions to speak in the foreign language and formal evaluation of this effort—indirect techniques must be used. Rather than reacting to student use of English with an exasperated, "In German, please," responses that amuse or cajole students are preferable. A teacher can say:

"My, what a bizarre language you are talking," or "What? I can't understand a word you're saying," or "You are speaking French with an extreme *western* accent." An indirect approach more often than not results in students laughing and switching into the foreign language. Direct criticism, on the other hand, tends to make students feel defensive and resentful.

If students do not immediately cooperate by using the foreign language as much as they should, the teacher should not give up in despair. Speaking ability includes extremely important affective elements in addition to necessary cognitive skills. While a specific body of knowledge can be acquired in several days or weeks, attitudes often take months or years to form. A patient and determined teacher can be rewarded when classes suddenly "bloom" two-thirds or even three-quarters of the way through the school year. Persistence, encouragement, and praise can play major roles in successfully maximizing use of the foreign language. When students respond, they can be complimented on having created original sentences that are comprehensible, even if not completely correct. Praising instances of desired behavior while withholding attention from undesirable behavior can have a strong positive influence in promoting increased foreign-language use in the classroom, as well as oral comprehension.

16.2.12 *Oral Speeches*

After students have mastered a grammar topic (that is, they have completed drills and oral and written tests), they may prepare speeches of one to two minutes duration in which they use a specified number of examples of the new structure. Speeches can hold class interest if they are based on a magazine picture, an original drawing, or a photo from the student's family album. They can also be spaced over a week, with part of the class reciting each day. This activity can serve to bring the class together and relieve the monotony of working on learning packets day after day.

Since many students become nervous if they have to stand in front of the class, students can give their speeches from their places. This is facilitated if students sit in a circle. Though speakers may want to use notes, they should learn to do without them. Otherwise, the assignment is reduced to reading aloud rather than speaking. If students seem unusually unsure of themselves, particularly at the beginning of the year, when adjustments to a new class situation may be difficult, they may be permitted one key word—but no more—per sentence to help them remember. Pictures accompanying the speech also may serve as memory aids. If a nervous student suddenly goes blank, he may be allowed to consult his notes, then resume talking without looking at them. Tension can be greatly relieved if speeches are graded "pass" if they are comprehensible, even if there are errors, which might best be corrected in private conferences rather than in front of the class. Extra-credit points may be awarded for extreme accuracy. A relaxed, accepting class atmosphere and a tolerance for occasional pauses for thought are important in making this assignment work successfully. Comprehensibility, originality, and good humor need to be stressed more than grammatical accuracy and stage-perfect delivery.

The listening comprehension aspect of this activity can be further strengthened by having each speaker ask one or two questions about what he has said and call for volunteers to answer them.

16.3 READING

Reading lends itself naturally to individualization. Students begin foreign-language study possessing widely divergent reading levels; these differences soon become manifest to the sensitive and observant teacher. Beginning and intermediate courses normally require students to read basic texts as well as supplementary materials such as short stories, graded readers, and foreign-language newspapers and magazines. Methods for individualizing these types of reading material will be considered in this section.

16.3.1 *Basic Reading Tests and Retests*

Students develop reading skill as a result of being held responsible for understanding basic material as measured on tests of comprehension. Multiple choice reading tests may show that beginners have difficulty in understanding what they read because they ignore key words in the text, such as negatives, or because they skip over abstract words they do not understand: prepositions, conjunctions, and adverbs. Training students to read every word they see in the basic text involves several steps. First, the text is read aloud to the students who need the explanation, and difficult passages are clarified. Next, students orally answer specific questions on the material. They may look up details in their text (exact page and line numbers may be indicated on the question sheets) but may not look at their books while answering. If the passage introduces many unfamiliar words, students memorize the list of new vocabulary and pass a check on it. They are now ready for a written test.

Simple level-one reading texts may be tested through true/false questions. Lengthier, more complicated level-two passages can test comprehension through multiple choice items. Students who do not pass the test the first time discuss their papers individually or as a group with the teacher or an aide. They then retest up to two or more times until they pass.

A common method for teaching reading skill is to have students write the answers to questions on a reading text as homework. Though this technique may be useful in the development of spelling or writing, its value in improving reading skill is questionable. Some students perform this homework assignment by skimming through the text until they find the same words used in the question. The sentence is then diligently copied without necessarily having been read and understood. Oral answers, on the other hand, prove that the student has at least read the text in class, if not as homework —which has been rejected by many television-oriented learners.

16.3.2 *Oral Summaries and Dramatizations*

As reading texts become lengthier in intermediate courses, multiple choice comprehension tests become less practical. Since most students have by now developed ability to read closely, subsequent training needs to focus on developing their ability to read widely with comprehension. One method of accomplishing this is to have students summarize orally the short story they have read. Oral résumés are preferable to written ones, since summaries in writing tend to be mere carbon copies of key sentences. Students may present oral summaries to the teacher individually or as a group—with one person chosen by the teacher to begin and others asked at random to continue. A passing grade can be given to students who speak comprehensibly, with extra credit awarded to those who demonstrate grammatical accuracy and frequent use of new vocabulary words.

Instead of electing story summaries, more creative and more fluent students might choose to dramatize the story itself or amusing variations of it. Groups of three or four students work together during the period and present their dramatization to the entire class, in this way effectively combining reading, speaking, and listening. Since this assignment is somewhat more demanding than an oral summary, extra credit could automatically be awarded for satisfactory performance. Both résumés and summaries may be preceded by explanations of difficult passages if needed by some students, as well as by generalized question and answer practice and vocabulary checks of the word lists that are distributed.

16.3.3 *Out-of-Class Reading*

In addition to reading texts which are explained in class, beginning and intermediate students need the experience of figuring out meanings on their own. This out-of-class reading may be optional the first year or semester, but it should be required at higher levels. Materials suitable for this assignment include monthly magazines written for beginning language learners, graded readers, collections of short stories, and foreign-language newspapers and magazines. A wide selection of materials can be made available in the classroom where students might browse through them and select the most appealing ones for outside reading. Or books may be located in the foreign-language resource or materials center, which students visit during or after class.

If appropriate materials for level one are hard to find, they can be created by the learners themselves. Students who learn rapidly may, as an extra-credit project, write dialog variations and original stories using the new vocabulary and structure. After these are corrected, students might illustrate them with their own drawings or with cut-out pictures and assemble them into booklets. Few language experiences can be more exciting for beginners than picking up a foreign-language book and finding they can really understand it.

When students read a wide variety of material outside of class (either optional or required), they may keep their own vocabulary lists and pass oral checks as part of their assignment. If, however, one collection of readings is assigned to an entire class, the teacher might consider preparing vocabulary lists, if time permits. The advantage of prepared lists is twofold. Chronological page-by-page explanations of words as they are encountered promotes reading continuity and enjoyment. Most students do not like using end vocabularies because breaks in the story line are distracting and make reading slow and painful. In addition to saving students valuable reading time, teacher-prepared vocabulary lists can ensure that students learn valuable new words that they might otherwise ignore.

An additional check on comprehension of outside reading material can be a brief summary, either oral or written. Alternatively, if an entire class will eventually be required to read the same outside assignment, a teacher not wishing to read lengthy reports or summaries should consider preparing short tests—three or four questions—that ask for obvious information that anyone reading the book with comprehension would know. Several forms of the test need to be prepared so that students do not pass answers. No retests are offered. Book tests have proved effective in second- and third-level required outside reading assignments.

16.4 WRITING

For many students, writing is a difficult skill to acquire in their native language, let alone in a foreign one. In setting realistic, attainable writing goals, teachers need to bear in mind that written communication consists not only of strict grammatical accuracy but also of comprehensibility and originality. By recognizing and rewarding both these aspects, teachers can make writing bearable—and even pleasurable—for their students.

16.4.1 *Full-Class Compositions*

The transition from spelling to writing an original composition in a foreign language may be eased by having the first few compositions written by the full class. The teacher brings to class a picture clipped from a magazine and asks members to contribute individual sentences about it, either describing the physical setting of the picture or narrating the action in it. Sentences are clearly written on the blackboard or overhead projector and students copy them. Student errors are not corrected aloud—this can be discouraging in an initial effort—but the sentences are written correctly for students to copy.

16.4.2 *Small-Group Compositions*

In another activity during the initial stages of writing, students form groups of no more than three or four to work on a group composition. The subject may be any of the following: an overhead transparency (perhaps teacher-made from popular, preferably foreign-language, magazines), a magazine photo, a textbook illustration. Or students might be asked to incorporate a certain number of new grammar or vocabulary items into a narrative or dialog. As each group works, the teacher and aides circulate to offer help where needed. As a follow-up activity, each group can read what it has written to the rest of the class. (This adds a valuable listening dimension to the assignment.)

16.4.3 *Individual or Paired Compositions*

Once students feel comfortable writing compositions in groups, they should be ready to write individually. Students still wishing some support may choose a partner with the understanding that the assignment is doubled in length and the grade is shared. Individual or paired writing is appropriate at the end of the beginning course if students have had considerable practice, or toward the beginning or middle of an intermediate course. Topics that are imaginative and fun are instrumental in developing student enthusiasm for writing. Stimulating topics include: satirizing a story or inventing a new ending for it; rewriting a story from the point of view of a character or inanimate object; writing a new ending to a story, expanding it, or continuing it. Compositions need not be dialogs or narratives exclusively; students enjoy other forms such as letters, diaries, poems, and newspaper articles. Open-ended sentences can also stimulate creativity: "The animal I would most like to be is . . . "; "I believe . . . "; "I feel happy when . . . ."

16.4.4 *Pass/Fail Grading and Composition Conferences*

Students will hesitate to write freely and creatively if they are penalized for grammar and spelling errors. Also, if they receive low grades, they will not enjoy writing. On the other hand, teachers do need to establish minimal standards of accuracy and comprehensibility for compositions. One way of resolving this dilemma is to pass all compositions that fulfill the basic requirements of the assignment and are comprehensible. For example, a minimum number of examples of new vocabulary or grammar must be written with no more than one or two errors in them allowed in order to pass. Still, *all* writing mistakes are marked (but not corrected) using an abbreviation system for agreement, word order, and so on, that has been explained to the class. (A sample of such abbreviations is in Appendix D.) Students do not receive credit for passing until *all* errors have been corrected on their first draft (double spacing helps) or second draft (if the first is illegible). If students cannot self-correct, they meet in class with the teacher or an aide who helps them. Extremely original and accurate first-draft compositions may be awarded extra credit. These individual student conferences can be instrumental in helping students to improve their writing ability as well as to review previous grammar topics. Students whose first drafts do not pass confer with the teacher and hand in a new composition the next day. Frequent composition assignments can result in marked improvement in writing ability. Teachers concerned about the heavy burden of paperwork can limit composition length to fifty or seventy-five words. Students will rarely object.

16.4.5 *Illustrated Stories*

Beginning students enjoy writing simple storybooks illustrated either with their own hand drawings or with magazine pictures. After students have created their booklets, they may spend a period exchanging them and reading what others have written. In addition to building students' pride in what they have created, this assignment can be extremely helpful in providing suitable reading material for beginners.

NOTES

[1] Excellent sources of ideas for combining affective training with free communication exercises are: Virginia Wilson and Beverly Wattenmaker, *Real Communication in Foreign Language* and *Real Communication in Spanish* (Upper Jay, N.Y.: Adirondack Mountain Humanistic Education Center, 1973); Phyllis S. Stoller and Joanne Tuskes Lock, *Real Communication in French* (Upper Jay, N.Y.: Adirondack Mountain Humanistic Education Center, 1974); and Stefano Morel, *Human Dynamics in French* and *Human Dynamics in Spanish* (Upper Jay, N.Y.: Adirondack Mountain Humanistic Education Center, 1974).

[2] Gerald E. Logan, *Conversations in German* (Rowley, Mass.: Newbury House Publishers, 1973).

CHAPTER SEVENTEEN
TECHNIQUES OF INDIVIDUALIZATION III: CULTURE, CIVILIZATION, LITERATURE

17.1 WAY-OF-LIFE CULTURE

At the beginning and intermediate levels, way-of-life culture may be treated in brief, full-group presentations, in independent study activities, or by a combination of these two techniques. Specific ways of applying these approaches in beginning and intermediate courses are considered in this section. At advanced levels, mini-courses can treat areas of special interest to students. This topic has been discussed in Chapter Six.

17.1.1 *Full-Class Activities*

Most students need and want a break from working every day on packets designed to improve their language skills. Brief, ten- to fifteen-minute cultural mini-lessons can serve this purpose quite well. Subjects may include recent news or magazine articles, slides or filmstrips relating to textbook material, song sheets for choral singing, and records or tapes of current hits in the foreign country. Students, as well as the teacher, may take responsibility for these presentations.

Students can tell of their experiences abroad and show slides or photos. They can read to the class the letters they have received from pen pals (through correspondence promoted and arranged by the teacher). They can present to the class the results of their individual study, such as reports, skits, and projects. Warning: Unless it is made completely clear from the beginning that these lessons are important (even though not always graded) and will occur a certain number of times per week, students will resent the teacher's using what they consider to be "their" class time.

17.1.2 *Individual Study Projects*

Students who consistently work faster than the class and those who enjoy independent study can select projects according to their individual interests. Or the entire class may be assigned a project. Dittoed lists of possibilities may be distributed, posted on bulletin boards, or written on indexed file cards. Students can consult with the teacher about these or about their own ideas. In order for this technique to work, reference materials must be available for student use in the library, resource center, or the classroom itself. These materials may include post cards from the foreign country, overhead transparencies with pictures to stimulate conversation or writing, foreign-language magazines and newspapers, pictures of works of art, outline maps to be filled in, cultural readers, records or tapes of songs, or *any* realia from the foreign countries—ticket stubs, menus, theater programs, games, subject-matter flashcards or study guides, city and road maps, cookbooks, and so on. If the teacher has not been abroad recently, students or friends who are traveling might be asked to bring back realia.

A convenient way of handling realia is to place related items in a large envelope or a box—such as a shoe box—along with questions about them. For example, an empty perfume bottle (which probably retains some of the original fragrance, thus furnishing a pleasant sensory as well as intellectual experience) can be accompanied by questions (ideally, in the foreign language) such as: Where is perfume made in France? What are some of the best-known manufacturers and perfumes? What perfumes are advertised in the newspaper you read at home? How is perfume made? How does the scent of the bottle make you feel? Why? A list of resources where answers can be found may be included.

Students may be encouraged to contribute materials to the culture envelopes or boxes and to make up study guides and resource lists. In this way they take an active and useful part in developing the curriculum as well as pursuing their individual interests regarding the foreign language and culture. In fact, creating a culture envelope or box can be counted as a project. A related activity could require that one or more students (they need not necessarily work alone) invent a game based on the foreign language and culture. It may take the form of a board that lights up or buzzes when items are matched or questions answered correctly. It may be a panel game modeled after those on television. Or students can make a board game in which players advance only if they demonstrate their knowledge of cultural material.

Students with special talents and interests should be encouraged to develop them. A ham radio operator may report his conversation with a ham abroad. Short-wave foreign-language programs can be recorded and explained to the class.[1] Students interested in drafting may construct plans of typical foreign homes. The artists in the class can elect to create maps, scenes from daily life, or attractive illustrations of grammar principles. Dancers can demonstrate folk dances, musicians can sing and play modern or classical music of the culture and offer explanations to the class. Art history buffs may analyze a work of art or outline major characteristics of a certain art style or movement. Students may choose to paint in the style of a favorite artist. Creative writers may enjoy imitating the style of a poem or story they have read or writing new captions for cartoons found in the daily newspaper. Film buffs can create their own original movie or videotape with foreign-language soundtrack. The family cassette player can be used to create man-on-the-street interviews of classmates speaking about topics of current interest. Similarly, family photos or slides can be used as the basis of a foreign-language program or narrative. Computer programmers can write material in the foreign language.

In order to ensure that projects are educationally worthwhile, the teacher and student need to confer often about the nature of the work and the rate of progress. In the beginning stages of language learning, short projects are most suitable for teaching students how to work well independently of the teacher. In this situation the teacher's personal guidance regarding choice of project and individual prescriptions for resources are instrumental in creating positive relationships with students. If students feel that the teacher cares about them as individuals and is willing to go out of his way to help them with their personal projects, they too will feel obligated to put forth their best efforts. In cases where the teacher feels that his personal expertise and knowledge of resources is inadequate, another member of the faculty—perhaps in another department—might also help guide an individual project. This interdisciplinary study can be highly beneficial to students and should be encouraged.

In case students in some classes claim that they have no ideas and no talents, the teacher might try a brainstorming session in which students throw out possible ideas as they occur to them. If this too should fail in a highly passive class, the teacher can offer a lengthy list of possible activities from which students may choose. Once students become accustomed to doing creative assignments, they will gradually learn to invent their own ideas.

17.1.3 *Culture-Based Mini-Dramas*

In preparation for culture-based mini-dramas, the teacher presents a brief (ten- to fifteen-minute) lecture or series of lectures about an aspect of the foreign culture: what people eat, how they entertain, the holidays they celebrate, ways they greet each other or make apologies, how they shop, how parents or teachers administer discipline, and so on. Or students might read cultural material in basic or supplementary texts, or on teacher-prepared fact sheets. Then in groups of two to four people they present skits where they play the roles of natives of the foreign culture or of Americans traveling abroad. Points of cultural conflict are especially appropriate for dramatization. This technique can be successful with both junior high school students and high school students.

17.1.4 *Magazine and Newspaper Projects*

Foreign language newspapers and magazines offer the advantages of being relatively inexpensive classroom accessories, of offering current, relevant, and *real* information, usually in appealing and attractive formats. Some limitations are that the reading level is usually beyond the abilities of most students, and it is difficult to obtain enough copies of one article or one issue for each member of the class. Nevertheless, there are several ways of incorporating these high-interest publications into worthwhile learning activities.

Beginning students can browse through magazines in search of something specific: vocabulary items, examples of American-made products advertised abroad, uses of a particular grammar topic that has just been studied, articles or advertisements that reflect cultural values or cultural differences. If a considerable number of issues from previous years are available, students can cut out items related to their chosen topic and assemble them in scrapbooks to be exchanged in class. Or students can assemble bulletin board displays with their materials.

More advanced students can analyze how ads use cultural values to appeal to consumers and convince them to buy the product. If students have read about an important recent news event in their own language, then chances are they will be able to understand, in general, a foreign-language article about that event. Students who elect this type of assignment may list a certain number of new vocabulary words learned and take an oral test on them. In the event that a short, interesting, and fairly easy article is found, it can be photocopied onto Dittoes and distributed to the entire class for discussion.

Advanced students can search for articles related to their own particular interests—dance, rock music, auto racing, oceanography, computer science, ecology, and so on—and report on them orally or in writing. Though these students may not understand every detail, their basic interest in the topic can provide them with sufficient motivation to read through a fairly difficult article.

17.2 CIVILIZATION AND LITERATURE

Although the study of the literary and cultural accomplishments of the past seems currently to have fallen into temporary disfavor when compared to student interest in what is current and relevant, there are nevertheless students who will enjoy courses in these areas if they are well presented and take into account individual differences and interests.

17.2.1 *Differentiated Assignments*

Though all members of the class may be required to read the same work of literature, study the same period in art or music, or attend a lecture about the same historic event, there is no need for them to take the same short-answer or essay test on the new material. Rather than passing a formal test, there are several other more stimulating, interesting, and creative ways for them to show that they have learned the new material. Students can write a diary from the point of view of the author, artist, composer or historical figure under study. They can create an imaginary newspaper account of events surrounding the appearance of a major literary or artistic work or a historical turning point. Alternatively, these events can be dramatized in front of the class. Students can pursue additional independent research on a related topic that interests them. Some students may be inclined to emulate the artistic, literary, musical, or rhetorical style of the people under study.

17.2.2 *Mini-Courses*

In this area too, mini-courses, as discussed in Chapter Six, have proven a popular and well-received alternative to the standardized lockstepped curriculum. The mere fact that the students know that they themselves have selected the subject matter—rather than having it imposed upon them as a matter of course—creates a positive climate for learning. Since they are limited in scope, mini-courses offer the double advantage of providing variety in the curriculum as well as the chance to study several topics in depth, rather than in the superficial survey manner. Mini-course topics could include: The Historic Role of Women; Romantic Poetry; Impressionism in Art and Music; Architectural Styles—Past and Present; and so on.

17.2.3 *Interdisciplinary Studies*

With the decline of the reading of foreign literary works as the primary reason for learning a second language, new justifications need to be found for foreign-language study in addition to its potential career or travel value. In order to combat declining enrollments, new courses have been developed that cross traditional discipline boundaries and present regular high-school or college subject matter in a foreign language. Courses such as science in German, history in Spanish, or art in French can be instrumental in providing students who are not language majors with the opportunity to maintain their skills while pursuing courses in areas of personal interest. Examples of this approach are described in the professional literature.[2,3]

17.2.4 *Foreign-Language Literature*

Reading foreign language literature can be facilitated by providing students with vocabulary lists and discussion questions focusing on major issues or ideas. If students must read a considerable number of pages before a worthwhile discussion can take place, the class can divide into reading groups that meet only two to three times a week, with the days that are not given over to discussion being devoted to in-class reading instead. By alternating discussion groups and offering a choice of assignments, teachers can meet the needs of students with different interests and reading levels.

NOTES

[1] Melvin G. Therrien, "Learning French via Short-Wave Radio and Popular Periodicals," *French Review*, vol. 46 (May 1973), pp. 1178–83.

[2] William V. Gugli, "Multi-Track Options for French Study," *French Review*, vol. 46 (May 1973), pp. 1184–91.

[3] William V. Gugli, "Total Immersion Language Program (TIP)," in F. William D. Love and Lucille J. Honig, *Options and Perspectives: A Sourcebook of Innovative Foreign Language Programs in Action, K-12* (New York: Modern Language Association of America, 1973), pp. 243–52.

APPENDIXES

APPENDIX A
Individual Interest Inventory	190
Example of Year-End Goals for a Foreign-Language Curriculum	192
Learning Packet Instructions for a Dialog	196
Learning Packet Instructions for a Reading Text	200

APPENDIX B
Learning Packet Instructions for a Grammar Topic	202
A Shortened Version of Learning Packet Instructions for a Grammar Topic	205
Sample Lesson Plan for a Flexibly Paced Grammar Unit	206
Learning Packet Instructions for a Culture Topic	211

APPENDIX C
Ten Criteria for Evaluating Commercially or Locally Prepared Learning Packets	212
Ideas for Developing Communicative Competence	214
Grammar-Based Exercises to Develop Speaking Ability	215
Ideas for Elective Enrichment Assignments	217

APPENDIX D
Form for Planning an Individualized Curriculum	223
Topics for Student Orientation	225
Foreign-Language Game Expressions (French)	226
Composition Correction Symbols	228

APPENDIX E
Self-Grading Form for Students	229
Program Evaluation Questionnaires	231
Useful Foreign-Language Classroom Expressions (French)	235
Evaluation Sheet for Oral Communication in the Foreign Language	236

APPENDIX A

NAME _____

INDIVIDUAL INTEREST INVENTORY

Please answer the following questions as well as you can. Your teacher is interested in the information so that the course can become more relevant for you. If you consider any question too personal, please feel free not to answer. Your answers will IN NO WAY influence your grade or your teacher's opinion of you. The information will be used solely to incorporate your interests, if possible, into the curriculum.

Check which of the following activities you participate in:

_____Dancing. Circle one: modern   ballet   tap   other_____

_____Singing. Where? What?

_____Art. Medium? Subjects?

_____Electronics. What?

_____Sports. Which?

_____TV. Favorite programs?

_____Hobbies. What? (collections?)

_____Play an instrument. Which?

_____Music. What kind? (listening/writing)

_____Acting. In what? What roles?

_____Cooking. What?

_____Sewing/Needlework. What?

_____Handcrafts. Which?

_____Reading. What type?

_____Creative writing. What?

_____Photography. Kind? Subjects?

_____Carpentry. What?

_____Travel. Where?

_____Mechanics.

_____Attend plays. What kind?

_____Attend films. What kind?

_____Volunteer work. Where?

_____School Clubs.   Which?

_____Pets.   What kind?

_____Attend concerts.   What kind?

_____Boating/Sailing.   Where?

_____Fishing.

_____Hunting.   What?

_____Work after school.   Where?   Doing what?

_____Speak foreign language at home.   Which?   With whom?

_____Science projects.   On what?

_____Gardening.   What?

_____House chores.   Which?

_____Other.

What are your career plans, if you know them?
What is your favorite subject?
What is your favorite activity?

EXAMPLE OF END-OF-YEAR GOALS FOR A FOREIGN-LANGUAGE CURRICULUM

COGNITIVE GOALS

Level I. A student who succesfully completes the course will be able to do the following activities:

SPEAKING

1. Pronounce the sounds of the foreign language and its intonations and liaisons in a manner comprehensible to a native speaker.
2. Use the active vocabulary and grammar presented during the year in comprehensible sentences.
3. Speak for one minute on any of the topic areas (such as the home, family, sports, food, leisure activities, and so on) he or she has studied.
4. Carry on a spontaneous conversation for two minutes with the teacher or a peer on a familiar topic studied during the year.
5. Use familiar foreign-language expressions for carrying out daily class activities (ask for explanations, directions, and so on).

LISTENING

1. Indicate whether groups of sounds and sentences heard are the same or different.
2. Understand all familiar directions in the foreign language used in classroom management, as demonstrated by appropriate behavior.
3. Demonstrate understanding of sentences containing the vocabulary and grammar taught either by selecting appropriate answer choices or by giving comprehensible oral responses.

READING

1. Read with comprehension the written foreign-language instructions in learning packets for completing course requirements, as demonstrated by appropriate classroom behavior.
2. Read with comprehension the dialogs and narratives presented in class, as evidenced by response to oral questions or to true-false or multiple-choice open-book reading tests.
3. Read simplified, unfamiliar material in magazines or readers, as demonstrated by brief English summaries of content.

WRITING

1. Spell accurately all words presented during the year.
2. Demonstrate understanding of sound-letter correspondences of the foreign language by spelling accurately from dictation words that have not been formally taught.

3. Write comprehensible sentences of at least five words using any of the active vocabulary words presented during the year.
4. Use the appropriate written grammar forms learned to respond to statements or questions presented orally or in writing.
5. Write a coherent and comprehensible five-sentence paragraph of 25 to 50 words on a topic studied during the year.

CULTURE

1. Demonstrate a knowledge of the location of countries in which the foreign language is spoken by identifying them on outline maps.
2. Complete at least four elective assignments (one per grading period) relating to the culture and civilization of the foreign countries under study.
3. Present original skits either in English or in the foreign language demonstrating instances of cross-cultural differences between Americans and natives of the foreign countries.
4. (Optional) Write letters to a foreign pen-pal.

Level II. In addition to maintaining the language skills of the previous course, a student who successfully completes Level II will be able to do the following:

LISTENING

1. Understand cultural information communicated slowly and limited to familiar vocabulary and structure.
2. Understand three- to six-sentence narrative paragraphs or dialogs based on recombinations of vocabulary and grammar learned, as demonstrated by performance on multiple-choice comprehension tests.
3. Understand whatever the teacher says when he or she speaks slowly and uses familiar vocabulary and structures.

SPEAKING

1. Speak for at least two minutes about personal interests in past, present, future, or conditional tenses comprehensibly and with acceptable pronunciation.
2. Carry on a spontaneous conversation for at least two minutes with the teacher or with peers on a topic of personal interest.
3. Make all classroom and learning needs known in the foreign language and use the foreign language to obtain what is wanted (such as explanations, tests, and so on).

READING

1. Read with understanding texts based on all the vocabulary and grammar studied, as well as others containing some cognates and unfamiliar

material. Comprehension is demonstrated by responses to oral questions or to multiple-choice, open-book tests.
2. Read with comprehension simplified stories and articles not explained in class as demonstrated by English summaries of content and oral tests on new vocabulary words.

WRITING

1. Write a comprehensible and generally accurate composition of 50–75 words in any of the verb tenses presented. There should be no more than two errors per sentence involving Level-II grammar.

CULTURE

1. Demonstrate knowledge of the foreign culture by satisfactorily completing the worksheets in at least nine of the culture packets (about one per month) available in the classroom. (Topics include: major cities and products, famous people, daily life, and so on. Materials may include: slides, filmstrips, written texts, maps, and so on.)
2. Present foreign-language skits demonstrating an aspect of the way of life in the foreign countries.

Level III. By the end of this level the successful student will be able to:

LISTENING

Comprehend in a general way taped stories and rapid oral speech.

SPEAKING

Express himself freely on everyday topics with a considerable amount of comprehensibility, fluency, and accuracy.

READING

Comprehend short stories of 5–10 pages containing unfamiliar structures and vocabulary words, as well as scripts from films and filmstrips and also slide soundtracks, as demonstrated by answering oral or written questions.

WRITING

Express himself comprehensibly in 75–100 words on any given topic (with no more than 10 errors) in the grammar that has been presented so far.

CULTURE

Demonstrate knowledge of the foreign culture and civilization by completing worksheets or tests on foreign-language films, filmstrips, slides, cultural reading texts, and classroom lectures.

Level IV. At the end of this level, the successful student will be able to:

LISTENING

Understand rapid oral speech and film, filmstrip, or slide soundtracks.

SPEAKING

Express ideas on complex, abstract, or technical topics (literary or cultural) with considerable fluency, ease, and accuracy.

READING

Read with understanding unedited foreign-language material such as novels, plays, poetry, magazines, and newspapers, as evidenced by his ability to analyze and evaluate their contents during oral discussions in class.

WRITING

Write coherent, comprehensible analyses or evaluations of the foreign-language literature or culture with a high degree of grammatical accuracy.

AFFECTIVE GOALS FOR FOREIGN-LANGUAGE TEACHERS

1. To improve attitude toward foreign-language study by:
   a. offering a free, relaxed, open-classroom environment
   b. allowing students to control a portion of what they learn
   c. offering individual help to each student according to his or her needs
   d. encouraging students to communicate freely without fear of penalty or correction
   e. allowing each student to experience success in the foreign language
2. To develop appreciation of the intrinsic worth of foreign-language study by:
   a. encouraging ties with foreign pen-pals and by making trips to museums, films, plays, and so on
   b. enabling students to experience the satisfaction of communicating in the foreign language
   c. discussing the nature of language and the difficulties and rewards of learning it (in individual conferences)
   d. modeling behavior of someone who enjoys communicating in a foreign language

LEARNING PACKET INSTRUCTIONS FOR A DIALOG
(Approximately 4- to 6-day unit)

Comments

Performance Objective: Show that you can pronounce the dialog acceptably, can spell all the words correctly, and can use the new vocabulary words (orally or in writing) in original sentences (5 words minimum) by completing the following activities satisfactorily.

Learning Steps

PRONUNCIATION

1. Attend a dialog presentation by the teacher or by a tape or cassette.

In beginning classes and in those flexibly paced, the teacher is more likely to do the first presentation.

2. Practice pronouncing the new dialog with the teacher, with the aides, with tapes, or with a friend. When you are ready, present yourself to the teacher or to an aide for an oral pronunciation test. You will be asked to read several dialog sentences aloud. To pass, you must speak fluently (though not rapidly) with little hesitation and with no major pronunciation errors. ("Major" errors interfere with the understanding of what you say.) If necessary, seek extra pronunciation help (by using language master cards or working with the teacher) and retest (within the deadlines, if any) until you pass.

This pronunciation objective is set at Stage 1, *Mechanical Skills*, of the subject-matter taxonomy.

SPELLING

_____3. Copy the dialog sentences once in order to learn the foreign-language spelling. Write out each sentence again, this time without looking at the original while you write. Check your copies for accuracy against the dialog in the text. Ask the teacher or an aide to check your work. If there are still errors in it, you will be asked to write the dialog once again.

The spelling objective in steps 3 and 4 is primarily for Level I students. Once the students have mastered the sound-letter correspondences of the foreign language, the spelling objective may be eliminated.

_____4. In class, attend the teacher's presentation of the foreign-language spelling system as well as the practice dictation sessions. When you are ready, take a dictation test administered by the teacher, an aide, or a tape. You will hear several sentences, each said three times. You are to write accurately what you hear. To pass, you must make no more than _____ (number) errors. Retest as needed.

The dictated sentences may be exactly the same as the dialog sentences studied—particularly at the beginning of Level I. As students progress, the dictated sentences may be variations or recombinations of those in the text. This objective may be set at Stage 2, *Knowledge*, or Stage 3, *Transfer*.

VOCABULARY

_____5. Memorize the vocabulary words on the list provided. With a friend, practice using each word in an original sentence. When you are ready, ask the teacher or aide for an oral test. You will hear 5 words. You must supply a foreign-language sentence for at least 4 of them. Your sentences must be fluent (not rapid) and comprehensible. Grammar accuracy does not count. Retest if necessary. You must use a minimum of 5 words in each sentence.

The vocabulary list may provide pictures or foreign-language or English equivalents of the new words. The number of words on the text may be less than 5. This step may also be done in writing, but then the vital oral dimension is sacrificed and the teacher's paperwork is considerably increased.

SPEAKING

_____6. Participate in at least two oral question-and-answer sessions to practice using the new vocabulary words. Practice with the teacher, an aide, or a friend. When ready, take an oral text given by the teacher either individually or in small groups. Retest as needed within deadlines. You will have 3 questions to answer on each test you take. To pass, your 5-word sentences must be fluent and easily comprehensible. Grammatical accuracy does not count if your response is understandable.

This sheet should be teacher-prepared if the material in the text is inadequate. Oral test questions may be the same as or different from those studied. The number of test items may be reduced to 1 or 2 if classes are large and sufficient personnel is lacking.

198 APPENDIX A

IRREGULAR VERB (GRAMMAR)

_____7. (If applicable to a particular unit) Look at the irregular verb forms on pages _____. Memorize them and do the exercises on pages _____. Correct your answers with the key and have the teacher or an aide sign this step.

One or more irregular verbs in one or more tenses are often included in Level II and Level III units.

_____8. (If applicable) Do the pattern drills on pages _____ and take an oral test on them with the teacher or an aide.

No conversation questions are provided here because they have been included in step 6 (Stage 3, *Transfer*).

_____9. On a sheet of paper write out the forms of the irregular verb(s) and check your work against the forms in the book. Show this material to your teacher or to an aide for a signature. In the testing area, write out the irregular verb forms on a blank sheet of paper and submit it to the teacher for correction. To pass, you must make *no* errors. Retest if necessary.

This test is harder for some students than it would appear to be. This behavior is at Stage 2, *Knowledge*.

COMMUNICATION ASSIGNMENT BASED ON THE DIALOG

SPEAKING

a. With two or three friends, prepare a variation of the dialog you have just learned. Have your work corrected by the teacher and present your dialog to the class.

The objectives here are at Stage 4, *Communication*.

b. Tell the class about a similar experience you have had. Be sure to have your work corrected before your oral presentation to the class.

These assignments may be optional for extra credit or students may be required to choose one of them.

WRITING ACTIVITIES

c. Use at least _____ (5 to 10) new vocabulary words in a unified paragraph of 5–10 sentences or 50–75 words. To pass, your work must be comprehensible. To receive credit in the teacher's gradebook, you must correct all your errors.

d. Write a dialog, narrative, news article, poem (and so on) about an experience you have had similar to the one in the dialog.

Note: Depending on the level of the students, this dialog unit may take from 3 or 4 days (at Levels II and III, with the spelling steps omitted) to perhaps 6 or 8 days or even more at the initial stages of foreign-language learning. More time should also be allowed for students who are just learning how to work in an individualized classroom.

Grading: Depending on the teacher's individual preferences, one grade may be assigned for the whole topic or separate grades may be assigned for one or more of its parts (pronunciation, vocabulary, spelling, speaking, and irregular verb).

LEARNING PACKET INSTRUCTIONS FOR A READING TEXT
(Approximately 4- to 6-day unit)

Objectives and Learning Steps

Performance Objective: Show that you can speak about the reading text and that you can read it with comprehension by completing the following activities:

Learning Steps

SPEAKING

1. At home, read the text at the end of the unit on pages _____. Use the accompanying vocabulary list to help you understand what you read. In class ask the teacher, an aide, or a friend to explain the sentences that cause you difficulty in understanding.

_____2. At home (or perhaps in class with a friend, if necessary) memorize the meanings of the words provided on the vocabulary list. When ready, sign up on the board for an oral test with the teacher or with an aide. You will hear 5 words in the foreign language for which you are to supply the meaning of at least four.

_____3. In pairs or in small groups of 6 to 8 with the teacher or an aide, practice answering orally the questions based on the reading text. These questions are found on pages _____. Practice these questions at least twice, answering the second time without looking in the book. When you are ready, sign up on the board for a speaking test. The teacher will ask you 2 or 3 questions and you are to answer fluently and comprehensibly in order to pass. (For students beyond the

Comments

Stage 3, *Transfer*, though there are elements of Stage 4, *Communication*, in the oral part of the objective.

This step is not signed. At this point, it is hard for the teacher to be absolutely sure that students have indeed read the assignment.

Students may supply meanings in English or may offer a foreign-language sentence. Though the latter test is "traditional," it offers the advantage of speed and effectiveness. If students do not know vocabulary they have great difficulty reading. Furthermore, students have opportunities to speak in the next step.

If questions in the book are not suitable, teachers may write their own. It is helpful to supply students with an answer key showing them on what page and line the answers may be found. The questions on the test may be the same as or different from those studied. This step may beginning stages, the oral test may consist of an oral resumé of the story—presented either individually (a time-consuming practice) or in groups of 4 to 6 students (one student begins the story and chooses a student to continue it, and so on.)

be done in writing, but then the oral practice would be sacrificed.

READING

4. You will have a multiple-choice (4 choices) reading test of 8 items. You must have your books open in order to answer, but you may not use notes or vocabulary lists. You are to indicate by an X which of the 4 response choices best completes the sentence or best answers the question given. To pass, you may make no more than 2 errors. You may retest up to 3 times.

The numbers presented here are merely suggestive. Different situations and levels will require variations from what is listed here. Stage 3, *Transfer*.

COMMUNICATION ASSIGNMENTS BASED ON THE READING SELECTION

a. Retell the story you have just read from the point of view of one of the characters or from the point of view of an object.

b. Which of the characters in the story is most like (or unlike) you? Why?

c. Expand the story to include more events and more details than those already given. Or, tell what happened before the story begins in the text. Or, tell what happens after the story ends in the text.

These assignments may be optional or students may be required to choose one of them. They may be carried out either orally or in writing. Orally, students may speak one or more minutes depending on their level. In writing, from 50–100 words is often a suitable length.

APPENDIX B

LEARNING PACKET INSTRUCTIONS FOR A GRAMMAR TOPIC (Approximately 5- to 6-day unit)

Performance Objective

Show you know how to use the new grammar to express yourself comprehensibly both orally and in writing by completing the following learning steps.

Comments

This is an objective that takes roughly one week. It is set at Stage 4, *Communication*.

LISTENING AND SPEAKING

_____1. Ask the teacher for an explanation, or read pp. _____ in the text, or read the explanation sheet prepared by the teacher, or listen to the explanation on the tape or cassette #_____. If you do not understand after the first explanation, seek further help from the teacher, an aide, or from a friend.

These learning activities are daily objectives. One or more of these alternatives may be offered. This one-day objective is set at Stage 3, *Knowledge*.

_____2. Using a tape or cassette or with a friend, or in a group of 4–8 with the teacher, practice the pattern drills on pp. _____. Ask the teacher or an aide for an oral test. You will see a model sentence and answer. When given a new cue, answer according to the model. You will have one item from each drill. To pass, your answers must be fluent with *no* mistakes in the new grammar forms. Retest as many times as needed to pass.

This is a performance objective for one day. It is set at Stage 3, *Transfer*. Satisfactory completion is indicated by a signature next to the number 2. Small groups of 4–8 are easily managed. Upward or downward revisions are also possible.

_____3. In a small group with the teacher, with an aide or with a friend, practice the questions and answers based on the new grammar. After practicing at least twice, take an oral test either individually or in a small group with the teacher who will give you 1–3 questions. To pass, your answers must be fluent (though not necessarily rapid) and easily comprehensible, and you must make *no* mistakes in the new grammar. You may retest as needed within the deadlines established.

Stages 3 and 4, *Transfer and Communication*. This sheet may be teacher-prepared if the text lacks this material and may be included in the packet. The questions asked on the test may be the same as or different from those practiced. The number of questions will depend on student ability and on time and personnel available for testing. Only an adult (as opposed to a student aide) should

WRITING ACTIVITIES
(Stages 3 and 4, *Transfer and Communication*)

_____ 4. Write out the pretest exercise and check it with the key (provided either at the bottom or back of the sheet). Correct your errors and have the teacher or aide sign this step. Ask for help on what you do not understand.

5. Take the written test when you are ready (within established deadlines). There will be _____ (number) of items on the test such as: (Examples, if needed). To pass, you must make no more than (number) of errors on the new grammar and your sentences must be comprehensible. You may take up to 3 tests in order to pass. When you have passed, show the signatures on this sheet to your teacher who will record your credit in the gradebook.

This assignment is due in class on: (date)

It expires out-of-class on: (date)

administer this test. Satisfactory completion is indicated by signature.

This pretest is actually an exercise that is an alternate form of the test students are to take. It may, however, be longer; 10–20 items is a manageable number.

From 5–10 items is a manageable number. The number of errors allowed depends on the mastery level the teacher decides to set. The number of retests can vary according to teacher preferences. The teacher may record either one total grade for the grammar topics or one grade for the oral work and one for the written work.

This information is for courses that are flexibly paced. If the dates are written in by students (as opposed to being printed) the learning packet sheet (if successful) may be reused in succeeding years. The out-of-class expiration date may be set one or two weeks after the in-class expiration date. This extra time period is for absentees or slower students.

COMMUNICATION ASSIGNMENT BASED ON THE NEW GRAMMAR

A. Write a composition of 40–60 words or 5–10 sentences using at least 5 different

Stage 4, *Communication*. The numbers presented are

examples of the new grammar. It may be a dialog or narrative, as you choose.

B. Make a chart for the bulletin board illustrating the new grammatical forms you have learned.

C. Design a game based on the new grammar that your classmates may play. Discuss your ideas first with your teacher before beginning.

suggestive. They will vary with the level and ability of the students, and with the time the teacher has for grading papers. This assignment might be required of all.

A few students may elect this assignment.

A few students may elect this assignment.

Other communication activities are possible—diaries, poems, skits, speeches, and so on. These are but a few suggestions.

A SHORTENED VERSION OF LEARNING PACKET INSTRUCTIONS FOR A GRAMMAR TOPIC

Once students have become accustomed to working in an individualized classroom and have become used to what the teacher expects from them and how they will be graded, the instructions in the learning packet can be shortened considerably. This is extremely important for teacher survival—particularly during the first year of individualization. After students have worked through one or two highly detailed units of study, the learning packet instructions can be as brief as the following:

Objective: Show that you can use the new grammar both orally and in writing.

1. Grammar explanation pp. _____, or see teacher in class, or use cassette #_____ or tape #_____.

_____2. Take the oral test on the patterns, pages _____.

_____3. Practice the questions and answers at least twice and sign up for the oral test.

_____4. Do the pretest exercise, page _____. Check it yourself and have an aide or the teacher sign this step.

_____5. Take the written test up to 3 times; 8 items; 2 errors allowed.

COMMUNICATION ASSIGNMENT

Use five different examples of the new grammar in a composition of 50 to 75 words. Be sure to remember to skip lines to allow room for teacher corrections. Pass: Comprehensible; no more than one error on new grammar.

SAMPLE LESSON PLAN FOR A FLEXIBLY PACED GRAMMAR UNIT

The following lesson plan suggests what activities might occur during a six-day flexibly paced grammar unit. The double horizontal lines separate the activities of each day. The vertical lines divide the activities into three types: Full-class, small-group, and independent. Basically, the classroom is organized so that the teacher has nearly all the time during the first days and students have nearly all the time during the last days. The first three days are used primarily for presenting grammar, drills, and conversation questions and for oral practice. The last three days are used primarily for testing, extra help, and individual conferences as needed.

No such lesson plan can be presented for continuous-progress classes, since each student may be at a different point in the course.

Each lesson is 40–45 minutes in length

	Full-class presentation by teacher	Small groups led by teacher or aides	Oral and written tests, individual conferences, independent work
Day 1 10–15 mins.	a. Oral comprehension exercise from preceding unit of study or current events or cultural talk or students' skits or speeches		
10–15 mins.	b. Explanation of new grammar topic and requirements of the learning activities		
10–15 mins.	c. Explanation and presentation of pattern drills. Students may or may not have a chance to practice the drills.		*** Homework: Study new grammar and pattern drills in preparation for oral test.

	Full-class presentation by teacher	Small-groups led by teacher or aides	Oral and written tests, individual conferences, independent work
Day 2 5–15 mins.	a. Continuation of a. activities from previous day or announcements, attendance, and so forth.		
10–20 mins.		b. Students form small groups with the teacher or aides or pair off to practice questions and answers on the new grammar.	
15–20 mins.		c. If necessary, the teacher offers a second explanation of the grammar to small groups of students who need it.	d. Students practice pattern drills or Seek additional explanations of grammar from teacher or aides or Peers help each other or Students confer with teacher over previous work—such as composition correction and test errors or Rapid learners pass test on pattern drills.

*** Homework: Study pattern drills and questions and answers in preparation for oral tests on each.

	Full-class presentation by teacher	Small-groups led by teacher or aides	Oral and written tests, individual conferences, independent work
Day 3 5–15 mins.	a. Announcements, or culture, or speeches, as in preceding 2 days.		
10–20 mins.		b. Students practice conversation material (question and answer sheets) for the second time.	
10–20 mins.	*** Homework: Continue studying for oral test on patterns or questions and answers, as needed. Write out pretest exercise, if ready to do this step.		c. More practice of pattern drills; most students pass oral test on drill or More individual conferences with teacher, as needed.
Day 4 5 mins.	a. Announcements of day's activities, attendance, and so on.		
40–45 mins.		b. Students sign up on blackboard for oral test in small groups (4–6) (after passing drills) or Students practice drills with aides or friends before signing up for oral test.	

	Full-class presentation by teacher	Small-groups led by teacher or aides	Oral and written tests, individual conferences, independent work
			c. Most students pass oral test on drills.
			d. Fast students pass oral question and answer test.
	*** Homework: Study for question-and-answer test, if needed. Complete pretest if not already done. Do an extra-credit communication assignment, if required work is complete.		e. Many students have pretest exercise signed.
			f. Fast students pass the written test on questions and answers (leaving them 2 unstructured days).
Day 5 5 mins.	a. Announcements and so on.		
40–45 mins.		b. More students complete activities as above.	c., d., e., f. More students (average learners) complete activities as above (leaving them 1 unstructured day).
	*** Homework: Extra-credit or required assignments as needed.		
			g. Fast students work on extra-credit assignment.
			h. Fast students tutor, play games, or work on projects.

	Full-class presentation by teacher	Small-groups led by teacher or aides	Oral and written tests, individual conferences, independent work
Day 6 5 mins.	a. Announcements and so on.	b. Nearly all students complete all oral testing.	c. Nearly all students complete written activities (slower learners).
	*** Homework: Extra-credit or required assignments, as needed.		d. More students work on extra-credit communication assignments.
			e. Those not finished complete activities out of class.
			f. Fast students peer tutor, play games, work on projects.

Note: The lesson plan above was created for ninth-, tenth-, or eleventh-grade students of average ability. Older or brighter students will take less time.

Conversely, younger students or those not yet accustomed to working efficiently in an individualized classroom may need a few more days in order to complete all the activities described. The amount of time particular students choose to spend on homework will also be a determining factor in the length of the unit.

APPENDIX B   **211**

LEARNING PACKET INSTRUCTIONS FOR A CULTURE TOPIC

Performance Objective: Demonstrate knowledge of _____ (an aspect of the foreign culture) by completing the following learning steps satisfactorily.

Learning Steps	Comments
1. Attend the culture presentation.	A behavior at Stage 2, *Knowledge*. The presentation may be of any of the following types: lecture by teacher; reading in a text; slides, filmstrips, or films with written or taped explanatory material presented either to the full class or on a small-group or individual basis.
____2. (If applicable) Write out the work sheet or the exercises on page ____ and check with the answer key provided. Have your work signed by the teacher.	Behavior at Stage 2, *Knowledge*. This activity may involve questions to answer—fill-ins, multiple-choice, matching, and so on. The material may be prepared by the teacher or commercially prepared material may be used.
____3. (If applicable) Take the test on the cultural material. There will be ____ (number) items. To pass, you may make no more than ____ (number) errors.	Tests are particularly appropriate for Levels III and IV, when culture is taught more formally than is usually the case in the preceding levels.

Performance Objective: Demonstrate your understanding of the foreign culture by using your knowledge in an original situation.

____4. (If applicable) Present an original skit in which you dramatize characteristics of the foreign culture or instances of cross-cultural conflict due to inadequate understanding of the foreign way of life. You will receive credit if your presentation is authentic.	Alternative assignments may be: written papers analyzing the foreign culture; research into topics of personal interest to students; plans for imaginary trips to the foreign countries, and so on.

APPENDIX C

TEN CRITERIA FOR EVALUATING COMMERCIALLY OR LOCALLY PREPARED LEARNING PACKETS

1. CLARITY. Are instructions clear? Can students follow them easily? Is the level of language suitable to the age and maturity of the students? Is the format clear? Is the printed matter easy to read? Are grammar explanations (if included) easy for students to understand?

2. SPECIFICITY. Are instructions sufficiently specific? Do students always know what they are to do? Do they know where to locate needed materials? Do they know how they will be tested? Are they aware of deadlines?

3. BREVITY. Are instructions sufficiently brief so as to be read easily? Is the writing style economical? Are the instructions in later packets more brief than those in earlier ones?

4. PERFORMANCE OBJECTIVES AND LEARNING STEPS. Do the packets clearly communicate the following information to students: the purpose of their assignments; the behaviors desired of them; the conditions under which they are to perform; the criteria used to evaluate their performance? Are the packets more than mere checklists? Do the behaviors represent at least the first four stages of the cognitive taxonomy?

5. VARIETY AND APPEAL. Is the format of the packets flexible? Are the optional and required activities varied from one unit to the next? Are the packets attractive? Do they look appealing?

6. LEARNING ALTERNATIVES. Do the packets present learning alternatives? Can students choose, for example, between oral and written assignments? Can they choose among various testing methods? Can they select some activities according to personal interests? Can they work either alone or in small groups? Can they select their preferred methods of learning?

7. BALANCE OF SKILLS. Is the amount of attention paid to each language skill appropriate to the particular course level? Are there sufficient opportunities for listening and speaking practice? Are pronunciation and speaking tests provided?

8. COMMUNICATION ACTIVITIES. Do the learning activities provide sufficient opportunities for free oral and written self-expression? Are students encouraged to do independent reading? Are there tests of communicative competence? Are there sufficient activities at stage four of the cognitive taxonomy? Are original and creative uses of the foreign language encouraged?

9. CULTURE. Do the packets provide cultural assignments? Are the amount and nature of the cultural materials appropriate to the particular

course level? Do the culture activities call for more than mere knowledge of facts? Can students demonstrate their understanding of the foreign culture in creative ways?

10. BALANCE OF CLASSROOM ACTIVITIES. Do the packets provide for large-group, small-group, and individual activities? Are there sufficient checkpoints? Is the amount of checking and testing manageable? Are there opportunities for retesting? Are tests and retests sufficiently brief so that they do not dominate class time?

IDEAS FOR DEVELOPING COMMUNICATIVE COMPETENCE

In order to develop students' ability to "think on their feet," as opposed to offering prepared oral answers, the following activity can prove effective. In small groups of 4 to 8, led by the teacher or an aide who speaks fluently, the students listen to the ideas presented (in the foreign language), choose roles, and dramatize the situation. The group leader may offer ideas or needed vocabulary words, but participates as little as possible. The dramatizations may be closely related to the content, vocabulary, and structure of dialogs or readings already learned; they may concern problems or conflicts that students often face; or they may involve cross-cultural differences presented by the teacher or textbook. Some examples follow:

1. You and your friends are part of the crowd enjoying (the Tour de France, a bullfight, a Fasching celebration, and so on). What are some of the things you see? What are your reactions? What will you all do after the presentation is over? Do you all agree or do you have different ideas? Must you call your parents? Do you have to be home by a certain time?

2. You have received a low foreign-language grade on your report card. What do your parents say to you? How do you explain the grade, and whose fault is it? Do your parents punish you? How? Can you talk your way out of the punishment by making certain promises?

3. You come home from a date at three in the morning and your parents are waiting for you. How do you explain staying out so late? Do your parents believe you? How is the matter settled?

4. You are living abroad with a family and are not yet used to the foreign culture. Act out a conflict you might expect to experience—perhaps regarding what is served at mealtimes or at what times certain activities (like siestas) take place. How do you adjust to the conflict? How do your foreign hosts explain their way of life?

5. A student from the foreign country is staying at your house. What aspects of American culture may be unfamilar to him? How do you and members of your family try to make him feel more comfortable?

6. A foreign exchange student is attending your school. At lunch time she asks about things she does not understand: grading system, amount of homework given, relationships between teachers and students, extracurricular clubs, and so on. She tells you how her school in the foreign country is different from yours. If she feels like it, she talks about teenage social life in her country as compared to what it is like in the United States.

GRAMMAR-BASED EXERCISES TO DEVELOP SPEAKING ABILITY

A. The following questions may be used to review the irregular present tense. Verb forms are underlined, some answers are suggested, and students are provided with an answer key on the reverse of the exercise sheets. Later in the course, the key becomes unnecessary. This approach may be adapted to any new vocabulary or structural items that require oral communication practice.

Questions

1. What instrument do you <u>play</u>? (piano? violin? guitar? clarinet? drums?)
2. To whom do you <u>write</u> letters? And your sister or brother?
3. What subject do you <u>like</u> the most? why? the least?
4. What time does your father <u>go</u> to work? Does he take the bus? train? his car? What time does he <u>come</u> home?
5. How do you <u>go</u> to school? on foot? by bicycle? What time do you <u>come</u> to school? What time do you <u>leave</u> school?
6. What do you and your friends <u>do</u> after school? What do you and your family <u>do</u> during the weekend?
7. What <u>is</u> your favorite meal—breakfast, lunch, or dinner? Why?
8. What do you have (<u>take</u>) for breakfast? for lunch?
9. How many telephones do you and your family <u>have</u>? What colors <u>are</u> they?
10. What newspapers or magazines do you <u>read</u>? And your mother and father?

B. For some grammatical topics, such as the conditional or subjunctive tenses in French and Spanish and word order in subordinate clauses in German, open-ended or incomplete statements are effective for stimulating personalized and meaningful oral communication. Each student in the conversation group may supply an original completion for sentence stems such as those that follow. Active listening may be encouraged by having other members of the group recall and repeat the answers of each student. This exercise may also offer an important affective dimension.

1. I believe that . . . /My parents believe that . . .
2. I want my parents to . . . /My parents want me to . . .
3. I am glad that . . . /I regret that . . .

4. If I were married . . . /
5. To be happy, one must . . .
6. When I was younger, I used to . . .
7. I think that our school is . . .
8. When I am twenty-one, I will . . .
9. Last night, my (mother/father) said . . .
10. I am annoyed when my (parents/brothers/sisters) say to me that . . .

IDEAS FOR ELECTIVE ENRICHMENT ASSIGNMENTS

Grammar-Related Assignments

1. *Develop your own original idea and secure your teacher's approval.*
2. Make an attractive, understandable, instructive chart illustrating your *least favorite* area of grammar: formation of *any* tense, word order of object pronouns, word order of negatives, meanings of prepositions, irregular adjective forms, agreement of past participles, question formation, use of narrative vs. descriptive past tenses, verbs of motion that take "to be" as a helper in past; expressions requiring the subjunctive; words of negation
3. Invent a board game, quiz program, or team game in which players must show they know specific grammar forms and how to use them in order to win.
4. Go through the foreign-language magazines available in the classroom and cut out interesting headlines or picture captions that illustrate a specific point (or points) of grammar in which you are interested. Assemble them in a scrapbook.
5. Prepare a grammatically correct but nonsensical story or poem in French that imitates Lewis Carroll's "The Jabberwock" in style.
6. Develop a grammar-based foreign-language project using the computer.

Vocabulary-Related Assignments

1. Prepare a word-study booklet or chart in which you show how various endings change the meanings of basic roots: *evidence, evident, évidemment*; *persuader, persuasion*; Show at least *five* examples of a pattern you have found.
2. Prepare a booklet or chart in which you relate French and English cognates: *diriger*/direct; *liberté*/liberty; Find at least *five* examples of each pattern.
3. Prepare a game—board, quiz, or team—in which a French definition of a word is given and players must supply its French equivalent.
4. Prepare a game in which players must supply antonyms or as many synonyms as possible for words presented in order to win.
5. Prepare a game in which players must supply rhymes in order to win.
6. Prepare a cross-stix puzzle and word definitions. Put it onto a Ditto master and reproduce it for distribution to your classmates.
7. Develop a vocabulary-related foreign-language project using the computer.

8. *Develop your own original idea and secure your teacher's approval.*

9. Follow the daily crossword puzzle in the newspaper. Mark (and fill in) all definitions that require supplying an item relating to French culture and civilization.

10. Translate a popular or favorite song into French. Reproduce it from a Ditto master and teach it to the class. Define difficult new words.

11. Play charades in French. Prepare words and play with class. Ask teacher for instructions.

12. In French, write an advertisement for any product—real or imagined. It may be illustrated. Or, present to the class a live commercial selling your product (or service).

Way-of-Life Culture Assignments

1. *Develop your own original idea and secure your teacher's approval.*

2. Using textbook reference sources available in the room, show that you have learned about the way of life in the foreign culture and ways in which it differs from yours by presenting in class a skit in French illustrating several cultural facts. (Negotiate number of facts, length of skit with teacher.)

3. Go through a year's issues of a foreign-language magazine in the room. In French, write out in which ways the articles and the advertisements differ from those found in an American magazine. Or, present your findings orally (in English) to the class.

4. For one to two months keep a scrapbook of news articles relating to the French-speaking world (France, French-Canada, Carribean countries, Africa). In French, orally or in writing, summarize your findings.

5. Create one or more culture boxes in which you put: realia, study questions, resource lists. Box must be clearly labelled. (Credit negotiable.)

6. Select a "culture box" that interests you and carry out research in French to find out more about it. (Negotiate credit with teacher.)

7. From a popular French record (or, preferably, a tape) transcribe the words of a song and type them onto a Ditto master. Gloss difficult words. (Excellent for listening comprehension. Teacher will help. Difficult assignment.)

8. If you have a short wave radio or operate a ham radio, tape a program broadcast in French, prepare a vocabulary list, and present it to the class for listening comprehension. (See the following list of frequency bands.)

"Foreign Radio Stations for Real Language—Where and When*

The following radio stations can be heard in the United States. They make an excellent source for recording "real" language activities for advanced students in Spanish or French.

49 Meter Band – 5950 to 6200 KHZ

TGNA	Guatemala City	5955 KHZ	2200 EST
HJCF	Bogota	5960 KHZ	2130 EST
YSS	San Salvador	5980 KHZ	0745 EST
XEUW	Veracruz, Mexico	6020 KHZ	0700 EST
OAX4Z	Lima	6082 KHZ	2300 EST
Radio Luxembourg		6090 KHZ	1645 EST
XEQM	Merida, Mexico	6105 KHZ	2100 EST
SEVDS	Hermosillo, Mexico	6115 KHZ	2000 EST
Radio Nac. de España		6130 KHZ	2030 EST
YVKG	Caracas	6170 KHZ	0700 EST
ORTF	Paris	6175 KHZ	0130 EST

also look for . . .

ORTF		15315 KHZ	1430 EST
Radio Nac. de España		11800 KHZ	2230 EST
Radio Nac. de España		9359 KHZ	2300 EST
XERMX	Mexico City	9705 KHZ	1000 EST

Extra-Credit Culture and Vocabulary Assignments

1. Construct a French store. In a "display case," put French products— labels, empty boxes, and cans—that have been imported from France: snails, wine, cheeses, perfume, clothes (designer labels?), and so on.

2. Pretend you import from France: What does your merchandise catalog look like? You might want to use newspaper ads for French products sold in the United States. You may include the price of each item.

3. Look through the old *Paris-Match* in the classroom. Make a scrapbook on any one of the following topics:
   a. American-made products sold in France.
   b. What strikes you as culturally foreign/different when looking at French ads? (Include a brief, written explanation.)
   c. *Grammar:* Cut out headlines and pictures centering on one topic— agreement of adjectives, irregular present, *passé composé*, reflexives or ANY grammar topic the class is studying.

---

* This list was compiled by Philip D. Smith, Jr., of West Chester State College. Reprinted by permission from *Language Association Bulletin*, vol. 24, no. 4 (New York State Association of Foreign Language Teachers: March 1973), p. 7.

4. Vocabulary game: Cut out from *Paris-Match* some commonly used words. Be sure to include all parts of speech: Nouns, adjectives, adverbs (negatives), prepositions, interjections (exclamations like *Tiens!*), and conjunctions (*and, or, but*). Place all the words in a box labeled with name of game, (original name). Game can be played several ways: Two or more players race to see who can make most *correct* sentences within a time limit. Or, each player keeps a pile of 20 words that he or she draws from pile and discards into pile in center. The person who finishes the sentence in the middle (each player adds a logical word) gets to keep that sentence. The player with the most sentences wins. (Cut-out words should be limited to masculine or feminine, singular or plural to avoid agreement problems.) Sentences may be nonsensical but must be grammatically correct.

5. Ask teacher for vocabulary list from a future lesson. Transfer the list onto flashcards: Write the French on one side and place the English equivalent, a picture, or a French synonym on the other. Put a rubber band around the packet and label it. Classmates may use the packet for vocabulary practice.

Civilization-Related Projects

1. Bring in a record of a French opera and play well-known arias from it. Explain the story to the class. Talk a little about the composer—in French!

2. Talk in French to the class about a favorite musical or artistic period of yours. Bring in examples to illustrate your talk.

3. Invent a game that requires players to know something about geography, history, art, music, or any interest of yours.

4. Make a list of French Proverbs and their English equivalents, if any. Illustrate them, if possible, and put them into a booklet or on a wall-chart.

5. Do an interdisciplinary project working both with your French teacher and a teacher from another subject area.

6. *Develop your own original idea and secure your teacher's approval.*

7. Edit a "newspaper" that comes from a period of French or French and American history. You and/or your "reporters" prepare editorials, political cartoons, "Dear Abby" letters, news items, interviews with important people, feature stories, and so on.

8. Write the imaginary diary of an important artist, writer, historic figure.

9. With your friends, put on a skit dramatizing an important historic event. Show that you know the facts and circumstances surrounding the event.

10. Imitate the style of one or more French artists. Tell the class about the artist's style and what you tried to accomplish in your work.

11. On a large map of France, draw in the various products produced in the country. Explain to the class the relationships between the geography of a region and its products.

12. Read some fables of LaFontaine. Make up your own fable—in either prose or poetry.

13. Read a novel, play, or poem of literary importance. Report on it orally or in writing. See your teacher if you want vocabulary lists or study questions for books available in school.

Diary Assignment

PURPOSE

To develop your awareness of instances of French culture and French language in our own culture.

ACTIVITY

Starting on Monday, Oct. 1, you are to keep a diary (on notebook paper) in which you record any instance of coming into contact with the French language or culture out of class. *Examples:* French words in a book you are reading, use of French on TV, newspaper advertisement of French products, hearing people talking French (outside of French class, of course!), seeing French-made products in stores, studying about France, French literature, or French history in another class, and so on.

EVALUATION

You *must* have an entry per day. If there was nothing for that day, write, "No entry." Your observations need not be long—a sentence or so per day. If you have completed this asignment according to instructions, you will receive 5 points. The people with the highest number of entries on French culture will receive a bonus of one point.

DUE DATE

The diary must be kept for each day from Oct. 1 through and including Tuesday, Oct. 23. It *must* be handed in on Wed., Oct. 24. Each day of lateness (except because of absence) will result in one point being subtracted from the total. After the diaries are handed in, a class period will be devoted to discussing the experiences you had during the three-week diary period.

Extra-Credit Activities—Foreign-Language Magazine

1. Find a large (nearly full-page) picture or advertisement. Using your dictionary, label in French the people, objects, and activities shown. The purpose of this exercise is to develop your vocabulary. Look up only commonly used words that you think will be useful. One point per 25 new words. Teacher will administer French-to-English oral test. Pass: 4 out of 5 correct. Be sure to mount each picture on colored paper for backing. Letter neatly. Be sure to include articles (masc. or fem. singular) for each noun you use. Verbs should be in infinitive form.

2. Look through the magazines to find examples of a grammar point being studied in class: irregular present, *passé composé*, reflexives, question words, and so on. Cut out the underlined examples (they will be attractive if accompanied by their picture) and assemble them into a scrapbook. One point per 10 correct examples.

3. Assemble a scrapbook of *new* vocabulary words and pictures illustrating those that have been cut from the magazine. One point per 25 new words (not the ones learned in French I). This will work best with words printed in large type.

4. Cut out words that rhyme and paste them (with pictures, if any) on one page of a scrapbook—one type of rhyme per page, at least 5 examples per rhyme. One point per 25 words (new or not).

5. Find short headlines, cut them out (with their pictures, preferably), paste them in a scrapbook. Then, using colored pen, write in a reversed meaning of the sentence. For example: You find *"Il fait chaud."*—You write beneath it, *"Il fait froid."* One point per 10 sentences.

6. Find a *new* vocabulary word for each letter of the alphabet—or at least 10 letters. Cut out each word and its picture and use it in a five-word sentence. Arrange the new words alphabetically. One point per 10 words in sentences.

7. Choose one letter of the alphabet as your theme. Try to find 20 new words that begin with that letter. Put them (and pictures) into a scrapbook.

8. If you don't like to make scrapbooks but like learning new vocabulary, study the vocabulary scrapbooks available in class and take an oral French-to-English vocabulary test on them. One point per 40 new words. Pass: 4 out of 5 right on oral test with teacher or aide.

APPENDIX D

FORM FOR PLANNING AN INDIVIDUALIZED CURRICULUM

During the preliminary stages of planning for individualization, it is helpful to clarify certain basic questions. Checkmarks in the appropriate spaces can offer a guide to what provisions will have to be made.

1. What language(s) will be individualized?
   ____French ____German ____Spanish ____Italian
   ____Other_____

2. To which level(s) will it apply?
   ____I ____II ____III ____IV ____V ____Other_____

3. How many classes will be involved?
   ____1 ____2 or 3 ____4 or 5 ____6–10 ____Other

4. Which teachers will work on individualizing instruction?
   _____ _____ _____ _____ _____

5. What new teacher-prepared materials will be needed?
   ____Learning packets ____Visuals ____Tapes ____Other_____

6. What additional equipment should be bought?
   ____Tape recorders ____Jack boxes ____Cassette players
   ____Duplicator ____Mimeograph ____Language masters
   ____Projectors (Type: _____) ____File cabinets
   ____Other_____

7. How should classroom space be rearranged?
   ____Materials center ____Tape/cassette area ____Testing area
   ____Small-group conversation space ____Individual study carrels
   ____Classroom library ____Open files ____Games/relaxation area
   ____Other_____

8. What enrichment materials will be required?
   ____Foreign-language newspapers and magazines ____Supplementary reading materials ____Slides ____Tapes/Cassettes ____Supplementary texts ____Programed materials ____Films ____Culture Capsules ____Filmstrips ____Foreign-language games ____Other_____

9. Who will teach in the classroom?
   ____Certified teacher ____Student teacher ____Paid teacher aid or native speaker ____Adult volunteer from college or community ____Student aide ____Peer teachers

10. How will classes be grouped?
    ____Heterogeneously ____Homogeneously: honors
    ____Homogeneously: regular ____Homogeneously: slow
    ____Nongraded ____Other_____

11. In what way will courses be individualized?
    ____Objectives of learning ____Rate of learning ____Method of learning ____Content of learning ____All of the above ____Other_____

12. How will credit be awarded?
    ____Traditionally, according to school procedures ____As earned, upon completion of a block of work ____Pass/fail (Passing level:____) ____No grades, sentence description of achievement ____Other_____

13. What type of scheduling will prevail?
    ____Traditional periods of 40–50 minutes, five days a week
    ____Flexible scheduling with large- and small-group instruction
    ____Demand scheduling based on time needs ____Frequent rescheduling based on past achievements and prescribed needs ____Other_____

14. How will the program be evaluated?
    ____Students' grades ____Comparison of failure statistics from year to year ____Standardized tests ____Teacher questionnaires ____Student questionnaires ____Staff conferences ____Supervisory personnel ____Outside observers ____Other_____

15. When will work on the individualized program be done?
    ____Summer workshop ____Workshop after school hours during the year ____Regularly assigned curriculum development periods during school day ____During regular teacher preparation periods and at home ____Other_____

16. How long will preparation for individualized instruction take?
    ____A summer ____A semester ____A school year ____Other_____

17. Circle the number of questions that you were unable to answer. Why were you unable to answer them?
    ____Lack of knowledge ____Uncertainty over school policies ____Uncertainty over budget allocations ____Uncertainty over program design ____Other_____

18. What measures could you take in order to find answers?
    ____Do more reading in professional literature ____Give additional thought to program design ____Consult with department chairman/language coordinator/school principal ____Other_____

TOPICS FOR STUDENT ORIENTATION

1. Goals of the course
2. How class activities are structured
3. Reasons for individualizing instruction
4. Structure of learning packets
5. How to use time effectively in class
6. Policy on learning rates and deadlines
7. Types of tests to expect
8. How to study for tests
9. Location of available materials and rules for their use
   a. Tapes, cassettes, audio flashcards, or language masters
   b. Slides, filmstrips, film loops, films
   c. Foreign-language magazines, newspapers
   d. Articles, short stories, magazines, books for independent reading
   e. Realia from foreign country, materials for culture assignments
   f. Reference materials (encyclopedias, alternative texts, maps, charts)
   g. Games, flashcards, records
   h. Equipment (tape or cassette players or recorders, filmstrip and slide viewers, and so on)
10. Classroom personnel and functions of each
    a. Certified teacher
    b. Student teacher or intern
    c. Student aides (from more advanced levels)
    d. Peer teachers (from the same class)
11. Classroom management policies
    a. Tardiness, attendance, and absence
    b. Opportunities to make up work
    c. Teacher's conference hours after class
    d. Materials to be brought to class daily (texts, writing equipment)
    e. Acceptable and unacceptable behavior
12. Words of encouragement, assurance, and so on

FOREIGN-LANGUAGE GAME EXPRESSIONS (FRENCH)

If you and your friends play a game in class, you will receive oral credit for using the following expressions:

1.	Who's turn is it?	1.	A qui le tour?	
2.	It's my turn.	2.	C'est à moi/	C'est mon tour.
	your		toi	ton
	his		lui	son
	her		elle	son
3.	Come on!	3.	Allons/Allez-y.	
4.	Hurry up!	4.	Dépêche-toi.	
			Dépêchez-vous.	
5.	It's not fair.	5.	Ce n'est pas juste/	
			Ce n'est pas de jeu.	
6.	Take a card.	6.	Prends une carte.	
	Draw.		Tire.	
7.	Throw the dice.	7.	Jette les dés.	
8.	You can't do that.	8.	Tu n'as pas le droit de faire cela.	
9.	Move your man one space.	9.	Avance ton pion d'une case.	
10.	What's the score?	10.	Quel est le score?	
11.	How many points do I have?	11.	Combien de points est-ce que j'ai?	
12.	Go to "Prison."	12.	Va à la case "Prison."	
	Begin.		Depart.	
13.	I'm exchanging my letters.	13.	J'échange mes lettres.	
14.	Start over.	14.	Recommence.	
15.	I'm not lucky.	15.	Je n'ai pas de chance.	
16.	Darn it!	16.	Zut!	
17.	It doesn't count.	17.	Ça ne compte pas.	
18.	Let me see.	18.	Laisse-moi voir.	
19.	I won.	19.	J'ai gagné.	
20.	How much/How many ...	20.	Combien de/d' ...	

21. Who wants to play?
22. Shuffle the cards.

23. Deal the cards.

24. You shouldn't cheat.

21. Qui veut joner?
22. Mèle les cartes.
    Bats
23. Donne les cartes/Distribue les cartes.
24. Il ne feut pas tricher.

COMPOSITION CORRECTION SYMBOLS

A. The following abbreviations will be used when the teacher marks your compositions. Correct your paper and return it in order to earn credit for your work. If you cannot make certain corrections, see your teacher for an explanation.

m.	Make this word masculine.
f.	Make this word feminine.
pl.	Make this word plural.
sing.	Make this word singular.
ag.	Make the subject and verb of the sentence agree.
wo	Correct your word order.
ww	You have used the wrong word to express your meaning.
?	This does not make sense. Please rewrite.
t	You have used an incorrect verb tense.
form	Your verb form is incorrect.
sp	Correct your spelling.
prof.	Please see the teacher for an explanation of this grammar.
‾∧	Please insert missing word to make your sentence comprehensible.
nom.	Use the nominative form.
gen.	Use the genetive form.
dat.	Use the dative form.
acc.	Use the accusative form.

B. An alternative method of correcting compositions could involve writing the page numbers of the text where students may look up the rules needed to correct their errors.

APPENDIX E

SELF-GRADING FORM FOR STUDENTS

The following form is distributed to students at the beginning of the ten-week marking period in a flexibly paced French II class. All required assignments are worth five points, for a possible total of 75 points. In addition, students must earn points by completing culture assignments and communication assignments in areas of speaking, reading, and writing. The first deadline is the last date in class spent on a particular assignment. The second deadline is an extension for students who need more time to complete their work after class. The entire assignment expires (is no longer accepted) two Fridays after the original in-class deadline. In the last column students record their cumulative point total. A week before the teacher assigns grades, students hand in their own form and state the grade they have earned.

Self-Grading Form for French II Students:
Marking Period I—Deadlines

PTS.	ASSIGNMENT	LAST DAY ACCEPTED IN CLASS	LAST DAY RETESTS AND COMPOSITION CORRECTIONS ACCEPTED OUT OF CLASS	MY POINT TOTAL
5	Oral Test on Useful Expressions (Appendix D)	Fri., Sept. 14	Wed., Sept. 26	
5	Oral Present (Review)	Thurs., Sept. 20	Fri., Oct. 5	
5	Written Present (Review)	" "	" "	
5	Required Composition	Mon., Sept. 24	" "	
5	Oral Passé Composé (Review)	Wed., Oct. 3	Fri., Oct. 12	
5	Written Passé Composé (Review)	" "	" "	
5	Required Composition	Wed., Oct. 10	Fri., Oct. 19	
5	Vocabulary 17A (Interview)	Thurs., Oct. 25	Fri., Nov. 2	
	Communication Assignment	Mon., Oct. 29	Fri., " "	

PTS.	ASSIGNMENT	LAST DAY ACCEPTED IN CLASS	LAST DAY RETESTS AND COMPOSITION CORRECTIONS ACCEPTED OUT OF CLASS	MY POINT TOTAL
5	Vocabulary: C'est La Vie (Outside Reading)	Fri., Oct. 26	None	
5	Comprehension: C'est La Vie	" "	None	
5	Vocabulary 17B	Thurs., Oct. 25	Fri., Nov. 2	
	Communication Assignment	Mon., Oct. 29	" "	
5	Diary: Contact with French Culture (Appendix C)	Fri., Oct. 19	None	
5	Oral: Present Reflex	Thurs., Oct. 18	Fri., Oct. 26	
5	Written: " "	" "	" "	
5	Required Composition	Wed., Oct. 24	Fri., Nov. 2	

Up to 10 points credit: Reading (classroom library)

Up to 2 points credit: Letter in French to a pen-pal

Up to 5 points credit: Culture assignments (as in Appendix C)

None of these will be accepted for the first marking period after Fri., Oct. 26

Up to 10 points credit: Use of French in class Fri., Oct 26 (Appendix E)   None

The grade I have earned is: _____

PROGRAM EVALUATION QUESTIONNAIRES

A. Questionnaire for the Beginning of the Year

In each of the following lines, please circle the choice that best applies to you. Your honest answers wil help your teacher in planning and improving the French course.

Your grade level: French II   French III   Sophomore   Junior   Senior

Your class: French II   French III

Your class period: 1   2   3   4   5   6   7   8

You are a: girl   boy

Grade range last year in French: 60–70   65–75   70–80   75–85   80–90   above 90

1. At the end of last year my attitude toward learning French was:

    0 very negative   1 negative   2 neutral   3 positive   4 very positive

2. After 3 days of orientation, my attitude this year toward learning French is:

    0 very negative   1 negative   2 neutral   3 positive   4 very positive

3. Do you intend to take a French course next year?

    0 definitely not   1 probably not   2 uncertain   3 probably yes
    4 definitely yes

4. How do you react to this statement?: Being able to communicate in a foreign language is a valuable and worthwhile skill that can help you throughout life.

    0 disagree strongly   1 disagree   2 neutral   3 agree   4 agree strongly

5. How would you rate yourself on responsibility? (that is, doing homework regularly, being prepared for tests, turning in assignments on time, making up work missed)

    0 rarely do what is required   1 often do not do the work
    2 sometimes do not work   3 most of the time I do what is necessary
    4 always fulfill my obligations

6. Why are you enrolled in a French course this year?

7. What do you hope to gain from French this year? (aside from school credit or good grades)

8. My desire to visit a country where French is spoken is (Suppose you could go to Quebec with parents or classmates for a few days):

   0 nonexistent   1 slight   2 moderate   3 strong   4 very strong

9. My desire to correspond with a French-speaking pen-pal is:

   0 nonexistent   1 slight   2 moderate   3 strong   4 very strong

10. In my house, knowing a foreign language is considered:

    0 useless   1 a school requirement   2 useful for some
    3 pretty important   4 extremely important

11. How do you react to this statement?: I am interested in learning about how French people live, what their daily routines are like, whether they are like Americans or not.

    0 disagree strongly   1 disagree   2 neutral   3 agree   4 agree strongly

B. Mid-Year Questionnaire

Circle one:

1. At the end of last year, my attitude toward French was:

1	2	3	4	5
very negative		neutral		very positive

2. At the beginning of this year my attitude toward French was:

   1   2   3   4   5

3. At mid-year, my attitude toward French was:

   1   2   3   4   5

4. Three reasons for my answer to question 3 are:

5. If I were the teacher of this class, three things I would change to improve it are:

6. Three things I would be interested in learning more about next semester are:

7. My attitude toward my teacher is:

1	2	3	4	5
very negative		neutral		very positive

8. On *fairness* I would rate my teacher:

1	2	3	4	5
very low		average		very high

9. On understanding of students I would rate my teacher:

   1   2   3   4   5

10. On *ability to explain clearly* I would rate my teacher:
    1   2   3   4   5

11. In comparison to my other courses, French class is most of the time:
    1   2   3   4   5
    very boring   about average   very interesting

12. Use this space for additional comments and suggestions.

C. End-of-year questionnaire

Please answer each question carefully. Your responses will be useful for evaluating this course. Please circle your answers.

1. At the beginning of the year, my attitude toward French was:
   very negative   negative   neutral   positive   very positive

2. At the end of this year, my attitude toward French is:
   very negative   negative   neutral   positive   very positive

3. Do you intend to take a French course next year?
   definitely not   probably not   unsure   probably yes   definitely yes

4. Please explain your answers to the questions above.

5. My reaction to individualized instruction this year is:
   very negative   negative   neutral   positive   very positive

6. What three things did you like most about the course this year?

7. Make three suggestions for improving this course.

8. Please rate this course from 1 (low) to 5 (high) in each of the following areas:

   ____learning packets
   ____textbook(s)
   ____cultural materials
   ____audio-visual materials
   ____variety
   ____interest
   ____teacher preparation
   ____classroom organization
   ____appropriate pacing
   ____fairness of amount of homework
   ____clarity of directions
   ____clarity of grammar explanations
   ____opportunities for success
   ____amount of free speaking practice
   ____teaching aides
   ____fairness of tests
   ____treatment of culture
   ____small-group activities
   ____willingness of teacher to help with learning problems
   ____amount of material learned
   ____availability of needed materials
   ____availability of help when needed
   ____fairness of grading system

9. Assume that you have the choice between two different types of foreign-language classes. Both are taught by the same teacher, both require about the same amount of work, and both have the same grading system. Circle which class style you prefer, A or B.

A	B
The teacher directs the class most of the time, explaining grammar, conducting drills, offering culture lectures, and so on. All assignments and tests are required for each student and must be handed in on the same day.	After giving necessary explanations, the teacher provides for full-class, small-group, and independent activities. Flexibility is allowed in handing in assignments and in taking tests. Students have some choice in determining which assignments they do.

10. Why did you answer the above question as you did?

USEFUL FOREIGN-LANGUAGE CLASSROOM EXPRESSIONS (FRENCH)

You will find the following French expressions very useful in French class. They will be helpful in asking questions and obtaining what you need. If you speak English instead of French in the following situations, your teacher will "not understand" you, and you will not get what you want.

1. I don't understand
2. I forgot
3. I don't know
4. May I go to the lavatory?
   my locker?
   the clinic?
5. May I take the test on . . . ?
6. It's my first test.
   second
   third
7. Did I pass my test on . . . ?
8. Did you correct my composition?
   test?
9. How do you say . . . in French?
10. What does . . . mean?
11. I need a sheet of . . .
    . . . help on . . .
    . . . pass.
12. I don't have my homework.
    my textbook.
13. Can you sign my packet?
14. On what page . . . ?
    line . . . ?
15. I was absent.
16. When may I see you (teacher) after class?

1. Je ne comprends pas
2. J'ai oublié
3. Je ne sais pas
4. Est-ce que je peux aller
   à la toilette?
   à mon placard?
   à l'infirmerie?
5. Est-ce que je peux passer l'examen sur . . . ?
6. C'est mon premier examen.
   deuxième
   troisième
7. Est-ce que j'ai réussi à mon examen sur . . . ?
8. Avez-vous corrigé
   ma composition?
   mon examen?
9. Comment est-ce qu'on dit . . . en français?
10. Que veut dire . . . ?
11. J'ai besoin d'une feuille de . . .
    de l'aide sur . . .
    d'un pass.
12. Je n'ai pas . . .
    mes devoirs.
    mon livre de français.
13. Est-ce que vous pouvez signer mon paquet?
14. A quelle page . . . ?
    ligne . . . ?
15. Jai été absent(e).
16. Quand est-ce que je peux vous voir après la classe?

EVALUATION SHEET FOR ORAL COMMUNICATION IN THE FOREIGN LANGUAGE

NAME _____

The sheet outlines various standards of in-class communication during the eight full weeks of each grading period. During the last three to five minutes of each class period the teacher or his designated aides sign in the space for the particular week, attesting to the student's oral performance evaluated that day. No more than two signatures are awarded per session: one for student-teacher communication, the other for student-student communication. Signatures at more advanced levels of performance include the points awarded at lower levels of behavior. Before the end of the grading period, students hand in their sheets for evaluation. They may self-grade if the teacher has provided guidelines for converting signatures into points. The teacher, though, may choose to grade subjectively, using the signatures as rough guidelines.

		1	2	3	4	5	6	7	8
Student-Teacher Communication	Always employs useful foreign-language expressions that have been memorized (page 235) in talking to the teacher or to aides.								
	Expresses original ideas in talking to the teacher in class or out.								
Student-Student Communication	Expresses original ideas when talking to friends in class. Minimum: Sustained conversation of at least 10 minutes.								
	Speaks the foreign language *all* the time during class without any use of English. Note: Silent study will not earn a signature here.								
	Speaks fluently with a high degree of pronunciation and grammatical accuracy. (This step is not signed. Credit is awarded according to the teacher's subjective evaluation.)								

INDEX

Academic standards, humanistic considerations versus, 39–41
ACTFL Review of Foreign Language Education, The, 3–4
Affective behavior (goals), 43–44
Affective domain, 24, 43–44, 75
Affective success, 118
Affective taxonomy, 43–44
Agatstein, Michael, 94n
Allen, Edward D., 169n
Altman, Howard B., 8, 13n, 14n
Amity Aid Program, 72
Appreciation, definition of, 44
Aronson, Howard I., 46n
Audio equipment, 85–88
Audio-lingualism, 4, 16–18
  reactions against, 18–21
Audio-visual equipment, 75–76, 81–82, 85–92
Ausubel, David P., 23n
Automation, 10

Barbanel, Laura, 34n
"Basic needs" theory of motivation, 25–26
  meeting basic needs in the classroom, 26–30
Belongingness and love needs, as motivation, 25, 27–28
Berward, Jean-Pierre, 80n
Bockman, John F., 14n, 149n
Bockman, Valerie M., 35n, 149n
Bornscheuer, Joan H., 150n
Briscoe, Laurel A., 55n

Brod, Richard I., 14n
Brooks, Nelson, 18, 22n, 67n
Brown University, 41
Bull, William E., 55n

Cameron-Bacon, Susan M., 80n
Campbell, Bruce G., 56n
Cassettes, 75–76, 86, 162, 172
Chastain, Kenneth, 22n, 23n, 167n
Cheating, 142
Chomsky, Noam, 19, 22n, 23n
Civilization and literature studies, 186–88
Clarke, Katharine M., 55n
Classroom equipment, for individualized instruction, 81–94
Classroom management
  communicating regulations, 111
  determining quality of management in, 156–57
  efficient student use of time, 130–33
  efficient use of teacher's time, 134–35
  enlisting help for, 71, 129, 135
  eupsychian management versus current realities, 33–34
  furnishings, 92–94
  maintaining neatness and order, 136–37
  meeting basic motivation needs, 26–30
  open style, 6
  overcoming common management problems, 127

237

Classroom personnel
  native informants, 72
  personalizing relationships, 7
  personnel, 5, 71
  personnel working relationships, 76–79
  secretarial help, 75
  student aids and tutors, 73–74
  student teachers and teaching interns, 73
  technical assistants, 75–76
Clausing, Gerhard, 67n
Cognitive domain, 24, 43, 75
Communication, 50
  definition of, 43
  oral exercises, 50
  performance objectives at the stage of, 49
  supplementary material for developing competence in, 50–53
Compositions, 181–82
Computerization, 10
Continuous progress program, 5, 58, 60–61, 156
  grading and record keeping, 146
Conversation, 171–73, 175, 176
Course objectives, need for diversified offerings, 41–42
Criticism, definition of, 43
Culture
  mini-lessons, 183–84
  past and current, 186–87
  realia for study, 90, 184
  way-of-life, 183–86
Curriculum
  and education for the future, 11
  criticism of, 9–10
  defining goals, 42
  evaluation of, 155–56
  for individualized learning, 37–44
  need for diversified course offerings, 41–42
  single text versus multi-text program, 48–49

Dialogs, 173
Discipline, 7
Disick, Renée S., 34n, 46n
Dittoing, 82, 129
Dramatizations, 179
Dusel, John P., 14n

Elective assignments, 58, 64–65
Elkins, Robert J., 14n, 45n
Esteem needs, as motivation, 26, 28–29
Eupsychian management, 32–33
  versus current classroom realities, 33–34
Evaluation
  curriculum, 155–56
  feedback from students, 151–53
  program, 151–57
  student questionnaire, 153–55
Eyde, Albert C., 46n

Failure
  eliminating, 30–31
  pass-fail grading, 40, 129, 130 139–40, 181–82
Films, 76, 82, 91
Filmstrips, 76, 82, 91
Fitzgibbon, Nancyanne, 67n
Flanders, N. A., 126n
Flexible pacing program, 5, 58, 62
Flynn, Mary B., 13n
Foreign Language Annals, 4
Foreign-language literature, teaching of, 186–88
Foreign-language publications, 64, 89, 186
Freedom to Learn (Rogers), 30
Freilich, Joan S., 67n
Future, study of the, 10–11

Gabriel, Toni, 55n
Games, in an individualized classroom, 90
Garfinkel, Alan, 106n
Ginnot, Haim G., 39, 45n, 121, 122, 126n
Glasser, William, 30, 35n
Gougher, Ronald L., 13n, 14n, 45n, 55n
Grading
  changing policies, 104–05
  continuous progress, 146
  contracts, 147–48

developing efficient procedures, 129–30
establishing a system, 146–49
pass/fail, 40, 128, 129, 139–40, 181–82
self grading by students, 148–49
Grammar, teaching of, 166–69
Grittner, Frank M., 14n, 45n, 66n, 79n
Gugli, William V., 188n
Guidance counselors, orienting to individualized instruction, 114
Gunderson, Barbara L., 46n

Hallock, Marcia, 67n
Hammelmann, William M. R., 80n
Harmin, Merrill, 55n
Harrell, Marcia, 13n
Hellman, Sharon, 13n, 67n
Hentoff, Nat, 9, 15n
Herndon, James, 9, 14n
Holt John, 9, 14n, 111n
Honig, Lucille J., 66n, 67n, 68n, 94n
Howe, Leland, 55n
Human Side of Enterprise, The (McGregor), 31
Humanism versus academic standards, 39–41
Humanistic theories, of motivation and management, 24–34

Illich, Ivan, 9, 15n
Inattention, 7
Independent study, 5, 58–59
Individual study projects, 184
Individualized instruction
  avoiding pitfalls of, 53–54
  choosing a class for, 105–06
  course content of, 63–64
  deciding where to begin, 102–06
  defining curricular goals of, 42
  definition of, 4–5
  equipment for, 81–94
  evaluation of, 154–55
  gaining support for, 100–02
  humanizing and personalizing, 122–25
  limiting scope of program, 98–99, 128
  need for diversified course offerings, 41–42
  orientation to, 107–15
  philosophy of, 38–39
  problems resulting from student misjudgment, 135–37
  program evaluation based on student reaction, 151–57
  rationale for, 8–13
  reasons for initiating program, 6–7
  single text versus multiple-text program, 48–49
  staffing for, 71–79
  student dissatisfaction with, 137
  styles of, 58, 65–66
  supplementary material for, 50–53
  support for program, 100–02
  teacher preparation for, 128–30
  time priorities, 97–100
  transition to, 95–105
  See also Classroom, Learning packets, Management
Interdisciplinary studies, 58, 64, 105, 187

Jakobovits, Leon A., 20, 23n, 41, 46n, 106n

Kalivoda, Theodore B., 14n, 45n
Kentz, Rita O., 13n, 67n
Kirschenbaum, Howard, 55n
Knowledge
  acquiring, 96
  learning steps at the stage of, 50
  taxonomic definition of, 43
Kohl, Herbert, 9, 15n
Kozol, Jonathan, 9, 15n
Krill, Carole L., 13n

Lado, Robert, 18, 22n
LaFayette, Robert C., 45n, 67n
Laleike, Fred H., 66n, 79n
Lamadrid, Enrique E., 55n
Lange, Dale L., 13n
Langellier, Alice, 55n
Language learning
  behaviorist school of, 17–18
  choice of objectives of, 5, 58–59, 98–99, 155

content of, 5, 58, 63–65, 98–99, 156
  eliminating failure in, 30–31
  facilitation of, 30
  method (mode) of, 5, 58, 62–63, 98–99, 155–56
  rate of, 5, 58, 59–62, 98–99, 155
Language master, 75–76, 172
Learning packets, 5, 104
  components of, 48
  examining structure of, 133
  pitfalls in designing, 53–54
  shortening, 129
  supplementary material for, 50–53
  training students to work with, 112
Lenneberg, Eric, 20, 23n
Le Texier, Bernard, 56n
Levy, Stephen L., 66n
Linguistics
  and objections to audio-lingualism, 19–20
  descriptive (structural), 16–17
  in the 1970s, 21–22
Lippmann, Jane N., 45n
Lipton, Gladys, 45n
Listening comprehension, 170–71
Literature
  foreign language, 188
  past and present, 186–87
Lock, Joanne Tuskes, 55n, 182n
Logan, Gerald E., 41, 45n, 46n, 56n, 67n, 94n, 148n, 182n
Love, F. William D., 66n, 67n, 68n, 94n

Mc Luhan, Marshall, 10, 15n
McGregor, Douglas, 31, 35n
Management
  eupsychian, 32–34
  Theory-X and Theory-Y, 31, 116–17
Marshall-University High School, 41
Maslow, Abraham H., 12–13, 15n, 35n, 126n, 154n
  "basic needs" theory of motivation, 25–26, 31
  eupsychian theory of management, 32–33
Mechanical skills, 43, 50
Media center, 5, 5n
Mini-courses, 5, 41, 58, 63–64, 105, 187

Mini-dramas, 185–86
Monsees, Anita, 106n
Moeller, Jack, 55n
Morel, Stefano, 55n, 182n
Morrey, Robert A., 66n, 79n
Motivation
  "basic needs" theory of, 25–26
  meeting basic needs in the classroom, 26–30
Mueller, Klaus A., 67n
Multimedia program, 5, 58, 62, 104, 156

National Defense Education Act, 8
National Defense Education Institute, 16
Native informants, 72
Needs theory of motivation, 25–26
  meeting in classroom, 26–30
Neill, A. S., 9, 15n
Nielson, Melvin L., 80n

Objectives, choice of, 5, 58–59, 98–99, 155
Oral comprehension, 123
Oral proficiency, 7
Orientation to individualized instruction, 107–15
  for administrators, 113–14
  for aides and paraprofessionals, 112–13
  for guidance counselors, 114
  for oneself, 108–09
  for parents, 114–15
  for students, 110–12
  for teachers, 108–09
Ostyn, Paul, 56n

Papalia, Anthony, 45n, 46n
Paper and paper products for an individualized program, 82–84
Paraprofessionals, 5n, 79, 104
  orienting, 112–13
Parents, orienting, 114–15
Peer teachers, 75
Pen pals, 65, 90, 184
Performance objectives
  foreign-language goals, 42–43
  writing learning steps for, 49–50
  writing unit objecitves, 49

Phillips, June K., 14n, 45n, 94n
Physiological needs, 25, 27
Playback equipment, 86
Pronunciation, 161–63
Psychology
    and audio-lingualism, 17, 20–21
    and education for the future, 11–13
    behaviorist school of, 17
Public relations, 102

Quinn, Terence J., 21, 23n

Raths, Louis, 55n
Reading, 123, 178–80
Reading material, 89–90
Realia, 90, 184
Receptivity, 44
Record keeping, 143–44
Record player and records, 87
Reeves, Dona B., 106n
Reinert, Harry, 55n, 66n
Reinhold, Robert, 46n
Repeatcorder, 87
Resource center, 5, 5n
Responsiveness, 44
Richardson, Charles P., 94n
Rivers, Wilga M., 20, 22n, 23n, 94n, 169n
Rogers, Carl R., 11–12, 15n, 30, 35n
Role playing, 173–74
Ryberg, Donald C., 67n

Safety needs, 25, 27
Savignon, Sandra J., 21–22, 23n
Scholastic Aptitude Tests, 39
Self-actualization needs, 26, 29–30
Silberman, Charles E., 9, 15n
Simon, Sidney B., 55n
Single text versus multitext program, 48–49
Skills
    development of preferred language, 59
    guidance in specific areas, 123–26
Skinner, B. F., 17–18, 22n
Slides, 82, 91–92
Small-group work, 5, 103–04, 171–73, 181

Smith, Philip D., Jr., 45n, 55n
Speaking, 124, 171–78
Speeches, 177–78
Spelling, 163–64
Staffing, for individualized instruction, 71–94
Steiner, Florence, 67n
Stenciling, 82, 129
Stoller, Phyllis S., 55n, 182n
Storage facilities, 84–85, 136
Student aides, 73–74, 112–13
Student teachers, 73
Students
    as peer teachers, 75
    as teaching aides, 73–74, 112–13
    demands for attention, 134–35
    dissatisfaction with individualization, 137
    efficient use of class time, 130–33
    evaluation of individualization, 151–55
    feedback from, 151–53
    improving communication between teachers and, 118–22
    misjudgment problems, 136–37
    new breed of, 9
    orientation of, 110–12
    promotion of student involvement, 7
    questionnaire for, 153–55
    self evaluation, 51–52
    self grading, 148–49
    working with learning packets, 112
Success
    affective, 118
    encouragement of subject matter, 117–18
Synergy, 117–18

Tape recorders, 86
Tapes, 75–76, 86, 161–62, 172
Taxonomy, 43–44
Teachers
    certified, 72, 79
    efficient use of time, 134
    facilitating freedom to learn, 30
    humanizing relations between students and, 116–17
    improving communication between students and, 118–22

orienting, 108–09
peer, 75
preparation for individualized instruction, 128–30
reactions against audio-lingualism, 18–19
student, 73
Teaching interns, 73
Teaching profession, approach to individualized instruction, 3, 6
Teetor, Will Robert, 149n
Television, 10–11
Tests, 5
criterion referenced, 5, 139
guidelines for, 138–41
oral, 143–45
pretest exercises, 51
retesting, 140–41
written, 128–29, 141–42
Theory X and Theory Y, 31, 116–17
Therrien, Melvin G., 188n
Time priorities, in the classroom, 97–100

Toffler, Alvin, 15n
Transfer, 43, 49, 50
Transparencies, 76, 91, 166
Tutors, 73–74

Valette, Jean-Paul, 55n
Valette, Rebecca M., 46n, 55n, 169n
Visual equipment, 88–92
Vocabulary, 5, 123, 164–65

Wattenmaker, Beverly, 35n, 55n, 182n
Way-of-life culture, 183–86
Wible Language Institute, 169n
Wilson, Virginia, 35n, 55n, 182n
Wolfe, David E., 55n
Workshops, 99–100
Writing, 124–25, 180–82
learning steps, 49–50
unit objectives, 49

Zampogna, Joseph, 45n